Twenty Years of Jewish-Catholic Relations

EDITED BY

EUGENE J. FISHER

A. JAMES RUDIN

MARC H. TANENBAUM

PAULIST PRESS
New York/Mahwah

Copyright © 1986 by
Eugene Fisher, A. James Rudin and Marc H. Tanenbaum

Library of Congress
Catalog Card Number: 85-62880

ISBN: 0-8091-2762-8

Published by Paulist Press
997 Macarthur Boulevard
Mahwah, N.J. 07430

Printed and bound in the United States of America

CONTENTS

PART III

Introduction:
Nostra Aetate, For Our Times
and For the Future

EUGENE J. FISHER

On October 28, 1965, 2,221 Catholic bishops, assembled from every corner of the earth, added their signatures to that of "Paul, Bishop of the Catholic Church," officially promulgating the shortest and most controversial of the documents of the Second Vatican Council. That document was *Nostra Aetate* ("In Our Time"), the Council's Declaration on the Relationship of the Church to Non-Christian Religions.

The controversy had surrounded only fifteen Latin sentences of text, the declaration's fourth section dealing with Jews and Judaism. As late as the weekend before the vote, newspapers were speculating that the section on the Jews would be reduced to a single sentence, and that the whole of the declaration would be shelved. In the event, the bishops of the Council voted overwhelmingly in favor of the fifteen sentences that had seen so much clarification and debate since the meeting between Pope John XXIII and the French Jewish scholar Jules Isaac had occasioned in the Pope's mind the thought that "the Council ought to be occupied with the Jewish question and antisemitism." By their approval, however, the Council Fathers, in the words of Fr. Thomas Stransky who was then on the staff of Cardinal Bea, "committed the Roman Catholic Church to an irrevocable act, a *heshbon ha-nefesh*—a reconsideration of soul" (*Origins,* June 20, 1985).

This volume is about that commitment made by the Church twenty years ago, about what it meant in the context of the nineteen hundred years of often tragic Christian-Jewish relations leading up to it, about what has happened since, and about what it means for us today. Even more than celebrating and analyzing what has been done, however, the essays in this volume aim to inform us on what needs to be done to preserve and move forward what the Council only began—and that, as the reader will soon perceive, is a great deal.

Pope John Paul II, in a meeting with leaders of the American Jewish Committee held in Rome on February 15, 1985, called on Catholics to accept *Nos-*

tra Aetate "as an expression of the faith, as an inspiration of the Holy Spirit, as a word of the Divine Wisdom." *Nostra Aetate,* then, remains, despite the great progress made in the dialogue in the past two decades, as much of a present challenge to us as a record of one of the most glorious (because most humble) moments of Church history.

This point needs to be set clearly at the outset. *Nostra Aetate,* as Cardinal Johannes Willebrands, President of the Holy See's Commission for Religious Relations with the Jews, reminded his hearers during a celebration of the fifteenth anniversary of the document in 1980, can only be read properly within the context of subsequent statements of the Holy See, the Popes and Episcopal Conferences interpreting and implementing it. On many points, affirmations that were only implicit in the document itself have now been made explicit, and statements that might have been read ambiguously at the time have now been clarified. This process of step by step growth in understanding and clarification is the result of the dialogue between our two peoples.

The papers collected here provide a commentary, and something more than a commentary on those Church documents, important as those are. Rather, they chronicle and analyze the relationship itself, its spiritual breakthroughs, past and present travails, and its hopes for the future. Entering them will provide not only the beginner with a solid primer in the state of the dialogue today, but the practitioner and scholar of either tradition with a set of fundamental challenges and new perspectives on long held (and often cherished) presumptions that Christians and Jews have had about one another.

Rabbi James Rudin's opening reflection frame the pairs of essays that are to come. Rudin sketches dramatically what a Catholic or a Jew might have said about "the other" if awakened at 3:00 A.M. on the eve of the Council, portraits of the other essentially negative on the one side and essentially defensive on the other. The background of the portraits, the tragic history of centuries of abuse culminating in the Holocaust, is filled in with broad and dark, but deftly fair strokes. Adding bright touches to the new images that the dialogue enables us to draw of our relationship and one another, however, are several recent events; the relatively benign experience Catholics and Jews have had in America, the rebirth of a Jewish state in the Land of Israel, and the Second Vatican Council and its aftermath in a new mode of Christian-Jewish relating.

In the first pair of essays, two of the greatest pioneers of the dialogue, both of whom were actively present at the Council, Msgr. George Higgins and Rabbi Marc Tanenbaum, give retrospectives on the significance of what took place then and what has happened since. Here, as in Rudin's overview, the reader will discern the emergence of key themes of the dialogue, and the differing but creatively diverse perspectives that Catholics and Jews bring to them. Even the toughest issues, the essays show, can be tackled in the dialogue, e.g., anti-Judaism in the New Testament, the relationship between the ancient Christian "teaching of contempt" and modern antisemitism, biblical interpretation and liturgical sensitivity, convergence, and the "agenda issues," such as the State of Israel on the one hand and the "seamless garment" of life issues on the other.

The second pair of reflections takes up directly the question of the Jewish people's religious attachment to the Land of Israel as the significance of the modern Jewish State for the people Israel as people of God. Rabbi Robert M. Seltzer evokes the inner Jewish longings over the centuries and the history of Zionism that made of this impossible dream of liberation a living reality in our time, as well as the tensions within the Jewish community between normalization and uniqueness that give the internal debates on the meaning of Zionism their distinctive richness and creativity. Fr. Edward Flannery likewise records a range of views within the Catholic community in response to the existence of the State of Israel. The Christian cannot, he argues, understand Israel except in the context of a renewed theological appreciation of the Jewish people as God's chosen. Thus the internal Christian debate on Israel, always to be conducted with dialogical openness to Jewish self-reflection, has much more at stake than mere diplomatic relations or political options. It touches a mystery the Church as Church needs to ponder prayerfully.

Rev. Lawrence Boadt, C.S.P. and Dr. Michael J. Cook move to a matter externally central to the relationship between the Church and the Jewish people: how do we read and interpret the Bible we share (the Hebrew Scriptures) and the Christian Scripture we do not share (the New Testament). In what may be seen as a bit of playful irony, the Catholic of the pair is primarily a scholar of the Hebrew Scriptures and the Jew a New Testament scholar. There is in the pairing, then, a rather unique opportunity for both Jewish and Christian readers to see ourselves as "the other" views us in dialogue.

Fr. Boadt's article surveys the changes that have occurred in the methodology used by Christians for the interpretation of the Scriptures, with consequent radical change in understanding, and in a final section frames concisely the state of the question on key perennial issues: the common worship of the same God, revelation, covenant, Christology and messianic hopes. This essay will be especially helpful for homilists and religious educators as well as students of the bible, whether professionals or beginners.

Rabbi Cook, in what can serve as an introduction to New Testament studies for Jews as well as an eye-opening look at the New Testament for Christians from a scholarly point of view, concentrates on the need to frame the biblical insights discussed by Boadt in such a way that they can be effectively conveyed to the Christian laity, developing a rationale for its need and a pedagogical method for the use of educators. Cook lists ten "anti-Jewish impressions demonstrably inherent in centuries of Christian Biblical exegesis," and argues that "each would become cast in a significantly different light were Jewish perspectives only incorporated into Catholic pedagogical discussion of Judaism," a proposition with which Boadt's essay agrees completely.

The third pairing complements the scrutiny of biblical sources and interpretation by surveying what has been done since the Council in religious education and the renewal of Catholic liturgy. Judith Hershcopf Banki summarizes the studies of the treatment of Jews and Judaism in American and European Catholic teaching materials that have been made and the areas that are still in need of significant work. As with two of the other Jewish papers (Rudin, Greenberg), Banki does not hesitate to cast the light of rigorous scrutiny on Jewish understandings of Christianity, and to show areas where real improvement is needed. She notes, for example, that many Jews remain basically ignorant of the changes in Catholic thinking since the Council. It is the hope of the editors that this book, if read widely within the Jewish community, will help to fill that need.

Eugene J. Fisher discusses changes that have been made in Catholic liturgy since the Council, for example during the Holy Week services, and problems that remain (for example, the Holy Week services) still to be faced and resolved in satisfactory manner. Samples of guidelines for Christians celebrating the seder and for the memorial of Yom Ha Shoah, as well as more detailed guidelines for homilists on Sundays throughout the year, are offered.

The next article responds to the question of what the local religious community is to do with all the new insights and richness of perspectives opened up by the dialogue on the national and international levels. Rev. Msgr. Royale M. Vadakin and Rabbi Alfred Wolf narrate the remarkable story of a decade of dialogical encounter in one such area. Theirs is a story of hopes fulfilled beyond expectation, and of the dynamic creativity latent in the Catholic-Jewish encounter. Modest projects open new vistas which, in turn, create new possibilities and wider areas of involvement.

Again, this is a section that speaks for itself, illustrating some of the many fruits of local dialogue as it gives life to the official pronouncements, and also, it may be said, spurring the national and international bodies to new efforts just to "catch up" with what the communities themselves are already achieving. This section will give readers a wide range of practical models to adapt to their own particular circumstances and needs.

The final pairing joins two of the leading theologians of the dialogue in an effort to assess current trends in theological understanding of "the other's" religious claims by each tradition. Both essays, it is safe to say, not only assess but also will significantly move forward the dialogue on the deepest theological level. Here we have major statements from the "cutting edge" of the best thinking about the relationship between the Jewish people and the Church that our two communities have to offer. Both Rev. John T. Pawlikowski, O.S.M. and Rabbi Irving Greenberg offer insights from within the integrity of their own respective traditions on how those traditions can affirm positively the central revelational and covenant claims of the other. Given the precise nuancing and delicate sensitivities of each to the double vision of self and other demanded by this task, it is best that no introductory summary be here attempted. Each author should be allowed to speak for himself unfettered from editorial second-guessing.

It would be useful in reading this book to have as a companion piece the two volumes of Helga Croner's *Stepping Stones to Further Jewish-Christian Relations* (Stimulus, 1977; Paulist Press, 1985), which provide much of the necessary documentation.

Finally, four important documents not found in Croner are provided here because of their special importance for the dialogue. These include the two key statements of Pope John Paul II and two especially valuable statements by recent Presidents of the United States Bishops' Conference, Archbishop John Roach and Bishop James Malone.

We stand "in our time" at the brink of the third millennium of a relationship at once uniquely fruitful in what it has given the world and uniquely tragic, all too often, in its internal relations between the two communities. The first millennium (if one can oversimplify for the sake of the schema) was characterized by ambiguity of understanding on both sides. As late as the ninth and tenth centuries, one finds bishops complaining that Christians persisted in going to the rabbis for blessings, indicating in a small way that on the community level relations were perhaps as positive as negative. By the middle of the second millennium, however, with the Crusades, expulsions, the institution of the ghetto, and the Inquisition as a background, the ambiguity seemed to have been resolved in favor of the negative. The Second Vatican Council, which the 1975 Vatican Guidelines declare found "its historical setting in circumstances deeply affected by the memory of the persecution and massacre of Jews which took place in Europe just before and during World War II," broke through the brooding darkness of centuries to provide the possibility of a third great age, this time one of dialogue and mutual respect.

This new stage, set against the millennia preceding it, is very much in its infancy, and very fragile. It needs nourishing and constant, central concern on the part of both of our communities if it is to grow robust and fulfill our hopes for it. But, to judge from the following essays, it is alive and well and, typically, bellowing for our attention. Nothing like this reconciliation of two ancient, mutually suspicious yet umbilically bound religious traditions has ever been attempted in all the generations that preceded this one. To this generation falls the task of framing the way our communities may relate for the next millennium. It is to the generations of the future that this volume is dedicated.

PART I

The Dramatic Impact
of Nostra Aetate

RABBI A. JAMES RUDIN

There is certainly good reason to commemorate the dramatic improvement in Roman Catholic-Jewish relations since 1965. It is no small thing when two of the world's great faith communities systematically and actively set out to repair the enormous damage that has taken place over the centuries.

To understand the full impact of the Second Vatican Council, it is necessary to recall the relationships that existed prior to 1965, both in the United States and throughout the world. And it is necessary to go beyond the animosities and mutual suspicions that Catholic and Jewish leaders often maintained toward each other. We need to recall what ordinary Catholics and Jews (if there be such persons!) were thinking throughout history, what a Catholic or Jew would have said about the "the other" if he or she had been rudely awakened at 3:00 A.M.

I will try in a brief way to summarize that painful history, and then describe what Vatican II has meant and what it can mean to Catholics and Jews in the future. Both faith communities need to clear away the enormous debris that has tragically accumulated over nineteen hundred years.

First, a 3:00 A.M. Catholic view: the Jews were a great spiritual people of the Biblical period who brought to the world a magnificent monotheistic religion, Judaism. Because of this religion, the Jewish people provided the milieu for the Savior, Jesus of Nazareth. But by the time of Jesus, the Jews as a people, and Judaism as a religion, had both become brittle and dry, spiritually exhausted, emptied of vitality and meaning. After the first century of the Christian era, Jews were no longer a people of God, no longer a people blessed by God.

The Old Israel along with its Old Testament was, of course, to be honored and remembered with gratitude by Christians, but Jews and Judaism had been succeeded, fulfilled, completed, replaced, and/or displaced by the New Israel, the New Testament, the Christian Church, the new people of God.

The ancient Hebrews and Israelites were to be revered for having blazed

9

the way in ancient religious thought and they were to be honored because God had placed his only begotten son in their midst. But to the Jews who came after the rise of Christianity, and to Judaism, Catholics at first showed impatience, then contempt, and finally hostility. For many Catholics in history the only good Jew was a converted Jew.

It was as if a child scorned, then hated, and finally attempted to destroy its parent, both spiritually and physically. Many of the early Church fathers exhibited a venomous attitude toward Jews. The teachings of the fathers formed the foundation for the infamous "teaching of contempt" about Jews and Judaism that has poisoned so much of Christian thought and belief.

A basic Catholic perception was that Judaism, as it emerged after the time of Jesus, was deficient in spiritual values. The many books of Jewish teaching, including and especially the Talmud, were often objects of contempt and derision. Indeed, with the founding of Christianity, the old Israel was no longer a source of religious vitality. It had completed its historic mission, and it should have disappeared from the stage of history. In effect, Jews and Judaism "dropped out" of Church history after the first century. Little if anything was taught in Christian schools about the rise of rabbinic Judaism. The richness of Judaism as a living faith simply disappeared, and it was usually replaced with highly negative images of the Jewish people and their religious faith.

But sometimes, depending upon the time and place, the historic Catholic attitude toward Jews and Judaism went even further than contempt and hostility; enter the monstrous "deicide" charge. "Deicide" is such a cool technical term, just as "genocide" is. But as it was played out in nineteen hundred years of tortured history between Catholics and Jews, "deicide" was neither cool nor technical. For what "deicide" proclaimed was that the Jews at the time of Jesus had willfully, consciously, and conspiratorially murdered the Son of God!

To murder God: the very phrase is chilling! The charge was hurled at an entire people, and not solely at the Jewish people who were alive at the time of Jesus. The charge was branded upon all Jews since the first century, down to the present day. To be guilty of murdering God staggers the mind in its enormity and in its potent power to profane, to poison, and to persecute.

That the Jewish people then, now, and forever is guilty of the greatest crime of all, the murder of God, must bring all of us up short as we recognize the gruesome and bloody effect of that teaching. But for some Catholics, the "deicide" charge provided a kind of divine license, a religious mandate to forcibly convert, and often to kill Jews. Jews became a surplus people, and Judaism became a surplus religion; neither had any positive role to play. Jews represented a system of religious belief and thought that was superseded by Christianity. Jews and Judaism had become excess baggage after the events of that spring day in Jerusalem in the year 30: the death and resurrection of Jesus.

The historic 3:00 A.M. Jewish view is almost the mirror image of the Catholic view. We well know that the perceptions people maintain are often more important and more decisive in the shaping of lifelong attitudes than are facts. What we think or feel about someone or some group is more crucial than what we truly and accurately know about the same person or group.

Jews never lost belief in their unique spiritual vocation. This may sound academic and devoid of flesh and blood reality. Let me be quite specific: Jews never lost their belief in the reality and the eternal validity of the covenant between them and their God. Even Jewish agnostics and atheists, those Jews who wandered far from the comforting fires of the spiritual hearth, always knew, they always believed that the Jewish people had a special destiny in history—not one of superiority or mastery over others, but a particular destiny unlike any other people in the world.

Strengthened with this unshakable belief, Jews never regarded the rise of the Roman Catholic Church and of Christianity as a form of divine punishment upon them nor as a judgment upon their faith. Indeed, Jewish religious thinkers accorded Christianity full credit for being a monotheistic faith, a faith whose followers were bound to the God of Israel.

But Jews early on had a difficult task, one that finally became impossible as a result of the brutal historic realities of Catholic-Jewish relations. How could one distinguish the high moral and ethical teachings of the Catholic Church, teachings that were not too dissimilar from some of those expressed in Judaism, from the murderous, hateful, and contemptuous behavior of Catholics toward Jews and Judaism. The nineteen hundred year record of Catholic attitudes and actions directed toward the Jewish people is, by and large, a tragic one, filled with suffering and persecution.

Jews wondered: which was paramount? Christian creed, which was noble and uplifting? Or Christian deed, which was bloody and ruthless?

For the Jews of the West, of Europe, the Roman Catholic Church became THE Christian presence, THE Christian reality that Jews experienced first-hand. At first there were verbal and rhetorical criticisms of Jews and Judaism, followed by book burnings, including the bonfires in medieval Paris that destroyed the precious handwritten folios of the Talmud.

But rhetoric soon became in some places a demand for conversion to the true faith, particularly in Spain and Portugal during the fifteenth and sixteenth centuries. No longer were burning books sufficient to assert the truth of the Christian faith; during the Inquisition human beings, many of them Jews, were burned alive for their alleged "heresies." The Crusades of an earlier period, had also been a deadly period with thousands of Christian soldiers marching off to the Holy Land to "redeem" it from the Muslims. These same soldiers usually stopped along the way in Europe while en route to Jerusalem in order to butcher and massacre helpless Jewish communities.

The Inquisition was followed by the physical expulsion of Jews from Spain, and even those Jews who were baptized were sometimes hounded and assaulted for being "New Christians." They were accused of not being faithful enough to their new religious faith.

For Jews it took more than a bi-focal vision to maintain a balance: Catholicism, rich in pageantry and in dramatic power, possessed a moral base that ran counter to actual Catholic behavior. In time, the attempt to balance professed beliefs with actual conduct collapsed and finally, especially after the Inquisition, most Jews came to view the Roman Catholic Church as an eternal adversary, a powerful enemy—a Church that spoke in the name of Jesus, a Jew from the land of Israel, while at the same time it was a Church that vilified the Jewish people.

Could any two peoples have been further apart? Catholics saw Jews as a spiritually and sometimes physically surplus people, unworthy of God's love because of the sin of stubbornness in not recognizing and accepting the longed-for Messiah, a people cursed for having killed Jesus, the Son of God.

And Jews, always a minority in Catholic lands, saw Catholics as people who were their potential or actual murderer, both physically and spiritually. Jews saw a Church that professed love, but whose members practiced hatred and violence.

Simply put, Catholics believed that the extraordinary ministry of Jesus should have brought the religious vocation of the Jewish people to an end, but it didn't. Even though Christianity won the minds and souls of millions of men and women throughout the world, somehow Jews and Judaism still persisted, still existed as a spiritual aberration.

On the other hand, Jews did not believe that Jesus was the Messiah, for he did not fulfill the Messianic expectations and criteria as articulated by the Jewish religious tradition. Despite a generally hostile environment, Judaism not only survived, but it continually renewed itself throughout the long centuries of the dispersion. But the Jewish people became a permanent minority, overwhelmed in size first by Christians and later by Muslims who were the followers of another daughter faith.

Of course, because this is a story about human beings, there were many close personal friendships between Catholics and Jews, and there were many acts of loving-kindness. The historical picture was never totally dark. For example, we are aware of the fruitful and enriching cross-fertilization between Church and Synagogue musicians in the Middle Ages. The works and teachings of religious thinkers sometimes transcended the distinct boundaries that had been established between Catholics and Jews. There are recorded instances when a Catholic Emperor or a Church official befriended a beleaguered Jewish community. But these instances were far from the norm in Europe. Fortunately in the seventeenth century a new and more hopeful chapter in Catholic-Jewish relations emerged in the New World.

The first immigration of Catholics and Jews to America, began in the 1600s. Jews arrived in New Amsterdam in 1654 as refugees from the Inquisition. At about the same time the colony of Maryland became a haven for Roman Catholics who were not welcome in other parts of the new English colonies. Later in the nineteenth and twentieth centuries, millions of Jews and Catholics came to the United States, That mass movement changed some long held perceptions and stereotypes, but it did not fundamentally alter the basic outlook and teachings about each other.

Irish Catholics, Italian Catholics, and Polish Catholics began to meet Jews, often in the same schools and workplaces. Indeed, that encounter usually took place in the neighborhoods of many American cities including New York City, Boston, Chicago, Philadelphia, Detroit, Baltimore, Pittsburgh, Cleveland, and a host of others.

A pragmatic co-existence set in thanks to the expanding American economy and thanks also to the unique American experiment in religious pluralism. There is, by Constitutional law and practice, no established religion in this land, no control of the religious communities by the government, and, conversely, no control of the government, especially its police and educational institutions, by any religious group. Government, though neutral in law, is, however, most hospitable to religions in America.

Catholics and Jews were often the victims of prejudice and discrimination in the United States. Living in the same poor urban neighborhoods, and usually surrounded by hostile elite ruling groups, Catholics and Jews formed a mutual bond of friendship in the face of a common adversary. The shared immigrant experience drew the two communities together.

But the perceptions that had been shaped in nearly two thousand years of history still existed in America. Mutual suspicion and theological bias still combined to keep Catholics and Jews separated and distrustful.

The catastrophic events of the Nazi Holocaust in the years 1933–45, the systematic destruction of six million Jewish men, women, and children in the heart of Christian Europe, staggered both Catholics and Jews. The loss in human terms is beyond measurement, and many believe the moral questions raised by the Holocaust are beyond human comprehension or meaning.

When it became clear that hundreds of thousands of baptized Christians had committed murderous acts against the kinspeople of Jesus, and that Christian churches had been mainly silent in the face of Nazism, it was apparent that a line of cosmic importance had been irrevocably crossed. Systemic evil had triumphed over Christian moral teachings.

Only three years after the end of the Holocaust, an independent and democratic Jewish State emerged in the Middle East. The rebirth of Israel in 1948 was for many Christians a refutation of a long held theology. The despised surplus people had risen from the actual ashes of Auschwitz and had re-entered history as a free and sovereign people in their own land.

The creation of Israel meant that Jews and Christians had crossed into a new and uncharted relationship. Before 1948, Christians could still maintain that Jerusalem, the Holy City, was a heavenly, an abstract reality. But after 1948, and surely after the 1967 Middle East war, Jerusalem, the Holy City, had clearly entered into the earthly realm as the capital of Israel, a city under the sovereignty of the Jewish people. And Rome, the Eternal City, the city of the Vatican, the city of Peter was once more inextricably linked to Jewish Jerusalem in ways it had never experienced since the time of Jesus and Paul. Clearly, as the popular expression goes, "something had to give." Roman Catholic-Jewish relations were on the verge of a tremendous breakthrough, and it was not long in coming.

Only three months after his coronation, Pope John XXIII had a captivating thought. "Without ever having thought of it before . . . the words 'ecumenical council' (were) contrary to all my suppositions or imaginations on the subject. The first to be amazed by this proposal of mine was I myself . . ." The date was January 20, 1959, and the Pope referred to the idea as "a little holy madness." The rest, as they say, is history.

On October 28, 1965 after three years of intense work, debate, and struggle, the world's Catholic Bishops at the Second Vatican Council issued the landmark *Nostra Aetate* declaration dealing with the Jewish people. Before and during the Council's deliberations, the American Jewish Committee played a prominent role. The AJC provided Vatican officials with scholarly documentation that traced the nearly two thousand years of the Catholic teaching of contempt toward Jews and Judaism, and the Committee made many other significant contributions as well. The AJC record was a positive and constructive one.

It is always important to stress that *Nostra Aetate* is directed at Christians, not at Jews. It does not, as some critics in 1965 charged, "forgive" the Jews for their alleged "crime" of deicide. The text says no such thing! *Nostra Aetate* does not forgive anyone, but lays down an authoritative teaching and repudiates the false belief that Jews are collectively guilty of deicide and doomed to wander the face of the earth for their "sin."

Since 1965 many important and far reaching Roman Catholic statements and guidelines on Christian-Jewish relations have been promulgated. Catholic Bishops in Latin America, the Netherlands, Belgium, France, Switzerland, West Germany, and Brazil (the country with the world's largest Catholic population) have all issued strong statements going beyond *Nostra Aetate* in calling for improved relations. The German Bishops confessed: "We turned our backs . . . and were silent about the crimes" committed against the Jewish people during the Holocaust. The Brazilian Bishops called for a safe and secure State of Israel. The Vatican published an important set of "Guidelines" in 1975 that gave specificity to the pronouncements of ten years earlier.

The post-1965 documents have broadened and strengthened Catholic-Jewish relations, but they were all set in motion by *Nostra Aetate*. Like the Magna Carta, the Declaration of Independence, and the U.S. Constitution, *Nostra Aetate* broke new ground and provided the mandate for constructive change. Pope John Paul II, in a February 1985 meeting in Rome with an American Jewish Committee delegation, declared that "relationships between Jews and Christians have radically improved" since 1965. Mutual stereotypes and caricatures have been shattered. There have been more positive encounters since 1965 than there were in the first nineteen hundred years of the Church.

Think back the way it was before 1965. In most communities Catholic clergy would not attend or participate in a non-Catholic religious service. The Church often appeared to sympathetic non-Catholics as distrustful, suspicious, even fearful of the outside world. But Vatican II broke down the self-imposed ghetto walls and allowed the Church to enter and to engage the modern world.

In 1967 the American Catholic Bishops established a Secretariat on Catholic-Jewish relations. Its first Executive Secretary was Father Edward H. Flannery, truly a legend in his time, and the current Executive Secretary is the extremely gifted Dr. Eugene J. Fisher. Courses of Jewish instruction are now a regular part of many Catholic colleges and universities, and great progress is currently taking place in major seminaries.

Jewish and Catholic seminary students, the men and women who will be the religious leaders of the twenty-first century, are gaining mutual respect and understanding as part of their theological training. What Christian seminarians learn about Jews and Judaism will profoundly affect their future ministries. Courses of instruction that stress post-Biblical Judaism, Jewish religious thought, the Holocaust, the State of Israel, and the contemporary interreligious encounter will enrich the Christian clergy of the future. Conversely, rabbinical students need to learn more about Christians and Christianity during their seminary years. We are all residents of a rapidly shrinking and increasingly pluralistic "global village." It is crucial that religious leaders gain an accurate picture of the "other."

In addition, most American Catholic textbooks used in parochial schools have been purged of anti-Jewish material, and anti-Semitic prayers are being removed from the Church's liturgy.

A nun, Sister Ann Gillen, leads the National Interreligious Task Force on Soviet Jewry. Jews teach about their religion and history in Los Angeles parochial schools. American Catholics and Jews work jointly on shared concerns: immigration, refugees, preventing nuclear war, aiding the poor and homeless, religious liberty, human rights, combating hunger.

Since Vatican II, thousands of lay Catholics and Jews have participated in intensive "livingroom dialogues" throughout the United States. These dialogues have focused on classic interreligious themes like Scripture and theology, as well as on contemporary questions. A network of Catholics and Jews has developed a deep trust relationship in many American communities.

Vatican II, although a Roman Catholic Council, has also had a profound impact upon the Protestant Christian community. Enormous energy has been released as Protestants and Catholics have drawn closer together, and Vatican II has provided a major impetus for improved Protestant-Jewish relations. Vatican II was everyone's council. Its influence and impact have been universal.

Of course, Catholics and Jews still differ on deeply held theological issues, as we will continue to do until the end of time. And as members of the same family, equally beloved by God, we also differ on some other issues as well. But isn't that the way it always is with members of the same family? We love each other, but we are also quite different from one another.

Catholics and Jews need to jointly address what Cardinal Joseph Bernardin of Chicago has so felicitously termed the "seamless garment" of life; those issues of life and death that affect all of us. The Cardinal's language allows us to move away from a fevered discussion of a single issue, be it abortion, birth control, or capital punishment. The "seamless garment" approach permits us to face awesome bio-ethical questions together. Should life sustaining equipment be removed from a terminally ill patient? What do Catholics and Jews believe about embryo transplants? What are the moral implications of medical "triage"? These questions, and many others, demand a compassionate and informed response from the religious community, and Catholics and Jews need to be at the forefront in shaping public policy on these issues.

Questions of church and state including possible tuition tax credits for parents who send their children to private or parochial schools, prayer in the public schools, sectarian symbols such as a crèche that are placed on public property—all these and more need to be addressed by Catholics and Jews together.

The American Bishops' Pastoral Letters on peace and war and the U.S. economy have stimulated important Catholic-Jewish discussions on these vital themes. Once again, the religious communities are asserting their moral authority on issues of transcendent importance.

The ever present pathology of anti-Semitism is unfortunately still a part of Christian-Jewish relations. Pope John Paul II, citing the teachings of *Nostra Aetate*, sharply attacked the evil of anti-Semitism in his meeting with the AJC leaders in early 1985: "Anti-Semitism . . . has been repeatedly condemned by the Catholic tradition as incompatible with Christ's teaching . . . Where there was ignorance and . . . prejudice . . . there is now growing mutual knowledge, appreciation, and respect.'' One of the lasting major achievements of Vatican II has been the affirmation of Judaism as an eternal living faith by the Catholic Church.

Despite the extraordinary gains in building positive relationships, many Jews believe that Roman Catholics do not yet fully grasp the profound meaning that the State of Israel has for Jews everywhere. A free Jewish State with Jerusalem as its capital represents the core of Jewish existence and aspirations. Today Israel is at the center of every serious Christian-Jewish encounter.

Israeli Prime Minister Golda Meir formally met with Pope Paul VI, and in 1985 Prime Minister Shimon Peres met with Pope John Paul II. A de facto recognition currently exists between the Vatican and Israel. There is a great deal of communication and contact between Rome and Jerusalem. Nonetheless, the Vatican has not yet established formal diplomatic relations with the Jewish State.

Many Catholics and Jews believe that such an act would be a major contribution to the Middle East peace process. Formal relations would give a strong signal to Israel's enemies that the Roman Catholic Church has fully affirmed the permanence and the legitimacy of Israel's membership within the family of nations.

The Vatican's role during the Holocaust and in the years immediately following World War II remains a focus of controversy. Charges and countercharges swirl about, centering on what the Vatican allegedly did or did not do in that tumultuous period. Critics have charged that the Vatican could and should have done much more to combat the anti-Semitism of Nazism. They have further charged that the Vatican provided a haven and a means of escape for Nazi war criminals after 1945. Catholic and Jewish scholars need to work together in a cooperative effort to study that crucial period of history. An intensive joint effort is clearly called for, and Vatican II has provided the mandate for such a serious and systematic study.

Until the liberating force of Vatican II and *Nostra Aetate,* the Catholic Church was locked into a self-imposed ghetto, a barrier against the modern world. Vatican II broke down the ghetto walls, or, to use Pope John XXIII's striking imagery, the Church opened a window to the world.

Both Jews and Catholics suffered because of this self-imposed ghetto. Jews often suffered with the loss of their lives, while Roman Catholics often suffered a spiritual deprivation. Victim and victimizer—both suffered, but in different ways.

How painful it was for my people! Their cries and whispers still haunt us and drive us forward in the work of improving interreligious relations. How painful it must have been for Catholics, who were trapped in a theology that often had to defame and sometimes even physically attack another people to legitimize its own existence. As God's children both communities deserve better.

Even though we will continue to hold different theological beliefs, and even though we may differ on certain contemporary issues and questions, *Nostra Aetate* has freed Catholics and Jews from the tight chains of the past. We can now move together to higher ground. This generation has the rare opportunity to chart the course of Catholic-Jewish relations for the next century, and perhaps beyond.

We are all children of Vatican II. It has irreversibly changed the way we look at one another. We commemorate the Council's twentieth anniversary not as an exercise in nostalgia, but rather as a mandate for further positive change.

Twenty Years of Catholic-Jewish Relations
Nostra Aetate in Retrospect

REV. MSGR. GEORGE G. HIGGINS

Early in the first session of Vatican II, a copy of a vicious anti-Semitic tract, running to several hundred pages and expensively printed and bound, was distributed out of nowhere to each of the two thousand-odd Bishops attending the Council. Entitled "The Plot Against the Church," it was written in Italian and bore the imprint of an Italian publishing house which no one had ever heard of before. The Bishops never found out where the book came from or who wrote it, for there was no return address on the wrappers, and the name of the alleged author, Maurice Pinay, like the name of the alleged publisher, was obviously a pen name.

Most of the Bishops with whom I was in personal contact at the Council disgustedly threw the book in the wastebasket once they had discovered, in leafing through it, that it was the work of a paranoid or a group of paranoids who had an almost psychopathic hatred for Jews—and not only for Jews, but also for an alleged fifth column of traitorous cardinals, archbishops and bishops "who are the unconditional tools of Communism and of the secret power directing it (and) . . . form a kind of 'progressive' wing within the Council (and) . . . will attempt to bring about a breakthrough of shameful reforms, whereby the good faith and eagerness for progress of many devout Council Fathers will be deceived."

As a matter of fact, so few of the English-speaking Bishops saved their copies of the book that I had great trouble in salvaging one for future reference. I finally ran into a Bishop who still had a copy of the book in his room at the hotel in which we were both staying at the time, but who hadn't even bothered to unwrap it. When he discovered what it was about, I think he would have been happy to pay me to get it out of his sight, although he must have wondered why I or anyone else would want to keep a copy of the book under any circumstances.

To make a long story short, when I eventually got around to reading the book, I realized, as never before, why the Jewish community, even in a plur-

19

alistic society as free and open as our own, is still deeply concerned about the threat of anti-Semitism and has yet to be persuaded that this threat was ended, once and for all, with the downfall of Hitler and the collapse of Nazism. The fact is that Hitler and his Nazi gauleiters had nothing on the group of fanatical anti-Semites who put this miserable tract together and then didn't even have the courage to sign their name to it.

These were sick people—very sick indeed. They had convinced themselves and tried desperately to convince the Council Fathers that "behind Communism, Freemasonry and behind every action which is directed at the destruction of Christian civilization stands Jewry as head of the octopus, which must be destroyed if one wishes to effectively defeat the arms—Communism, Freemasonry, Socialism, and the other sects. For if the head of the octopus is not attacked, the arms can grow again." This, being translated into basic English, meant that "Jewry" must be completely destroyed in the name of Christianity.

Those Gentiles in the United States who may be inclined to make light of the Pinay book on the grounds that it was published in Europe more than twenty years ago by a small group of obviously unbalanced extremists and was therefore irrelevant to our own situation in the United States will want to know that an English-language edition of the book is still circulating under the imprint of the St. Anthony Press (obviously another false front) and is being distributed by the "Christian Book Club of America."

The moral of all this is that, while some Gentiles may complacently think that there is no market in the U.S. for this kind of psychopathic anti-Semitism, the anonymous authors and promoters of the Pinay book and similar screeds see the situation differently. They are still intermittently carrying on an advertising campaign and obviously hope to be able to sell at least enough copies of their wares to get back the tainted money which they have invested in this obscene operation.

The best way for American Catholics to counteract this sort of anti-Semitic propaganda is to concentrate on implementing the Vatican Council's Declaration on Catholic-Jewish Relations promulgated twenty years ago this fall. This Declaration is by far the shortest of all the documents voted on by the Council Fathers. And yet, in the long run, it may well prove to be one of the most important documents of the entire Council.

The very fact that it ran into so many obstacles and nerve-wracking delays during the four suspense-ridden years that it was on the agenda of the Council is one more proof that it was badly needed.

From the very beginning there was never any doubt as to how the overwhelming majority of the Council Fathers would vote on the Declaration, but so persistent was the behind-the-scenes opposition to it on the part of certain political forces in the Near East and, from the theological point of view, from a minority of theologians and Council Fathers, that one could never be absolutely certain, until the very end, that it would ever come up for a definitive vote.

In any event, on the occasion of its twentieth anniversary, Catholics and Jews alike will want to see it in the long perspective of the future. In other words, they will want to bear in mind that when Pope Paul solemnly promulgated the Declaration on October 28, 1965, he was, in effect, writing finis, not to a book, but only to the preface of the first of a long series of volumes which will not be completed for many years.

This is merely another way of saying that, while the Declaration, alas, cannot undo the past, with all its bitter memories of hatred and persecution of Jews by Christians, it can, by the grace of God, help to usher in a new era of "mutual knowledge and respect which," in the words of the Declaration, "is the fruit, above all, of biblical and theological studies as well as of fraternal dialogues."

If our Jewish neighbors and friends will bear in mind that this is the long-range purpose of the Declaration, perhaps they will find it easier to live with the fact that, from their point of view, it is not a perfect document. Of course it isn't a perfect document. The fact remains, however, that, in spite of its imperfections—which were just as disappointing to this writer and to many of the Council Fathers as they are to our Jewish friends—it is, on the whole, a good Declaration and one which, to repeat, holds out great promise for the future.

This promise will only be fulfilled, however, if Catholics, too, bear in mind that the solemn promulgation of the document was not the end of the story, but only the beginning. It is up to us to take the lead in fostering "mutual knowledge and respect" and in looking for opportunities to engage in fraternal dialogue with our Jewish fellow-citizens.

In saying this, I mean to stress the fact that the Declaration was addressed to Christians. It was intended to clarify Christian teaching in areas where, in a more or less remote past, an anti-Jewish tone had deformed the pure presentation of the Gospel. The statement, therefore, was a Christian affair and represented an examination of the Christian conscience.

Misleading newspaper headlines to the contrary notwithstanding, the Declaration did not "absolve" the Jewish people of anything. That would have been an unconscionable insult to the Jewish community. Moreover, as Gregory Baum points out in his excellent commentary on the Declaration, the Council "had no intention of telling the Jewish people who they are. There would have been something aggressive, or at least condescending, about a Christian Church intending to tell the Jews whether or in what sense they were God's chosen people . . . . If Jewish readers understood the text as addressed to them, it is not surprising that some of them were disturbed and slightly insulted."

My own experience in meeting in recent years with a representative cross-section of Jewish leaders leads me to believe that some of them do think that the Declaration was addressed to the Jews.

This is rather disturbing, for if Jews mistakenly think that the Declaration was addressed to them and was meant, insultingly and condescendingly, to "absolve" them from responsibility for the Crucifixion, they will understandably be very reluctant to enter into dialogue with Christians. And, by the same token, if Christians fail to understand that the Declaration was meant to be a sincere examination of the Christian conscience—which has so much to answer for in this area—they will be ill-prepared for the kind of dialogue which is so strongly recommended in the document.

Fortunately, however, popular misconceptions about the nature and purpose of the Council's Declaration are gradually being cleared up as time goes on. Although the wording of the Declaration leaves something to be desired, many Jews would agree with Baum when he says that it "may well turn out to be a turning point in the history of Jewish-Christian relations."

The Declaration stresses the spiritual patrimony common to Christians and Jews. Since this patrimony is so great, the Council, by means of the Declaration, "wants to foster and recommend that mutual understanding and respect which is the fruit, above all, of biblical and theological studies as well as of fraternal dialogues."

From time to time in the past, there had been Christian-Jewish dialogues in this country on social and cultural issues of mutual interest, but rarely, if ever, until after the Council did Christians and Jews get together at any level to talk about biblical and theological matters. They are doing so frequently at the present time and are likely to do so much more frequently in the future, for there is a growing awareness on the part of both groups that if each is to be fully itself, Judaism and Christianity must meet on the plane of theological encounter.

One of the first fruits in the United States of this growing awareness, which, in a limited way, antedated the Council, was a book, *Torah and Gospel: Jewish and Catholic Theology in Dialogue,* edited by Philip Scharper and published by Sheed and Ward. This book grew out of a symposium of Catholic and Jewish scholars held in January 1965, at St. Vincent's Abbey, Latrobe, Pennsylvania. The papers delivered at that historic meeting were reprinted in *Torah and Gospel,* with an Introduction by Mr. Scharper.

Mr. Scharper also attempted "to convey to the reader . . . something of this warmth as well as the wisdom" of the Latrobe symposium by reprinting Bishop William C. Connare's welcome to the participants and the remarks with which the late Rabbi Arthur Gilbert brought the meeting to a close. Each stressed "the importance of the climate of comradeship which made this symposium not merely an academic exercise but a shared religious experience."

The appearance of *Torah and Gospel* several months before the Declaration was promulgated was a publishing event of great importance. We owe Mr. Scharper and his associates a vote of sincere thanks for their initiative in moving ahead so rapidly to implement both the letter and the spirit of the Declaration.

We are also indebted to the now defunct Bruce Publishing Company for the timely publication shortly thereafter of an equally important book, *The Star and the Cross: Essays on Jewish-Christian Relations,* edited by Mother Katherine Hargrove, R.S.C.J., then associate professor of religion at Manhattanville College, Purchase, New York. Mother Hargrove, like the Fathers of the Council and the participants in the Latrobe symposium, was convinced that the time had come for Christians and Jews to begin the dialogue at the level of biblical and theological studies as well as at the level of civic and social matters. She was persuaded that Jews will become better Jews and Christians would be stronger in their own faith if each made a genuine effort to understand the religious beliefs of the other.

With this end in view, she brought together a series of essays written by prominent Christian and Jewish authors, including some of the contributors to the Sheed and Ward volume, *Torah and Gospel.*

In the book's first part (Unity), the essays stressed the bonds that link Jews and Christians together especially in the pluralistic society that is America. These essays served as an introduction to the second part (Tension), where the gloves were taken off, so to speak, and some extremely frank comments were made on issues which then divided Jews and Christians and were causing animosity and hostility between the two groups.

Among the topics discussed were anti-Semitism, Christian teachings that instill contempt for the Jews and vice versa, the apathy of Christians during the Nazi persecution, and the touchy subjects brought to light in Vatican II during the debate on the Declaration. Here, too, Mother Hargrove skillfully included essays probing inter-marriage between Gentiles and Jews, religious authority, secularism and Jewry.

The book's final part (Toward a Deeper Unity) offered several perceptive essays stressing better relations between Christians and Jews. Highlighting this section was a moving essay by Mother Hargrove that will impress the reader with its depth of knowledge resulting from months of research by its author.

The simultaneous publication of these two very important books—*Torah and Gospel* and *The Star and the Cross*—got us off to a running start in the implementation of the Council's Declaration on Christian-Jewish Relations and served to indicate that the pessimism of those who feared that American

Catholicism was going to lag behind Europe in carrying out the aggiornamento was not well founded.

In this connection, I might add, to the best of my knowledge, the United States is doing far more than any other country in the world to implement the Declaration. We are not doing enough, of course, but, in any event, we have made a good beginning. Suffice it to mention, merely by way of example, the effective work of the Secretariat for Catholic-Jewish Relations of the National Conference of Catholic Bishops, so ably administered by Father Edward Flannery and Dr. Eugene Fisher, respectively; the scholarly writings of Msgr. John Oesterreicher, Father John Pawlikowski, Father Ronald Modras, Dr. Leonard Swidler, and many others; the proliferation of diocesan, regional, and national Christian-Jewish workshops; several scholarly studies on the strengths and weaknesses of Catholic textbooks in the area of Catholic-Jewish relations; and similar scholarly studies on ways and means of reforming certain liturgical practices in the light of *Nostra Aetate.*

Another book published shortly after the Council that dealt with the Christian-Jewish dialogue in the United States was a controversial sociological study by Charles Y. Glock and Rodney Stark of the University of California, Berkeley, entitled *Christian Beliefs and Anti-Semitism.*

In summary, Glock and Stark concluded in this work that there is a significant correlation between religious beliefs and anti-Semitism. They also seemed to assume that anti-Semitism, if conjoined with religious opinions unfavorable to Jews, is always the result of the latter. A number of competent scholars, both Catholic and non-Catholic, questioned this assumption and, beyond that, questioned the overall methodology of the Glock-Stark study.

As an amateur sociologist, I, too, had certain reservations about the methodology employed by Glock and Stark. On the other hand, I had no reason to think that they exaggerated the extent of Christian anti-Semitism in the United States. On the contrary, it appeared that, if anything, their findings on this score may have been somewhat conservative.

Be that as it may, the continuing controversy over the Glock-Stark study quickly took a potentially dangerous turn. Two well-known Protestant commentators publicly stated that the Gospels themselves were the root cause of Christian anti-Semitism. And at least one of them concluded, in doctrinaire fashion, that the only way to eliminate Christian anti-Semitism was to rewrite the New Testament. The two men in question were Professor Roy Eckhardt of Lehigh University, Bethlehem, Pennsylvania, and Dr. Donald S. Harrington, pastor of the Community Church, New York City.

Professor Eckhardt, speaking at an international Jewish-Christian conference in Cambridge, England, was reported to have attacked the Gospels rather bitterly. Indiscriminate denunciation of the Jews in the New Testament, he said, is linked inextricably with the most anti-Semitic diatribes of modern times.

Dr. Harrington went even further in his denunciation of the New Testament. In the very first sentence of his review of the Glock-Stark study Harrington asked: "Is there any way short of the complete rewriting of the Christian Gospels and recasting of Christian theology to eliminate the monstrous evil of anti-Semitism?" His own answer to this question was a very emphatic "No." "There is no possible hope of eliminating the evil of Christian anti-Semitism," he said, until "the poison in the Gospels is recognized as poison, even if it does occur in what is believed to be the Word of God."

Harrington did not indicate whether or not he himself believed that the Gospels are the Word of God, but I think it would be fair to infer that he did not. The New Testament writings, he said, must be read in "their historical context, for the valuable but limited, and often fallible and even destructive (sic) writings that they are."

Eckhardt and Harrington are to be commended for their vigorous, not to say violent opposition to all forms of anti-Semitism, the most monstrous of which, of course, is that diabolical contradiction in terms known as "Christian" anti-Semitism. On the other hand, their proposed remedy for this evil—namely, the complete rewriting of the Gospels—was almost too bizarre to be taken seriously. If they had been content to say, as Harrington did in passing, that the New (as well as the Old) Testament writings must be read in their proper historical context, they would have found widespread, if not universal, agreement on the part of Catholic and Protestant scholars alike. It is obvious, in other words, that our exegesis or explanation of certain New Testament references to "the Jews" is in need of refinement.

At long last, this problem is now being tackled seriously by Catholic and Protestant exegetes throughout the world. Hopefully the impetus given to biblical scholarship by Vatican Council II will embolden them to get on with the job without delay. Cardinal Bea, incidentally, set the pace for them with his semi-popular but scholarly commentary on the Council's Declaration on Christian-Jewish Relations, the English edition of which was published on or about the tenth anniversary of the Declaration.

But to exegete or explain the Gospels in their proper historical context is not to edit or rewrite them, nor is it to agree with the Eckhardt-Harrington assumption that the Gospels are the root cause of Christian anti-Semitism. As Dr. Albert Polack, a prominent Jewish scholar from Great Britain, told the Cambridge conference, in direct reply to Professor Eckhardt, any such accusation would do more harm than good for interdenominational relations.

It should be noted, in this connection, that Glock and Stark themselves did not make this accusation and did not advocate the rewriting of the New

Testament. On the contrary, they explicitly rejected the Harrington-Eckhardt thesis.

A number of Jewish scholars in addition to Dr. Polack—for example, Rabbi Marc Tanenbaum of the American Jewish Committee, speaking with Polack and Eckhardt at the Cambridge meeting—also rejected the Eckhardt-Harrington "solution" to the problem of Christian anti-Semitism.

The Glock-Stark study was also misinterpreted from the opposite point of view. John Birch officials severely criticized the study, saying that it told the public that "the more time Catholics and Protestants spend in church, the more anti-Semitic their feelings are."

"Nothing could be further from the truth," Arnold Forster, General Counsel of B'nai B'rith replied. "This was not a finding of the study," he said, "and the (Anti-Defamation) League never said it was." Forster charged that the Birch Society by its attacks on the study and on the ADL, is "not only contributing to anti-Semitism but is treading the path toward the lunatic fringe."

Mr. Forster's point was well taken. The Glock-Stark study most certainly did not say that "the more time Catholics and Protestants spend in church, the more anti-Semitic their feelings are." What it did say, in summary, was that an alarmingly high percentage of Christians are caught up in a process—"orthodoxy" to "particularism" to religious bigotry—which often culminated in secular anti-Semitism.

It is important to note that Glock and Stark did not maintain that there is an inexorable causal relationship between Christian beliefs and anti-Semitism. They merely said that their sociological studies indicated that for many Christians the relationship exists. Their book, as they clearly stated in the Introduction, "is not to be read as an indictment of religion." Moreover they readily admitted that the good will and serious concern of most Christian leaders has already been demonstrated. "It is not our intention," they said, "to castigate them if (our) findings implicate religion in contemporary anti-Semitism. Rather we hope to provide them with the necessary understanding to transform the churches into a reliable force in man's struggle to free himself from bigotry."

Meanwhile American Catholics at all levels will want to bear in mind that the Declaration is only the first step. As Gregory Baum points out in his commentary, "it now presents a challenge to the Church. What counts in the future is how soon the teaching of the Council enters our institutions and the hearts of our people, and how resourceful and enterprising we shall be in giving visible expression to the spiritual bond that unites the Church and the Jews."

Needless to add, this longed-for dialogue presupposes that Catholics, in the spirit of the Declaration, will first of all purge from their hearts any slightest trace of anti-Semitism—which, in any and all of its forms, is a blasphemous contradiction of both the letter and the spirit of the Gospel—and will forcefully reject, "as foreign to the mind of Christ, any discrimination against men or harassment of them because of their race, color, condition in life, or religion."

What a proud boast it will be for the Church in the United States, I wrote at the time the Declaration was promulgated, if our own bishops, priests, and faithful step out in front and set an example for the rest of the world in this regard. A year later, November 13, 1966, the late Cardinal Spellman pledged to a group of Jewish leaders that the Church in this country would do just that.

Cardinal Spellman made his remarks during an event, believed to be unprecedented in the history of America's religious communities, at which the American cardinals and some of the bishops assembled in Washington for the annual conference of the American Catholic bishops joined in a ceremony with leaders of the American Jewish Committee at a reception at the Catholic University of America in Washington, D. C.

The occasion was the presentation by the American Jewish Committee of commemorative plaques to the American cardinals and specifically to Cardinal O'Boyle of Washington, in his capacity as Chairman of the administrative board of the former National Catholic Welfare Conference (now the U. S. Catholic Conference) in "heartfelt appreciation" for the leadership given by American members of the Roman Catholic hierarchy in behalf of the passage by the Vatican Council of the "Jewish declaration," and of its implementation.

Cardinal Spellman's pledge that the Church in this country would do everything it possibly could to foster stronger and more extensive bonds of mutual understanding, respect and cooperation between Catholics and Jews was not an idle promise. The bishops of the United States had already established a special Secretariat for Catholic-Jewish Relations. This Secretariat shortly thereafter issued a set of practical guidelines aimed at fostering and promoting mutual understanding and esteem between Catholics and Jews, which, in the words of the Declaration, "will be the fruit, above all, of biblical and theological studies and of brotherly dialogues."

From time to time in the past, as noted above, there had been Christian-Jewish dialogues in this country on social and civic issues of mutual interest. This kind of cooperative effort, which was heartily endorsed and commended in the Secretariat's guidelines, is most heartening and undoubtedly will become even more widespread as time goes on. As already indicated, however, until very recently Catholics and Jews in the United States have rarely, if ever, come together at any level to talk about biblical and theological matters of mutual interest and concern. To repeat, however, they are likely to do so more in the future, for there is a growing awareness on the part of both groups that, if each is to be fully itself, Judaism and Christianity must meet, in a spirit of mutual respect and reciprocal love, on the plane of theology.

"It is evident," as the late Cardinal Bea pointed out in his book-length commentary on the Council's Declaration, "that such a dialogue requires not only a love of truth but also great humility and charity. One must not aim at triumphing over another or proving himself right, but simply at searching for truth and serving one's neighbor." The purpose of the dialogue, in other words, is not to proselytize or to "convert" the other party, but rather to help all of us, Catholics and Jews alike, to become more fully aware of our common spiritual patrimony.

In Bea's words, Christians and Jews "live by substantially the same faith (in the God of Abraham, Isaac, and Jacob) and shape their lives according to the same divine wisdom. They express their praise and adoration of God, their sorrow for their sins and their supplications in the same prayers inspired by the Spirit of God. They can both be said to follow, though in various degrees, the same course of divine instruction and education which is called the economy of salvation. Through it they come to a knowledge of the gradual revelation of the mystery of man's salvation, hidden in God throughout the ages, to long for and to seek its realization, though each travels towards it along a different road."

There is every reason to share Cardinal Bea's optimistic conviction that, with the help of God, "we can go the greater part of the way together." Indeed there is a growing consensus that we are under a solemn obligation to try to do so without delay.

Brotherly collaboration, at every level, between Christians and Jews, Bea pointed out, "is an urgent duty and necessity, both before God and before men. We have been given a talent which must not be buried but must be made to bear interest. In the Old Testament God had endowed us with a wealth of truth and wisdom about Himself, about man and about man's highest destiny, which he wishes to be shared by all men. No one who loves God and loves his fellow men can ever be resigned to the fact that hundreds of millions of men are still ignorant of these great truths and have no share in our inheritance.

"The task of dispelling this ignorance has become all the more urgent in view of the spread of both theoretical and practical atheism and of the systematic opposition to all religion, both of which imperil a man's hold on his most precious and sacred possession. The duty of those who have access to the treasure-house of the Old Testament is therefore all the more serious and urgent."

In the spirit of the Council's Declaration, the Church in this country has also vigorously opposed "as foreign to the mind of Christ, any discrimination against men or harassment of them because of their race, color, condition in life or religion." The Declaration, alas, cannot undo the past, with all of its bitter memories of hatred and persecution, but, by the grace of God, it can help to usher in a new era of "mutual knowledge and respect."

As I have already indicated, we can expect, as Cardinal Spellman pointed out, to encounter obstacles from time to time—as, for example, the misunderstanding which cropped up between some Christians and Jews in this country at the time of the six-day war. In the summer of 1967, in the wake of the Israeli-Arab War, it looked for a time as though we might be in for a major crisis in the area of Christian-Jewish relations and that the "dialogue" between Christians and Jews in the United States might have to be suspended indefinitely. A number of prominent Jewish spokesmen took the position that the "silence" of the Christian churches at the height of the Middle East crisis rendered any further dialogue between the two groups absolutely meaningless.

My own instincts told me at the time that the situation wasn't really as bad as all that and that the crisis in Christian-Jewish relations, however unpleasant it might prove to be in the short run, would probably do more good than harm over the long haul. If nothing else, I thought, it would help to clear the air and, hopefully, would also help to move the dialogue to a new plane.

I thought that in spite of the fact that a leading Jewish spokesman—Dr. Jacob Neusner, Professor of Religion at Dartmouth College—stated that "few, if any, serious Jews, excluding those whose professional responsibilities require them to engage in dialogue, are now prepared to renew the conversations (between Christians and Jews) which have flourished in the past."

These were strong words, but I was prepared to take it on the authority of Rabbi Arthur Hertzberg that they did not represent the dominant view among American Jews, once the dust had settled. The fact that a man of Rabbi Hertzberg's standing in the Jewish community publicly disassociated himself from Dr. Neusner's pessimistic point of view with regard to the future of the Christian-Jewish dialogue was most significant, for in the summer of 1967, at the height of the Middle East crisis, Hertzberg himself, by his own admission, was also strongly tempted to call it quits.

In the immediate aftermath of the crisis, however, he was much more optimistic than Dr. Neusner about the future of the dialogue. "The overwhelming majority of the very rabbis who pushed their Christian colleagues hardest in May and June, 1967," he wrote, "have come to a different view of both the usefulness and even the achievements of the dialogue. In the first place, that we could continue to talk at all, and that we kept coming back to talk some more, in the midst of a situation that was laden with deep and explosive emotions, was in itself a great new fact. Enough relationship had been built up in recent years between responsible Jews and Christians that we remained in the same rooms even when we were very angry with each other."

Rabbi Balfour Brickner, then with the Union of American Hebrew Congregations, Rabbi Marc Tanenbaum of the American Jewish Committee, Dr. Joseph Lichten of the Anti-Defamation League, the late Rabbi Arthur Gilbert and a number of other Jewish leaders tended to agree with Rabbi Hertzberg in this regard. In other words, they tended to go along with Hertzberg when he said that "the very fact that we were so angry in June of 1967 has convinced both Jews and Christians not to end the discussion but that it needs to be pursued in depth."

Richard L. Rubenstein made the same point in a remarkably frank article, "Did Christians Fail Israel?" in *Commonweal.* "I can understand those rabbis who lost their cool," he wrote. "Nevertheless, I think they were profoundly mistaken in their responses. If the recent events demonstrate anything, they exhibit the greater need for forthright Judaeo-Christian dialogue. Nothing in what has happened can justify an end to dialogue. As we get to know each other we will undoubtedly discover ever deeper layers of similarity and difference between us."

For my own part, I strongly argued then and would argue even more strongly today that the "silence" of the Christian churches in the summer of 1967 is an argument for rather than against the dialogue. By this I mean that one of the reasons that support by Christian groups for Israel of the type and to the extent that the Jewish community had expected, was not forthcoming is that Christians, generally speaking, did not then and do not now fully understand what Israel means to Jews in theological terms. Jews themselves are the only ones who can help us to overcome this gap in our knowledge. This means that we need more rather than less Christian-Jewish dialogue. It also means that the dialogue must, in the future, include a profound study of the theological meaning of Israel from the Jewish point of view. Unfortunately this issue was generally avoided or side-stepped in pre-1967 Christian-Jewish seminars. It is my impression, however, that both parties to the dialogue now agree that it must be placed at the very top of their agenda.

The willingness of so many distinguished Jewish leaders to begin the dialogue anew and to pursue it in even greater depth was a most encouraging development. In view of what happened in June 1967, and again, to a lesser extent, during the Yom Kippur war, they might have been tempted to cut their losses, so to speak, and to withdraw from the dialogue until further notice. Instead, they again extended the hand of friendship to their Christian colleagues. I admired them for doing so, and was pleased that so many of their opposite numbers in the Catholic community were equally ready and anxious to take up where we had left at the time of the six-day war and to make up for lost time as rapidly as possible. Rabbi Hertzberg warned us that we might find at first that the dialogue will now be "less agreeable." He was right about that, but he was also right when he added that it would also be "more open . . . and more constructive."

I thought it was most encouraging, too, that Rabbi Arthur Gilbert re-·flected this guardedly optimistic point of view in his book, *The Vatican Council and the Jews.*

Gilbert was critical of the Declaration in certain particulars, but, on balance, he thought it represented a most significant breakthrough and was a very hopeful omen for the future of Catholic-Jewish relations. To his credit, he consistently leaned over backward to be scrupulously fair in stating his disappointment with certain Catholic opponents of the Declaration and with certain Jewish critics of the finished product. He could not possibly have been more objective in his handling of such a controversial matter.

As I have already indicated, Rabbi Gilbert had certain reservations about the Declaration, but in spite of these reservations—and in spite of die-hard criticism of the document in certain Jewish circles—he was reasonably optimistic about the future of Catholic-Jewish relations. "The council's decree," he wrote, "must be seen as a moment in a dynamic process within the church, rather than as a fixed and frozen expression of Catholic policy . . . . The statement is a tool that can be used to fashion a more sophisticated theology of Jewish-Christian relations." He concluded his scholarly study of the Declaration with a fervent prayer that both Christians and Jews will be worthy of their calling "to repair the world" and to "increase the experience of godliness among men."

The Vatican's Guidelines on Catholic-Jewish Relations were intended to promote this long overdue objective. That is to say, they were intended to implement the Declaration. Like the Declaration itself, the Guidelines reaffirmed, in even stronger language, the Church's condemnation of anti-Semitism and called for sweeping action to eliminate all forms of discrimination against the Jews that might be found in the Church's worship and catechesis. The Guidelines also called for dialogue between Catholics and Jews, affirmation of a joint biblical and theological heritage, and a strong emphasis on "common elements of the liturgical life" as means for improving relations between Catholics and Jews.

Among other things, they appealed for Catholic respect for the "Jews' faith and their religious convictions," warned against comparing the Old Testament unfavorably to the New Testament, stressed that "it is the same God" who speaks through Abraham, Moses and Jesus, and urged a common quest for social justice.

The statement of response to the Guidelines issued by the International Jewish Committee on Interreligious Consultations was cautiously affirmative. On the one hand, it predicted that the Guidelines would lead to better understanding between Catholics and Jews. It also applauded the Vatican's stand on anti-Semitism. On the other hand, it noted with regret that the Guidelines failed to include a reference to Israel and left unanswered the question of whether Jews were to be viewed as needing conversion to Christianity.

I agree with the committee on the question of Israel. In other words, to return to a point I have already touched upon, I wish that the Vatican Commission, in calling upon Catholics "to learn by what essential traits the Jews define themselves in the light of their own religious experience," had openly declared that this admonition, in the words of the Jewish statement of response, "requires an acknowledgement of the central role of peoplehood in Jewish religious thought and of the consequent religious character of the historic attachment of the Jewish people to the land of Israel."

In this connection, let me quote briefly from Father Thomas Stransky's commentary on the Vatican Guidelines:

> Israel is not on the list. The omission is surprising. Since the guidelines insist that "Christians must strive to learn by what essential traits the Jews define themselves in the light of their own religious experience," then indeed we must see the Jews not as a church or a denomination but as a people sustained by a faith that Land is the visible expression of the Faithful God who wills by covenant the permanence of the Jewish people.
>
> Again a gulf in sensitivity? As the Christian sees the distinction in his own faith between the sacred and the political more clearly, his sensitivity to the place of Israel in Jewish belief and experience can become blunted.
>
> Theologically, what is the relationship between the People, the Land, the State of Israel, and specific political ideologies? There is certainly no Catholic consensus (nor Jewish?), and the guidelines chose deliberate silence. But a spectrum of varying Church views or pastoral worry about partisan political misinterpretations should not exclude the clear question. To be positive, the very highlighting of the omission will, I hope, prod the dialogue to give the question higher priority.

The need to do just that has been clearly acknowledged by Catholic leaders in the United States and other countries and will undoubtedly be strongly re-emphasized in future statements coming from official Catholic agencies in this country.

While I agreed with the authors of the Jewish statement of response on this particular issue, I thought they might have been unduly alarmed about the so-called "conversion" issue. The Vatican strongly denied that it had any intention of proselytizing in the "fraternal talks" between Catholics and Jews advocated in the Guidelines. I thought then, and still think, that our Jewish friends would be well advised to take the Vatican at its word in this regard. On the other hand, given the tragic history of Catholic-Jewish relations, I can readily understand why the Jewish people are so concerned about the conversion issue.

In any event, Catholic proponents of the dialogue most certainly do not see as one of its purposes the "submergence" of Judaism as a living faith or the "conversion" of Jews to Christianity. In the authoritative words of the late Father Cornelius Rijk, formerly in charge of the Catholic-Jewish desk in the Vatican's Secretariat for Christian Unity, "Israel has its own authenticity and identity which it preserves, and this it does according to the plan of God whose gifts are without repentance and whose call is irrevocable. . . . Israel has a concrete, complex, and religious reality outside the Christian order, has its own function in the plan of divine salvation. . . . In true fidelity to its vocation and election Israel will survive."

Conversion, Father Rijk continued, "is necessary for both Jews and Christians. It means the conversion of the heart to the Lord to obey his commandments more faithfully. It does not mean changing from one religion to another, but discovering more clearly God's plan of salvation, and following the ways of His providence. This teaching about conversion is certainly very much needed by Christians; particularly in their attitude and behaviour towards Jews is radical conversion needed. In such attitude of sincere conversion and real penance, we will, perhaps, receive the grace of discovering the mystery of Israel and its relation to the Church."

I am confident that all of the American Catholics who are promoting the dialogue completely concur in these forthright statements by Father Rijk on the nature and the purpose of the dialogue. I am certain that they would also concur with Father Rijk when he added, quoting a fellow Dutchman, that "for the first hundred years, Christians must be silent in their contact with Jews, and just listen and learn."

Returning to the Vatican guidelines, I also think that Rabbi Marc Tanenbaum of the American Jewish Committee, a good friend and highly esteemed collaborator, may have overshot the mark when he said in the course of a separate statement of response that the Vatican guidelines "implied a religious 'second class status' (for Judaism) in the family of faith communities."

I did not find any such implication in the guidelines although I must admit that the document was not as clear on this issue as it might have been.

Be that as it may, I fully agree with Father Edward Flannery that the guidelines do not impugn the integrity of Judaism and share his view that the document "will open new doors and give impetus to the course of the relations between the faiths."

In summary, while the Vatican guidelines may have been incomplete in some respects and ambiguous in others, I think they represented a significant step in the right direction and, in Father Flannery's words, provided "the basis for genuine dialogue between the Church and the synagogue." In the past, this dialogue, more often than not, has been initiated by the Jewish Community. The time has come for Catholics to reverse this process and to take the lead, vigorously and without further delay, in promoting better Catholic-Jewish relations on their own initiative. Catholics will want to do this in a spirit of deep repentance for past offenses and crimes committed by Christians against Jews and with profound respect for the Jew "as he is: above all, respect for his faith and his religious convictions."

In passing, let me touch upon two points of a more practical or, if you will, more political nature: (1) the attitude that Christians ought to take with regard to the State of Israel considered as a political entity, and (2) the attitude that the Jewish community ought to take with regard to certain so-called "Catholic" issues. Concerning the first point, suffice it to say that Christians must vigorously oppose the efforts being made by the Arab nations and some of their Third World allies to discriminate against Israel in the United Nations and other international agencies. More specifically, Christians in the United States must be prepared to urge the United States to walk out of the U.N. General Assembly if the Arab-Third World bloc persists in its efforts to expel the State of Israel.

To their credit, the members of the U.S. labor delegation to the 1975 annual conference of the International Labor Organization (the oldest of the U.N. specialized agencies) followed this course of action when the Arab-Third World bloc rammed through a vote granting official observer status at the Conference to the Palestinian Liberation Organization, an Arab terrorist group which, on more than one occasion, has called for the destruction of the State of Israel. The chairman of the U.S. labor delegation explained the American walk-out as follows: "Our position is clear: We have never opposed legitimate movements fighting for their freedom and independence. And our history and record have demonstrated our support for such movements in North Africa and Black Africa . . . but we oppose the admission of liberation movements to the ILO which do not represent an oppressed state and we oppose the admission of liberation movements which seek the destruction of another state as a prerequisite to achieve their goals, particularly when that threatened state is a member of the very organization that has voted in favor of admission of that group into its ranks. . . ."

That is a sound position and, in my opinion, the only one that is consistent with the purpose of the United Nations and its specialized agencies. Pope John XXIII stated that purpose as follows in his encyclical *Pacem in Terris:* "The United Nations Organization has as its essential purpose the maintenance and consolidation of peace between peoples, fostering between them friendly relations, based on the principles of equality, mutual respect, and varied forms of cooperation in every section of human endeavor."

The United States, as suggested above, will have no alternative but to live up to this statement of purpose, whatever the cost, if the Arab-Third World bloc is reckless enough to try to expel the State of Israel from the United Nations.

A growing number of theologians have helped to put the question of Israel in proper focus. I would cite in this connection, by way of example, a perceptive essay by Msgr. John Oesterreicher, one of the most influential pioneers in the field of Catholic-Jewish relations and one who played a decisive role in the drafting of the Council's Declaration. In the fifth volume of his series of Judao-Christian studies, *The Bridge,* Oesterreicher noted that there is ''a weighty difference'' between the Jewish and Christian approaches to the promised land. To the Christian, he wrote, no country is holier than the others; hence, ''no land plays a similar role in the religious experience of the Christian as does the land of Israel in the experience of the Jews. Though this lack of experience makes it difficult for the Christian to grasp the Jewish attachment to 'the land,' it certainly does not forbid him to respect this attachment. There is, in my opinion, no religious tenet that imposes on him a detached or neutral stance toward the reality that Jews have regained their ancient land and now live under their own flag.''

Taking the argument a step further, Oesterreicher pointed out that the living reality of the State of Israel should, for the most part, evoke the respect and admiration of the Christian theologian. ''For the theologian,'' he said, ''Israel's future cannot be a mere political problem. Heaven forbid that he allow the cry 'Politics!' to prevent him from taking a stand. Certainly, what the exact boundaries of the State should be, who would best succeed the present Prime Minister, and many similar questions are the kind of political problems that are fully outside his special competence. Not so, however, the question of whether the sovereign State should stay on, or be wiped off, the face of the earth; or whether its people should be drowned in the sea or live in peace. I, at least, cannot see how the renewal of the land could be anything to the theologian but a wonder of love and vitality, how the reborn State could be anything but a sign of God's concern for his people.'' An ever-increasing number of U.S. Catholics fully agree with Oesterreicher on this matter.

Concerning the approach that the Jewish community ought to take with reference to a number of so-called Catholic issues, let me quote Dr. Judd L. Teller, a prominent Jewish author and journalist, from a book entitled *Strangers and Natives: The Evolution of the American Jew from 1921 to the Present.* Dr. Teller says that American Catholic proponents of the dialogue expect Jews, because of the Vatican Council's Declaration, ''to abandon some of their most deep-seated principles'' on aid to parochial schools, textbook support for religious schools, and other controversial matters of public policy. I must respectfully disagree with Dr. Teller. I think I know almost all of the American Catholics who are actively promoting the dialogue and I am confident that they are not expecting a *quid pro quo* from the Jewish community. On the contrary, I think they would unanimously reject and repudiate any attempt on the part of any group of their fellow Christians to misuse the dialogue as a means of cajoling or subtly pressuring Jews on matters of public policy as the price of continued Catholic participation in the dialogue.

On the other hand, the time has come for Catholics and Jews to dialogue openly and frankly about any and all public policy issues on which they happen to be divided. The fact that this kind of dialogue has already begun on a number of controversial issues is a very hopeful sign. It means that both Catholics and Jews are beginning to achieve a greater degree of maturity and a greater degree of mutual trust and respect.

Let me cite but one example. Before Vatican II one could have taken it for granted, without giving the matter a second thought, that the Jewish community in the United States would almost unanimously oppose any expenditure of federal funds for the benefit of children attending parochial or other church-related schools. Less than two years after the Council, Rabbi Arthur Gilbert, then a member of the staff of the Anti-Defamation League, reported that "the united front usually maintained by the Jewish community on church-state issues is now torn asunder."

That was true, he wrote, in several fields, but particularly in the field of education where "the G.I. Bill of Rights, the availability of NDEA money, the Higher Education Facilities Act, as well as the newly enacted Poverty Education Acts, suggest that there is certainly a partnership, or at least a cooperative relationship, in the making between big government and the church-related institutions."

Rabbi Gilbert found this new trend to his liking and was convinced that it would not be reversed. He hastened to add, of course, that we must be vigilant so that tax funds are not misused or misappropriated and that direct grants are not given in support of specifically religious programs. On balance, however, he was satisfied that the present laws adequately assure a formal separation between church and state. "For those who are dissatisfied with this arrangement . . . and who dissent from this emerging pattern of cooperation," he concluded, "the Supreme Court will be available for final adjudication. It is important that Americans protect the right of this minority who will wish to engage in litigation. But I must admit that my own personal sympathies on this issue are with the Johnson consensus."

Shortly after Rabbi Gilbert's book was published, another distinguished Jewish writer, Milton Himmelfarb, made substantially the same point in a feature article in *Commentary,* of which he was and still is an associate editor. To judge from the overwhelmingly negative response to his article in *Commentary's* open forum, Mr. Himmelfarb (and Rabbi Gilbert) represented then (and probably still represent) a minority point of view in the more articulate segment of the American Jewish community. Nevertheless their flexible, undoctrinaire approach to the problem of church-state relations was significant and was not to be dismissed as the purely personal point of view of two isolated free-lance writers.

Mr. Dore Schary's keynote address at the 1967 meeting of the National Commission of the Anti-Defamation League was sufficient proof that Gilbert and Himmelfarb were not just a couple of unrepresentative mavericks in the American Jewish community. As chairman of ADL, Mr. Schary forthrightly called for a complete review of the League's traditional position on church-state relations. The need for such a review, he said, became evident with the passage of the Elementary and Secondary Education Act of 1965, which authorized the use of federal funds to provide special services to disadvantaged children regardless of whether they attend public or non-profit private schools, and also authorized the distribution of texts and resource materials for the use of these children.

"With this Act," he pointed out, "two cherished American traditions— and two convictions ADL, also, has held dear—came into sharp conflict. One is church-state separation; the other is the right of every American to an education which will equip him to take his just place in our democratic society."

Many strict constructionists, Mr. Schary continued, were disturbed by the ESEA of 1965. This he could understand. "But we live," he said, "in times of great ferment, of social and scientific revolution, and in such times we must pause to evaluate the appropriateness to our age of tenets we have held precious for centuries. . . . There is nothing, after all, sacrosanct about secular principles which may be outworn, if indeed they are." In delivering the answers to the complex questions raised by the enactment of ESEA and similar pieces of legislation, he concluded, "we should, I think, start from some basic premises and assure our friends of other faiths about the sincerity of our motives."

Mr. Schary had no reason for concern on this score. To my way of thinking, he had amply demonstrated the sincerity of his own motives and was to be congratulated on his willingness to face up to the thorny problem of church-state relations so realistically and with such complete openness of mind. American Catholics had reason to be very grateful to him—and to Rabbi Gilbert and Mr. Himmelfarb—for their statesmanlike initiative in this regard.

By the same token, however, Catholics will want to return the favor by making a special effort to try to understand why the vast majority of American Jews—including the three distinguished writers referred to above—are so passionately in favor of the separation of church and state. To be sure, the overwhelming majority of American Catholics are also completely in favor of separation, but less passionately so, I should think, than their Jewish fellow-citizens. Why should this be so? How is one to account for the fact that American Jews, by and large, are more deeply concerned about this issue than the majority of Catholics? In the words of Mr. Schary, the answer is that Jews have suffered so much at the hands of Christians in nations where the state was "the hand-maiden of the church—that is, the church of the dominant group in the population."

Father Edward Flannery, in a sermon delivered at the National Shrine of the Immaculate Conception in Washington just a few days before Mr. Schary spoke to this issue, pointed out that "from this dangerous and degrading situation in Christian society Jews were finally liberated in the eighteenth and nineteenth centuries by secular, even anti-religious, forces and governments." And yet, he concluded, Christians wonder why many Jews prize separation of church and state more than we do. Until Catholics in this country cease to wonder at this perfectly natural phenomenon and, instead, begin to understand it— and, if you will, to feel it in their very bones—little progress will be made in developing the kind of inter-religious dialogue which the Gilbert-Himmelfarb-Schary breakthrough made possible.

On the occasion of the tenth anniversary of the Declaration, Father Edward Flannery highlighted the subject of Catholic-Jewish cooperation on social issues, addressing it from a theological point of view and pointing out that the laicization process in Western culture has resulted in grave problems touching war and peace, poverty and plenty, freedom and oppression, and others again.

"Is it fanciful to believe," Father Flannery wrote, "that the healing of the cultural and philosophical breach that characterizes the Jewish-Christian relationship will bring a new measure of healing to these problems as well?

"Is it too Utopian to conclude that before the century ahead of us ends the world we live in will have experienced this healing touch and in consequence will have started out on a new path to health and wholeness, and to a pluralistic oneness, the like of which it has never before enjoyed?

"It is a grandiose dream that rises from the heart of our timid and faltering encounter. But then we come, both of us, from a grandiose past and tradition. To realize our dreams we have in the first place to draw upon them."

That says it all and says it very well indeed.

A Jewish Viewpoint
on Nostra Aetate

RABBI MARC H. TANENBAUM

It is appropriate, I think, to ask why it is that "the Jewish declaration," introduced at the second session of Vatican II, November 1963, and promulgated October 28, 1965 had elicited such widespread universal attention.

As Cardinal Bea said in his *relatio* September 25, at the time of his introduction of the "Jewish declaration,"

> I can only begin with the fact that this Declaration certainly must be counted among the matters in which public opinion has shown the greatest concern. Scarcely any other schema has been written up so much and so widely in periodicals . . . . Many will judge the Council good or bad by its approval or disapproval of the Declaration.

This decree had engaged the concern and the attention of twenty-three hundred Council Fathers in Rome over a period of three years. It involved the attention of the Protestant and Eastern Orthodox observers. Why is the issue of the relationship of Christianity to Judaism and the practical relations between Christians and Jews on a daily level of such central significance? Why did it attract such widespread attention?

It is my thesis that the issue of relations between Christians and Jews had reached the point of ripeness, of maturation, in a way that can be seen analogously in terms of the ripeness and the fullness which relations between the black and white societies have reached. The moment of crisis, or the moment of truth, in relations between black and white people is tested and resolved to the degree to which we overcome the contradictions between our professions of love, charity and justice and our practices which have often stood in flagrant opposition to our pious verbalizations. In the process of being confronted by blacks with a challenge to our moral claims, and our negative attitudes and behavior toward them, we have begun to find it necessary to face truthfully the fact that we have been dealing with blacks in the main as abstractions, as mythic perceptions, but not as real people, not as persons who have a human dignity that demands a certain response from us as brothers and sisters. One of the facts that has become very clear to us is that we have evaded our moral duties to blacks by substituting a series of myths for genuine confrontation. These myths have buffered us from encountering the reality of black people.

Now in many ways the mythology, the unreality, the capacity to abstract human relationships and to empty them of solid human meaning and feeling find an analogy in the relations between Christians and Jews. What we have begun to confront in the relationships between Christianity and Judaism and between Christendom and Jewry is the fact that there is a fundamental ambivalence historically and theologically within Christian teaching and within Christian social practice that has never been confronted before in any serious and systematic way in the past nineteen hundred years of the Christian-Jewish encounter. Just as the social revolution of the blacks has caused us to confront the race issue in a way that we cannot escape, so certain revolutionary facts of the twentieth century have made the Christian-Jewish confrontation inescapable.

I believe that the Nazi holocaust and all that has meant for the Christian conscience, as well as the tremendous needs of a new world of the twentieth century in which Christians and Jews together find themselves increasingly a minority in relation to a non-white, non-Judeo-Christian world, are compelling us to confront the deep realities of the relationship between Christians and Jews. Fundamentally, Christianity has never made up its mind as to where it stands in terms of its common patrimony with Judaism and its daily attitudes and relationships and behavior toward Jews. We find as we look into the history of the Christian-Jewish encounter for the greater part of the past two millennia that there have been teachings and episodes betokening the greatest of mutual respect and esteem between Christians and Jews. Thus, we find St. Athanasius, one of the early Church Fathers at the beginning of the fourth century, who said that "the Jews are the great school of the knowledge of God and the spiritual life of all mankind." St. Jerome, who lived in the fifth century and who spent forty years in Palestine where in Caesarea with Jewish scholars and biblical authorities he studied the Holy Scriptures and the Masoretic traditions—and from whom he obtained insights on which he based his translation of the Scriptures into the Vulgate—declared that "the Jews were divinely preserved for a purpose worthy of God."

This side of the affirmative attitude of the Church toward the Jews reflected the tradition of St. Paul in Romans 9 to 11, which speaks of Christians being engrafted onto the olive tree of Israel (11:17) planted by God. This tradition also found expression in positive behavior of popes even in the Middle Ages. Thus Callixtus II issued a bull in 1120 beginning with the words "Sicut

Judaeis'' in which he strongly condemned the forced baptism of Jews, acts of violence against their lives and property, and the desecration of synagogues and Jewish cemeteries. Gregory IX issued the bull "Etsi Judeorum" in 1233 in which he demanded that the Jews in Christian countries should be treated with the same humanity with which Christians desire to be treated in heathen lands.

Side by side with that tradition there existed a tradition of hostility and contempt which the late French historian, Professor Jules Isaac, has written about in his various studies.[1] This tradition was perhaps most explicitly embodied in the eight sermons of St. John Chrysostom, who in the year 387 spoke from the pulpits of the city of Antioch to the first congregations of early Gentiles who became Christians, saying:

> I know that a great number of the faithful have for the Jews a certain respect and hold their ceremonies in reverence. This provokes me to eradicate completely such a disastrous opinion. I have already brought forward that the synagogue is worth no more than the theatre . . . it is a place of prostitution. It is a den of thieves and a hiding place of wild animals . . . not simply of animals but of impure beasts . . . God has abandoned them. What hope of salvation have they left?

> They say that they too worship God but this is not so. None of the Jews, not one of them is a worshipper of God . . . . Since they have disowned the Father, crucified the Son and rejected the Spirit's help, who would dare to assert that the synagogue is not a home of demons! God is not worshiped there. It is simply a house of idolatry . . . . The Jews live for their bellies, they crave for the goods of this world. In shamelessness and greed they surpass even pigs and goats . . . . The Jews are possessed by demons, they are handed over to impure spirits . . . . Instead of greeting them and addressing them as much as a word, you should turn away from them as from a pest and a plague of the human race.[2]

Now, if one enters into the historic background and the context within which St. John Chrysostom made these remarks, perhaps one can understand a little better—one can explain but certainly not excuse—what led St. John Chrysostom to make these anti-Jewish polemics.[3] It may be useful to take a moment to observe that the Church in the first four centuries of this era was struggling for its existence as an autonomous, independent faith community. In the minds of the Roman Empire the early Christians represented another Jewish sect. Judaism was the *religio licita* (a favored religion), and for early

Christians to achieve any status, including the right to conduct Christian ceremonials, they had to come as Jews to achieve recognition by the Romans.[4] And so the early Church fathers found it necessary to separate Christians from the Jews. The early Christians felt very close to Jews; they observed their Sabbath on the Jewish Sabbath, their Easter on the Jewish Passover. At the time of the Council of Elvira (ca. 300) many Christians in Spain thought the Jews had a special charism as the People of God and therefore invited them to bless their fields so that they would be fruitful. To separate Christians from their associations with Judaism, to create a sense of autonomy and independence for Christianity, apparently in the wisdom of the early Church Fathers it became necessary to embark on a drastic effort to break the bonds between church and synagogue and to give Christians a consciousness of difference from the Jews. In the process of this disidentification, however, the pattern of anti-Jewish attitudes and of anti-Jewish behavior became so entrenched, that by the time the Church became the established religion of the Roman empire, these attitudes were reflected increasingly in ecclesiastical legislation. These laws subsequently led to the establishment of ghettos, the forcing of Jews to wear yellow hats and badges, and in general, this legislation reduced Jews to the status of pariahs throughout the Roman empire. As the Church became the major institution integrating the whole of medieval society, the perception of the Jew within medieval Christendom became the perception of the Jew within Western culture and civilization.

Lest one think that these attitudes are mainly of academic or historic interest, one needs to confront the following facts. A prominent Catholic educator has traveled around this country to various Christian seminaries and universities, to speak of the new understanding between Christians and Jews. As she sought to elaborate her thesis of the historical and theological factors which helped shape the conception of the Jew in the Western world, she received many questions from students at the end of her lectures. These are some of the questions that were asked of her by students in Catholic and Protestant seminaries and universities, and also on some secular campuses:

If the Jewish people did not kill Christ, who did?

You said that the high priest and the elders and not the Jewish people had a share of the responsibility in Jesus' condemnation. That is not true. The gospel says that the people clamored for his death.

I am a Catholic and I know what I have been taught when I went to catechism; and that is that the Jews killed Christ. That is what my Church teaches. I don't like it. I have several friends who are Jewish, but what can I do? I have to believe my Church.

Don't you think that in this country we are antagonistic to Jews because they are too successful in business?

Why are all Jews rich?

Why are the Jews better than anyone else in business?

I have heard it said that Hitler had to do what he did because Jews held all the money in Germany.

The St. Louis University study,[5] in its examination of Catholic parochial school textbooks, found that there are echoes and resonances of this tradition of contempt in materials used even to this day. Thus, for example, to cite some of the teachings which have an unerring echo from the teachings of St. John Chrysostom, it is written in some of the religious textbooks studied by Sister Rose Albert Thering:

The Jews wanted to disgrace Christ by having him die on the cross.

Show us that the Jews did not want Pilate to try Christ but to give permission for his death.

When did the Jews decide to kill Christ?

The Jews as a nation refused to accept Christ and since that time they have been wandering on the earth without a temple or a sacrifice and without the Messias.

The findings of the Yale University Divinity School study, published in book form as *Faith and Prejudice* by Dr. Bernhard E. Olson, have revealed analogous results in some of the denominational textbooks used in Protestantism. There have been significant revisions, as well as improved portrayals of Jews and Judaism, in Catholic and Protestant teaching materials since the publication of the St. Louis and Yale studies. Nevertheless, there is still a heavy residuum from the polemical histories of the past in far too many textbooks, and, above all, in sermons, religious radio broadcasts, Seminary Manuals, Bible commentaries, liturgical missals, catechisms, passion plays, and in fact in the daily attitudes of many professing Christians.

These studies, which are of interest, I think, to people who have professional religious and educational responsibilities, do not begin, however, to make us aware of the consequence of these generations of teachings in terms of the impact they have had on the attitudes toward Jews in Western society and culture. These views which began in a theological and religious matrix have penetrated into the marrow of Western civilization and continue to influence the Western world's attitudes toward the Jews to this very moment.

When you go home to your studies, if you will open any unabridged dictionary and look up the definition of a Jew, you will find the following:

Webster's Universal Dictionary:[6]
"Jew—to cheat in trade; as to Jew one out of a horse. To practice cheating in trade; as, he is said to Jew. To Jew down."

Funk and Wagnalls:
"Jew—(slang) to get the better of in a bargain; overreach: referring to the proverbial keenness of Jewish traders."

Merriam Webster:
"Jew—adjective, Jewish, usually taken to be offensive. "Jew—verb, to cheat by sharp business practice, usually taken to be offensive.
"Jew—noun, a person believed to drive a hard bargain."

Contrast this with the dictionary's definition of "Christian":

Webster's Universal Dictionary:
"Christian—colloquial, a decent, civilized, or presentable person, characteristic of Christian people, kindly."

If one looks at the general social reality in terms of the way the Jew is perceived by and large (with significant changes in recent years growing out of our greater contact with each other), one finds, for example, a striking double standard in the evaluation of the behavior of the Christian and the Jew in the world of commerce. When a Jewish business man is successful in a given business or industry, in the parlor rooms and in the bars where the "man-to-man talk" is made (and all of us have heard this enough to know that it is true and not a figment of one's imagination), one hears the "explanation": "Well, he's a Jew." There's something sharp, there's something cunning about his practices. It is the Jewishness of the man which leads to his success. But if a Christian or a Gentile is engaged in the same industry, using virtually the same business practices, achieves the same kind of success, then in the American mythos this is the result of "Yankee ingenuity." This is living out the Horatio Alger myth of rags to riches in American life. It is a consequence of living out the "Puritan ethic."

One must confront ultimately how as recently as the past forty years in a country—which, when it vaunted its great values and its great moral traditions, spoke of itself as a country of ancient Christian culture, which was in fact the seat of the Holy Roman Empire for almost a millennium beginning with Charlemagne—it was possible for millions of Christians to sit by as spectators while millions of human beings, who were their brothers and sisters, the sons of Abraham according to the flesh, were carted out to their death in the most brutal, inhuman, uncivilized ways. And one must confront as one of the terrible facts of the history of this period the conversation that took place between Adolf Hitler and two bishops in April 1933, when they began raising questions about the German policy toward the Jews and Hitler said to them, as reported in the book, *Hitler's Table-Talk,* that he was simply completing what Christian teaching and preaching had been saying about the Jews for the better part of nineteen hundred years. "You should turn away from them as a pest and a plague of the human race," said St. John Chrysostom, and fifteen hundred years later thousands of his disciples implemented his teachings, literally.

One must compel oneself to face these hard facts in our own time because there is a tendency to want to evade the reality of this problem, since in America both for Christians and Jews anti-Semitism is not much more than a social nuisance. It is not a serious problem of human deprivation, of human discomfort, or a clear and present danger. But it was not too long ago that in the city of Buenos Aires, for example, where 400,000 Jews live, Jewish merchants were packing guns into their business places and synagogues were being stored with armaments because the Neo-Fascist, ultra-nationalist movement called the TACUARA, consisting entirely of young well-to-do Catholic students, tramped through the streets of Buenos Aires spraying machine gun fire at synagogues and throwing bombs at Jewish businesses. The TACUARA apprehended a Jewish girl, Gracielal Sirota, as she came home from the university in the evening, kidnaped her and carved a swastika in her breast. The chaplain of this TACUARA movement was a Father Julio de Meinvielle, who has written a book called *The Mystery of the Jew in History.* Father Meinvielle has claimed that he bases his "ministry" to these students in the TACUARA movement on the fact that the tradition of St. John Chrysostom's views toward the Jews and Judaism and those who have repeated that tradition represent *the* authentic view of the Church toward the Jewish people and to Judaism.

Within the past twenty years since the close of Vatican Council II, all of us have lived through what in fact may be the most revolutionary period in the history of the Christian-Jewish encounter over the past two millennia. As in race relations, the churches have begun to seek to reconcile the ambivalences and the contradictions between theology and history. The Catholic Church, through Vatican Council II's approval of a declaration dealing with Catholic-Jewish relations, the World Council of Churches, in its very forthright resolution at New Delhi in December 1961, and American, West European, and

Latin American Catholic and Protestant bodies have all contributed dramatically to the powerful assault against anti-Semitism. Their wide-ranging programs of textbook and curriculum revision, teacher training, seminary education, retreats and adult education have been confronting increasingly the issues of responsible portrayal of Jews and Judaism.

If nothing else came out of Vatican Council II other than what took place in Rome on September 28 and 29, 1964, the Council more than justified its existence in terms of Jewish interests. On Friday, September 25, 1964, Cardinal Bea arose in the aula of St. Peter's Basilica to read his *relatio* to the "Jewish Declaration." After indicating the importance of this decree to the life of the Church, the importance of the Church's understanding of her true relationship to Israel, to the Bible, to the Jewish people, ancient and present (an understanding upon which is founded the whole future and prospect of the biblical, liturgical and theological renewals of the Church), Cardinal Bea declared before twenty-three hundred Council Fathers, "There are many historical instances from various nations which cannot be denied. In these instances this belief concerning the culpability of the Jewish people as such has led Christians to consider and to call the Jews with whom they live the deicide people, reprobated and cursed by God and therefore to look down upon them and indeed to persecute them." Then he described what he thought was authentic Church teaching about the role of the Jews in the passion and the mystery of the relationship between Christians and Jews. The moment of truth, as those of us who were privileged to be in Rome were able to observe, occurred on those two days when thirty-five cardinals and bishops from twenty-two countries arose on the floor of St. Peter's, and one after another, in terms more powerful and more committed than had ever been heard before, called upon the Catholic Church to condemn anti-Semitism as a sin against the conscience of the church. Thirty-one of the cardinals and bishops from every major continent of the world took positions regarding Catholic attitudes in relation to the Jewish people, Judaism, the role of Israel in salvation history, the synagogue and its continued relevance, conversion, anti-Semitism—positions that have never been heard before in nineteen hundred years of Catholic-Jewish history, positions articulated with such friendship, indeed, fraternal love, as to make clear that a profound turning point had taken place in our lifetime.

Cardinal Cushing, the first of the American hierarchy to speak out on the declaration on the Jews, called for a denial by the Council of the culpability of the Jews as a people for the death of Jesus. "Rejection of Jesus by the Jewish people is a mystery and is to serve to instruct us not to inflate us," Cardinal Cushing said.[7] He declared that the Catholic Church cannot judge the ancient judges of the Jews, as that is for God to do. At the same time, the Cardinal of Boston said Christians must be aware of the universal guilt of all men who by sinning crucified and are crucifying Christ.

Cardinal Meyer of Chicago stated that "it is not enough for the Church to deplore any injustices against the Jewish people. It must also point out the close relationship of the Church with the Jews." Cardinal Meyer pointed out that St. Thomas Aquinas taught that the Jews were not guilty of deicide.

Cardinal Ritter of St. Louis said that the declaration would repair injustices of past centuries. He said that it is often assumed that God abandoned the Jews, and the Jews were rightly to be accused of condemnation by Jesus. Now, he said, an opportunity had been offered to remedy these errors and to remove these injustices. Referring to the passage that spoke of the "reunion" of the Jews with the Church, Cardinal Ritter said that it sounds as if the Church envisions conversion of the Jewish people. He pointed out that the text did not speak of the Moslems, Hindus and Protestants in the same respect. Therefore he suggested that the final text find less offensive wording and include a paragraph expressing the biblical hope of the union of all men and women at the end of days.

Cardinal Leger of Canada called the declaration a necessary act of the Church's renewal.

Cardinal Lercaro of Bologna suggested that the declaration emphasize biblical discussions with the Jews. He said the Jewish people should not be regarded as having value only in the past. But the heritage of Israel, the institution of the eucharist within the Jewish paschal cycle, the relation between the Passover meal and the Mass, the common fatherhood of Abraham—all these should be emphasized in the declaration, Cardinal Lercaro said, in order to give witness in a pastoral way and to foster piety. He added that the Jews of today should not be called an accursed or deicide people, but rather that we should recognize that all of us "have strayed like sheep."

Archbishop Pocock of Canada said that the Church must acquit the Jewish people of all false accusations made in the past through the abuse of truth and charity.

Bishop Stephen A. Leven of Texas, in rejecting the ancient deicide charge against the Jews, declared:

Fathers of the Council, we are not dealing here with some philosophical entity but with a word of infamy and execration which was invented by Christians and used to blame and persecute the Jews. For so many centuries, and even in our own, Christians have hurled this word against Jews, and because of it they have justified every kind of horrible excess and even their slaughter and destruction. It is not up to us to make a declaration about something philosophical but to reprobate and damn a word which has furnished so many occasions of persecution through the centuries. We must tear this word out of the Christian vocabulary so that it may never again be used against the Jews.

During those two days of debate in Rome and in the final text that was promulgated by Paul VI on October 28, 1965, the Catholic Church took a great and historic leap forward in reconciling this ambivalence, affirming on the highest levels of its teaching authority the indebtedness of Christianity and the Christians to Judaism and the Jewish people, the rejection of anti-Semitism and an unprecedented call for fraternal dialogue between Christians and Jews. Later in this paper I should like to discuss the Declaration that was promulgated and both the Jewish and Catholic reactions to it.

There is a larger dimension to what took place in Rome at Vatican Council II that should be of as great significance to the Jewish people as the Jewish Declaration itself. The clue to that larger significance is suggested by the letter that Pope Paul VI sent to Cardinal Tisserant, dean of the Council presidency, on November 9, 1965. In that letter, Paul VI announced that Vatican Council II would end on December 8, "on the same date on which in 1869, there was solemnly inaugurated the first Vatican Ecumenical Council." The Pope then said that "our Council can well be considered under many aspects a worthy counterpart" of Vatican Council I. I need not belabor the point of how great an advance, indeed a revolution, Vatican Council II represents in contrast to Vatican Council I. As you well know, most objective, impartial historians have described Vatican Council I as that which marked the decisive victory of ultramontanism. The foundation stones of Vatican Council I were based on the encyclical *Quanta Cura* and the accompanying *Syllabus of Errors* issued by Pius IX in 1864.[8] J.B. Bury, regius professor of modern history at Cambridge, in his study *The History of the Papacy in the 19th Century* summarizes the contents of the encyclical and the Syllabus in this way:

The leading ideas which are associated closely with modern progress are described as *monstrosa opinionum portenta,* and those who propagate them are designated as slaves of corruption to design to demolish society, *civilis societatis fundamenta convellere.* . . .

He [Pius IX] begins his comments on this doctrine (of toleration) by quoting with approval a passage from *Mirari Vos* of his predecessor, where liberty of conscience and the right of each man to practice his own religion are described as *deliramentum.* Such liberty, says Pius, citing St. Augustine, is *libertas perditionis.*

Professor Bury concludes (p. 6) that "the general drift of the argument [of the encyclical] is: liberty, toleration, secularism, and democracy are closely bound together, and what they mean is materialism."

Wrapped up in religious phraseology, Bury adds, the encyclical "is really a political document, setting forth an ideal of civilization and declaring principles of political import."

> The positive principles which it asserts by means of condemning their negations may be summed up thus: The State must recognize a particular religion as regnant, and submit to its influence, and this religion must be Catholic; the power of the State must be at its disposal, and all who do not conform to its requirements must be compelled or punished. The duty of governments is to protect the Church, and freedom of conscience and cult is madness. Not the popular will, but religion, that is the papal authority, is the basis of civil society, otherwise it will sink into materialism. The Church is superior to the State, and therefore the State has no right to dictate to her, and has no power over religious orders. The family and the education of children belong to the Church, not to the state. The Pope can decree and prescribe what he chooses, without the State's permission, and his authority is not limited to doctrines and morals (p. 8).

The Episcopal scholar, the Rev. Dr. Frederick Grant, in his introduction to Professor Bury's study, described the mentality of Vatican Council I and of Pius IX as that which held that "the best safeguard of the Christian faith" against liberalism and modernism was to convert the Catholic Church into "a Maginot line of impenetrable defense." In the face of a series of shocks beginning with the Reformation in the sixteenth century and climaxed by the French Revolution in the eighteenth century, the Church became preoccupied with her own self-preservation and was relatively indifferent to the fate of those who were non-Catholic. This virtual obsession with the preservation of herself and her institutions made it possible for the Church to enter into concordats with the blackest forces of reaction, a tradition which led to tragic consequences in the twentieth century.[9]

As one reads the texts of the sixteen declarations promulgated by Vatican II and compares these with both the spirit as well as the rhetoric of the documents of Vatican Council I, there is no conclusion possible other than that the Catholic Church has undergone a revolution in terms not only of her self-perception but in her attitudes toward non-Catholics and her own responsibility for the welfare of other people. Nowhere is the new attitude of concern for others, involvement in their fate and destiny more clearly reflected than in the

Constitution on the Church in the Modern World, the *Declaration on Religious Freedom,* the *Decree on Ecumenism,* and the *Declaration on the Relationship of the Church to Non-Christian Religions.*

No person of good will can fail to be moved by these words contained in the *Constitution on the Church in the Modern World:*

> The joys and the hopes, the griefs and the anxieties of the men of this age, especially those who are poor or in any way afflicted, these are the joys and the hopes, the griefs and the anxieties of the followers of Christ. Indeed, nothing genuinely human fails to raise an echo in their hearts. For theirs is a community composed of men (art. 1).

> In our times a special obligation binds us to make ourselves the neighbor of every person without exception, and of actively helping him when he comes across our path, whether he be an old person abandoned by all, a foreign laborer unjustly looked down upon, a child born of an unlawful union and wrongly suffering for a sin he did not commit, or a hungry person (art. 27).

> Respect and love ought to be extended also to those who think or act differently than we do in social, political and even religious matters (art. 28).

This emergence from behind something of a Maginot line and the joining of a dialogue with the world was dramatically ratified as much for non-Catholics as for Catholics in the brilliant address of Pope Paul VI before the United Nations at the end of 1965. The Pope renounced for the Catholic Church any pretense to temporal power and then declared, "We make our own voice of the poor, the disinherited, the suffering, to those who hunger and thirst for justice, for the dignity of life, for freedom, for well being and progress." Pope Paul VI gave Catholic support to "the pluralism of states" and to "co-existence" between peoples. He said to the United Nations: "Your vocation is to make brothers not only of some but of all peoples." He then ratified "the formula of equality" saying: "Let no one inasmuch as he is a member of your union be superior to the others; never one above the other." The Pope then decried that "pride" which "disrupts brotherhood." Noting that the United Nations proclaims "the fundamental rights and duties of man, his dignity, his freedom—and above all, his religious freedom," the Pope declared that "the life of man is sacred; no one may dare offend it." Pope John Paul II has given vivid affirmation to those humanistic trends throughout his Papacy.

I believe that I speak the mind of most informed Jewish observers when

I say that if this mentality had been normative for the popes, the Vatican and the Catholic and Protestant masses over the past one hundred years, the incredible phenomenon of hundreds of thousands of so-called devout Christians becoming accomplices or passive spectators to the cruel slaughter of millions of men, women and children who happened to be born Jews—or Gypsies—would not have been possible. The pragmatic significance of this newly articulated humanitarian mentality has given birth, I have no doubt, to the magnificent involvement of priests, nuns and Catholic laymen who, together with ministers and rabbis, marched together through the streets of Selma, Alabama, or in the March on Washington as a powerful renunciation of that mentality which echoed in traumatic silence less than forty years ago in the cities of ancient Christian culture of Germany, Austria, Poland and elsewhere in Europe. The Pope cried out "No more war, war never again!" and moved the world when he pleaded. Vatican Council II has proclaimed to the whole of the human family: "No more indifference, indifference and silence no more!" as long as the dignity of a single human being is offended or is exploited.

The promulgation of the *Declaration on the Relationship of the Church to Non-Christians* on October 28, 1965 received a mixed reaction in the Jewish community. As a commonplace pun has it, "Where there are two Jews, there are three opinions"—which is a Jewish self-critical way of describing the deep-seated democracy and pluralism that exists in Jewish life. The Jewish reaction ranged across a broad spectrum. There were those who opposed the Declaration and, in fact, who resented it. There were those who were indifferent to it. There were those, including myself, who welcomed the Declaration as an important contribution to improve the future relations between Catholics and Jews. In my study of the Jewish responses, I became aware of how decisive a role mass media played in influencing relations between groups. A substantial segment of the Jewish community reacted not to the content of the Declaration as much as to the headlines which reported about the Declaration. The day following the promulgation, newspaper headlines throughout this country, and, in fact, throughout the world, carried such statements as "Vatican Council Exonerates Jews for Death of Christ"; "Catholic Church Absolves Jews of Crucifixion." The so-called Jewish man-in-the-street naturally responded to such presumptive formulations with resentment, if not worse. No Jew in my acquaintance has ever felt guilty for the death of Jesus. Therefore, no Jew felt in need of absolution. But the problem was created by the newspapers and the radio and television commentators who used those words. The text of the Declaration itself does not use "absolve" or "exonerate" even once. This is not to impute bad motives or incompetence to the mass media. The problem of reducing to headlines a complex historical and theological problem is one that I am glad I did not have to face. But again, the fact that such headlines and such radio and television reports were dinned around the world for days both prior to and following the promulgation led almost inevitably to a negative reaction of so many Jewish people.

A more substantive consideration is the fact that the Vatican Council, for whatever reasons, "backed and filled" over this declaration for some four years. And to many Jews it was as though the Jewish people were being subjected to a trial over this period of time. When you add to that a number of unfortunate episodes that took place during those four years (including the insulting articles and speeches by Bishop Carli of Segni, who said, in fact, the Jews and Judaism today are collectively responsible for the crucifixion and stand under God's reprobation because of it), then one has another insight into how the Jewish patience wore thin. Overriding all, however, was the absence in the Declaration of any note of contrition or repentance for the incredible sufferings and persecutions Jews have undergone in the Christian West. The Church's various declarations asked forgiveness from the Protestants, from the Eastern Orthodox, from the Moslems, but not from the Jews. Many Jews, especially those who lived through the Nazi holocaust, asked with great passion, "How many more millions of our brothers and sisters will need to be slaughtered before any word of contrition or repentance is heard in the seats of ancient Christian glory?"

The Jews who were indifferent to the Vatican Council's action believed that it was too little and too late. Within this group there was strong feeling that the Catholic bishops in Germany and Pope Pius XII himself could have spoken out decisively, unambiguously at a time when it would have meant something of profound importance to the Jewish people. That did not happen in terms adequate to the need and, therefore, the loss of confidence in the present usefulness of the Vatican statement is widespread among this group. In the perspective of history this group has also been aware that up until the time of the Enlightenment and the French Revolution, the Church contributed to the disenfranchisement of the Jewish people of the Western world and much worse. This group looked to the secular powers of the world for its political and civic salvation. In the view of this group history has outdistanced the Christian community, and such statements are only pleasant rhetoric and are really of no significant effect in terms of the security or fate of the Jewish people in the twentieth century. The reluctance of the Holy See to establish full and formal diplomatic relations with the State of Israel has provided confirmation for this skepticism.

In the view of the third group, the text of the final version of the Declaration that was adopted represented a compromise document compared to the text that was introduced at the close of the third session and which received an overwhelming majority vote of the Council Fathers. The earlier version was warmer, more generous, and less severe: it dealt explicitly with the "deicide" concept which became something of a symbolic test of good will. In that perspective, the failure of the Council to enact the majority will of the Fathers of 1964 was a disappointment. But in the view of this group, seen in the perspective of nineteen hundred years of Christian-Jewish history, this Declaration represents an incredible achievement.

As important as the Declaration itself is, the commitment of Catholic Church authorities and institutions to translate the teachings of *Nostra Aetate* and the 1975 Vatican Guidelines on Catholic-Jewish Relations into reality in the lives of some eight hundred million Catholics throughout the world was of even greater importance. That commitment was given decisive expression when the American Catholic hierarchy designated a special subcommission on Catholic-Jewish relations charged with the responsibility of implementing the objectives of the Declaration throughout every level of Catholic culture and society. The determined action of the Vatican shortly after the Declaration was promulgated which put an end to the veneration of Simon of Trent—that ritual blood libel episode which since the fifteenth century has been celebrated by annual procession through the streets of Trent, repeating an insult to the whole of the Jewish people—was another impressive demonstration of the commitment of the Catholic Church to express in deeds its new attitude of respect and esteem for the Jewish people. The instruction given by Cardinal Dopfner of Munich to the organizers of the Oberammergau Passion Play to revise the text so that all anti-Jewish references are removed is another earnest of the Catholic Church's commitment to the uprooting of the sources of anti-Semitism. (Tragically, the Oberammergau Passion Play remains "structurally anti-Semitic," our AJC studies revealed.)

In the face of the agonizing history that many of the people of the cross had wrought in the transformation of the Jews into a cross among the peoples, there should not be too great bafflement or wonder over some of the skepticism of a number of the Jewish people in this country and abroad as to the real meaning of the Vatican Council Declaration to them and their children. As long as hostile references to the Jewish people, Judaism and the synagogue continue to appear in Catholic textbooks, missals, liturgical commentaries, theological dictionaries, sermons, and passion plays, a great many Jews will continue to view the Vatican Council Declaration as a vain and even hypocritical show. Having worked closely with members of the Catholic community both here and abroad, especially in the fields of religious history and religious education, I am deeply persuaded that a vast and irreversible tide of self-purification and self-correction with regard to the portrayal of Jews and Judaism in the teaching process of the Catholic Church—nor should the Protestants be slighted—is under way and that the fruits of this process are already in evidence. That is not to overlook the hard reality that a great deal more needs to be done before the last weeds of anti-Jewish teaching and anti-Jewish poison are removed. But in my judgment, no Jew has a right to belittle the great advances that have been made already. I am persuaded that we are now going through a period of transition which will find both Jews and Catholics fumbling and stumbling as they seek to find appropriate new modes of relating to each other in a growing climate of mutual tolerance and esteem.

During the course of the deliberations of Vatican Council II in connection with *Nostra Aetate* the contradictory and at times confused views expressed with regard to the inclusion or elimination of a passage in the third version of the text relating the question of the conversion of the Jews brought into sharp focus the fact that the Catholic Church has done very little serious thinking about the place of Jews and Judaism in the divine economy. That episode alone underscored the need for Catholic theologians and scholars to develop a theology of Israel and the synagogue in salvation history that has some correspondence with the historic realities of the present-day living Jewish people. At the same time, the bewildering and bewildered response of many Jews to Vatican Council II, whose attitudes toward present-day Christians are based on old-world memories of Christians as persecutors, threw into sharp relief the critical need for Jews to develop a theology of Christians and Christianity that is consonant with the realities of an emerging "new Christian" society that is struggling in unparalleled fashion to uproot anti-Semitism and to restore her traditions to biblical modes of thought and practice.

At the heart of Christianity's problem of what to make of the Jew is the Christian's immense ignorance, if not illiteracy, regarding Judaism. If the Jews were supposed to have committed deicide against Jesus, then a great many Christians in fact have committed homicide against him. They have killed Jesus as a Jew and as a man. The weapon was ignorance of Jesus' Jewishness. But Jesus' life, his preaching, his teaching, his vision of the kingdom of God, the very ground of his messianism cannot be accurately or profoundly understood apart from his background in the synagogue, his life of worship and observance as a Jew, and his education with the Pharisaic rabbis of the first century. Indeed, the New Testament itself cannot be fully comprehended as other than a Jewish book, written almost entirely by Jews for Jews, and in the Jewish mode of exegesis, known as Haggaddah. Long passages of the New Testament are, indeed, actually nothing less than new and different exegesis of the Jewish Bible, the difference being determined by the belief in the divinity of Jesus, which stands in opposition to the uncompromising monotheism of Judaism.

The significance of this Christian amnesia regarding the Jewishness of the origins of Christianity is that the Christians who live in this ignorance are expressing the Marcionite heresy. Further, God bestowed promises upon the Jews and chastised them with curses, in order that they might repent. But a certain tradition of Christian teaching appropriated the promises for "the new

Israel'' and imposed upon the ''old Israel'' the left-over curses. In this way, many Christians found it possible to cease to identify religiously with Judaism and, worse, perceived the Torah and Judaism as ''stagnant'' and ''dessicated.'' From this conviction it was but a short step to the belief that the Church ''superseded'' Israel—despite St. Paul's admonition in Romans that God's call and promises to the Jews are irrevocable.

When one adds to this ignorance of first-century Judaism the even greater lack of knowledge about post-biblical Judaism, the ground of misunderstanding becomes an abyss. To most Christians, Judaism came to an abrupt end with the close of the canon of the Hebrew Scripture. But Judaism did not come to an end with the Old Testament. Just as a non-Catholic does an injustice to Catholicism by failing to take into account the significance of tradition, Church teaching and canon law, in addition to Sacred Scripture, so do non-Jews distort Judaism by failing to recognize that modern Judaism is the product of a long and rich development of post-biblical thought, devotion and piety that the great rabbis and sages of the Jewish people developed over the past fifteen hundred years. In the absence of that knowledge, the Christian pedagogues' continued use of the stereotypes of ''Pharisees'' for hypocritical post-biblical Jews, the false antinomy of Judaism as a religion of law and justice versus Christianity as a religion of love, mercy and compassion will only serve to perpetuate bias and know-nothingism in religion.

In this perspective, it has now become very clear that there are at least three major and decisive areas of scholarship that must be vigorously pursued by Catholic and other Christian scholars if the call of Vatican Council II for ''biblical and theological studies'' is to be translated into ''mutual understanding and respect.'' These are, first, critical commentaries and interpretations of the New Testament that will remove any possibility for bigots to exploit certain expressions in the gospels for anti-Semitic purposes. An excellent example of such studies is to be found in the essay ''Anti-Semitism and the Gospel,'' by Dominic M. Crossan, which appeared in *Theological Studies*. In that essay Crossan wrote that ''the often-repeated statement that the Jews rejected Jesus and had him crucified is historically untenable and must, therefore, be removed completely from our thinking and our writing, our teaching, preaching and liturgy.''

The second area is that of historical studies. If one reads Church histories and Jewish histories of the same events, it is as though Christians and Jews are being educated in different universes of discourse. A Christian historian, for example, Philip Hughes, writes of the Crusades of the eleventh and twelfth centuries as ''holy wars'' to free Jerusalem. ''Never before had Europe known such a vast and successful propaganda as the preaching of the First Crusade, and its success is a most eloquent proof of the reality of the new reform papacy's hold on the average man and of its popularity with him,'' wrote Hughes

in his *A Popular History of the Catholic Church*. To Jewish historians the Crusades "becomes a gory story of pillaging Jewish settlements, killing Jewish
people, looting Jewish wealth. Such serious restrictive legislation as the hu-
miliating garb, ritual-murder charges, Host desecration libels, and confine-
ment of the ghetto were not the heritage of the Dark Ages but the heritage of
the Crusades."[10]

As The Rev. Edward Flannery, author of *The Anguish of the Jews,* has
written, "most Christians have torn out of their history books the pages that
Jews have memorized." The time has come, perhaps, for a proposal to be
made for Christian and Jewish historians to join together in writing a common
history of the Jewish-Christian encounter which will fill in the blank pages.

The third area of much-needed scholarship is that of theological studies
in Jewish-Christian relations. Unless and until Christian scholars and people
develop theological conceptions regarding Judaism and the synagogue that reflect in some way the vital reality of the existence of present-day Judaism, very
little else of significance in Jewish-Christian relations will be possible. Gregory Baum has begun to point the way:

> The apostle tells us that the Jews of the Synagogue remain dear to
> God for the sake of the fathers (cf. Rom 11:28). Their election
> stands. Why? Because God is faithful, his gifts and call are irrev-
> ocable (Rom 11:29). His election cannot ultimately be undone by
> human decision against it. This scriptural theme is invoked in the
> conciliar text.

> What does this mean for the understanding of the Jews of our day?
> Giving this Pauline theme its weakest possible meaning, it asserts
> that God continues to be present and to address Jewish believers in
> their synagogue services. The testimonies of God's mercy in the past
> as celebrated in the synagogue worship remain a way of divine ac-
> tion, for "his gifts and call are irrevocable." We have here the an-
> swer to a question crucial to the Jewish-Christian dialogue. What is
> the present synagogue worship before God? Is the Christian forced
> to regard present Jewish worship as an empty form, as words and
> gestures without meaning? Or is he able to acknowledge in Jewish
> worship the presence of the living God? The conciliar text answers
> this question by its adoption and use of the Pauline theme. God re-
> mains present in his gifts to Israel.[11]

That new appreciation of Judaism and the Jewish people has come full
term in the latest declaration of His Holiness Pope John Paul II. In an audience
with American Jewish Committee leaders held on February 15, 1985, to com-

memorate the twentieth anniversary of *Nostra Aetate,* the Holy Father made this important statement:

> I wish to confirm, with utmost conviction, that the teaching of the Church proclaimed during the Second Vatican Council in the Declaration *Nostra Aetate* . . . remains *always for us,* for the Catholic Church, for the Episcopate . . . and for the Pope, a teaching which must be followed—a teaching which it is necessary to accept not merely as something fitting, but much more as an expression of the faith, as an inspiration of the Holy Spirit, as a word of the Divine Wisdom.

> I willingly repeat those words to you who are commemorating the twentieth anniversary of the Declaration. They express the commitment of the Holy See, and of the whole Catholic Church, to the content of this Declaration, underlying, so to speak, its importance.

> After twenty years, the terms of the Declaration have not grown old. It is even more clear than before how sound the Declaration's theological foundation is and what a solid basis it provides for a really fruitful Jewish/Christian dialogue. On the one hand, it places the motivation of such a dialogue in the very mystery of the Church herself, and on the other hand it clearly maintains the identity of each religion, closely linking one to the other.

> During these twenty years, an enormous amount of work has been done. You are well aware of it, since your organization is deeply committed to Jewish/Christian relations, on the basis of the Declaration, on both the national and the international levels, and particularly in connection with the Holy See's Commission for Religious Relations with Judaism.

> I am convinced, and I am happy to state it on this occasion, that the relationships between Jews and Christians have radically improved in these years. Where there was distrust and perhaps fear, there is now confidence. Where there was ignorance and therefore prejudice and stereotypes, there is now growing mutual knowledge, appreciation and respect. There is, above all, love between us, that kind of love, I mean, which is for both of us a fundamental injunction of our religious traditions and which the New Testament has received from the Old (cf. Mk 12:28–34; Lev 19:18).

There is no doubt that much remains to be done. Theological reflection is still needed, notwithstanding the amount of work already done and the results achieved thus far. Our Biblical scholars and theologians are constantly challenged by the word of God that we hold in common.

Education should more accurately take into account the new insights and directives opened up by the Council and spelled out in the subsequent "Guidelines and Suggestions for the Implementation of *Nostra Aetate* n. 4," which remain in force. Education for dialogue, love and respect for others, and openness toward all people are urgent needs in our pluralistic societies, where everybody is a neighbor to everybody else.

Antisemitism, which is unfortunately still a problem in certain places, has been repeatedly condemned by the Catholic tradition as incompatible with Christ's teaching and with the respect due to the dignity of men and women created in the image and likeness of God. I once again express the Catholic Church's repudiation of all oppression and persecution, and of all discrimination against people—from whatever side it may come—"in law or in fact, on account of their race, origin, color, culture, sex or religion" (*Octogesima Adveniens*, 23).

In close connection with the preceding, there is the *large field of cooperation* open to us as Christians and Jews, in favor of all humanity where the image of God shines through in every man, woman and child, especially in the destitute and those in need.

I am well aware of how closely the American Jewish Committee has collaborated with some of our Catholic agencies in alleviating hunger in Ethiopia and in the Sahel, in trying to call the attention of the proper authorities to this terrible plight, still sadly not solved, and which is therefore a constant challenge to all those who believe in the one true God, who is the Lord of history and the loving Father of all.

I know also your concern for the peace and security of the Holy Land. May the Lord give to the land, and to all the peoples and nations in that part of the world, the blessings contained in the word "shalom," so that, in the expression of the Psalmist, justice and peace may kiss (cf. Ps 85:11).

The Second Vatican Council and subsequent documents truly have this aim: that the sons and daughters of Abraham—Jews, Christians and Moslems (cf. *Nostra Aetate,* 3)—may live together and prosper in peace. And may all of us love the Lord our God with all our heart, and with all our soul, and with all our strength (cf. Dt 6:5). Shalom!

NOTES

1. *Jesus and Israel, Has Anti-Semitism Roots in Christianity?* and *The Teaching of Contempt* are all by Professor Jules Isaac, translated by Mme. Claire Huchet Bishop.

2. See Robert L. Wilken, *John Chrysostom and the Jews: Rhetoric and Reality in the Late 4th Century* (Berkeley: University of California Press, 1983).

3. Martin Luther appropriated these anti-Jewish polemics and incorporated both the images and rhetoric in his "The Jews and Their Lies." See *Luther and the Jews,* essays by Professor Eric W. Gritsch and Rabbi Marc H. Tanenbaum, published by the Lutheran Council in the U.S.A., 360 Park Ave. South, New York, NY 10010.

4. See James Parkes, *The Conflict of the Church and the Synagogue* (London: Soncino Press, 1934).

5. *Catechetics and Prejudice* by the Rev. John Pawlikowski (Paulist Press, 1973) summarizes the findings of the St. Louis textbook studies. *Faith Without Prejudice* by Dr. Eugene Fisher (Paulist Press, 1977) is also based on these studies.

6. See Jacob Chinitz, "Jews and Judaism in the Dictionary," *Reconstructionist Magazine* (June 1963).

7. These paraphrases of the interventions of the Council Fathers are based on the press reports issued by the Press Service of the National Catholic Welfare Conference and also on the summaries printed in the *Herder Correspondence.* The publication of the full texts of the interventions would be a valuable contribution, in my judgement, to a fuller understanding of the historic implications of the Council's actions for the future of Catholic-Jewish relations.

8. Whether the *Syllabus* possessed dogmatic character is a subject of controversy which Professor Bury discusses at some length. He cites critics, such as M. Dupanloup and others, who sought to minimize its binding import, but concludes from evidence contained in letters of Cardinal Antonelli "that the Syllabus was intended to have dogmatic value . . . on the subject of modern errors." Similarly, there is a deep divergence of views regarding ultramontanism itself. Paul Droulers, S.J., for example, writing in the *Journal of*

Rabbi Marc H. Tanenbaum

World History, characterizes the "ultramontanist" movement as one "impelled by the desire for greater purity and fervor" and constituted a "voluntary renunciation of local ecclesiastical particularism. It held up the pope, the head and center of the Church, as the visible source of Catholic vitality, while steadily consolidating his practical authority." Looking at the same set of "facts," the Lutheran church historian, Rudolph Sohm, in his book *Kirchengeschichte in Grundriss,* characterized ultramontanism as "the intolerant doctrinal Catholicism which with its lust of power demands once more the complete subjection of the individual, of the world itself, to the supreme authority of the Church."

9. Paul Droulers, S.J., writing on *Roman Catholicism in the 19th Century World,* states, "The diplomacy of the Court of Rome . . . was adapted to meet the varying circumstances of the individual countries, striving to obtain the fullest possible measure of civil liberty for the celebration of worship and the exercise of spiritual government . . . . The Bull *Sollicitudo Ecclesiarium* of August 7, 1831, contains an explicit reminder that in the cause of religion the Holy See will negotiate with any duly constituted government, though this does not imply recognition of its legitimacy before the law (293).

10. Max Dimont, *Jews, God and History* (New York: Simon and Schuster, 1962).

11. Gregory Baum in *The Ecumenist* (May-June, 1965).

The Jewish People,
the Land of Israel, Zionism,
and the State of Israel

ROBERT M. SELTZER

Through enormous effort and with great sacrifice, a Jewish common-wealth has emerged in the most volatile and sensitive region of the globe. Love for Zion (*ahavat Tsiyyon*) runs like a golden thread through the Jewish tradition—in the Hebrew Bible, rabbinic lore, the liturgy, medieval Jewish piety and mysticism, and a more recent literature in Hebrew and other languages used by Jews. Translation of this concept into reality as the new State of Israel in the old Land of Israel is certainly one of the most poignant dramas of modern history.

The land of Israel plays two crucial roles in Judaism: first, as the concrete homeland of the people, making possible the institutions of the Jewish religion; second, as a symbolic expression of the harmony and intimate love between God and the people. Zion is a territorial reality and an ideal condition in Judaism. The land of Israel subsists in Jewish history as a fact and in Jewish theology as the setting for our utopia.

First, the sheer historicity of the land in Judaism. For all the universalism of the Jewish conception of God, moral vision, conviction as to the unity of the human race and the cosmos and so forth, Judaism is the religion of one people. Without the matrix of a people (that is, without a specific language, sociology, and culture) there would have been no Hebrew Bible, hence no historic Judaism, hence no historic Christianity. Canaan became the land of Israel because it was located between the first historical civilizations, with the result that ancient Israel could both borrow from and negate central features of their world views.

We are told that the semi-nomadic ancestral clans of Israel abandoned Mesopotamia (the land of the tower of Babel) for Canaan where a yet unknown God guided and protected them. Their descendants entered into an irrevocable covenant with this God in the wilderness of Sinai, a no-man's-land between Egypt and Canaan. In the covenant God promised the Israelite tribes a per-

61

manent home as a collective inheritance. In biblical theology, God is the ultimate owner of the land and the children of Israel are his collective tenant (Lev 25:23); therefore in the holiness code Israel is to arrange a redemption of the land every forty-nine years to "proclaim liberty throughout the land to all its inhabitants" (Lev 25:10). The seasons of this particular land permeate Israelite worship, the pilgrim festivals being celebrations both of the formative events of Israelite history and of the natural cycle of springtime and harvest. The Deuteronomist summarized the people's tie to the land in the following manner: "You shall therefore keep all the commandments which I command you this day, that you may be strong, and go in and take possession of the land which you are going over to possess, and that you may live long in the land which the Lord swore to your fathers to give to them and to their descendants, a land flowing with milk and honey . . . a land which the Lord your God cares for; the eyes of the Lord your God are always upon it, from the beginning of the year to the end of the year" (Dt 11:8–12).

Two widespread ancient assumptions are avoided in the biblical conception of the tie between *Am Yisrael* and *Erets Yisrael:* that holiness adheres in certain sites as such and that the right of possession is based on conquest. The land was holy because God chose it as the place where ancient Israel could actualize the commandments and create a holy society. The people can jeopardize their occupancy by not fulfilling their covenantal obligations: "But you shall keep my statutes and my ordinances and do none of these abominations, either the native or the stranger who sojourns among you . . . lest the land vomit you out, when you defile it, as it vomited out the nation that was before you" (Lev 18:28). These forebodings were held out as warnings by the Torah and the pre-exilic prophets well before the actual exile. When the catastrophes of 722 BCE and 587 BCE occurred, their religious meaning had been fully articulated by the Torah and pre-exilic prophets. The Deuteronomist promises that future faithfulness will be acknowledged within the context of the eternal covenant: "The Lord your God will restore your fortunes and have compassion upon you, and he will gather you again from all the peoples where the Lord your God has scattered you. If your outcasts are in the uttermost parts of heaven, from there the Lord your God will gather you, and from there he will fetch you; and the Lord your God will bring you into the land which your fathers possessed, that you may possess it . . ." (Dt 30:3–5). The prophet of the exile reaffirmed this promise of salvation: "Fear not, for I am with you; I will bring your offspring from the east, and from the west I will gather you. . . . I am the Lord who made all things . . . and who says of Jerusalem, 'It shall be inhabited,' and of the cities of Judah, 'They shall be built, and I will raise up their ruins' " (Is 43:5–6; 44:24–26).

The return to Zion of the 530s and the reconstruction of the Jerusalem Temple in the 520s merely rounded out the paradigmatic cycle of settlement-commonwealth-exile-return. The land is not merely the place whence the people came, but the place whither they are to return. Zion—mountain, city, land—is the abandoned mother whose children are about to return, in the poetry of Deutero-Isaiah. The nations of the world shall march toward Jerusalem's light and the rebuilt Jerusalem shall herald the world's spiritual unification, for all mankind shall know that it is the Lord who ransomed Israel and reigns in Zion (Is 49:14–26; 54:1–17). In Zechariah the prophet exclaims: "Sing and rejoice, O daughter of Zion; for lo, I come and I will dwell in the midst of you, says the Lord. And many nations shall join themselves to the Lord in that day, and shall be my people; and I will dwell in the midst of you, and you shall know that the Lord of hosts has sent me to you. And the Lord will inherit Judah as his portion in the holy land, and will again choose Jerusalem" (Zec 2:10–12).

Necessary as the land of Israel is for the originality of Judaism, it is the setting for less than half of Jewish history. The diaspora as a permanent feature of Jewish life began with the Babylonian exile of 587–534 BCE. "Seek the welfare of the city where I have sent you into exile, and pray to the Lord on its behalf, for in its welfare you will find your welfare" (Jer 29:7). Persian rule over most of the Middle East made possible the return of many Judean exiles to Zion where they rebuilt the Jerusalem Temple; at the same time the Persian empire facilitated the growth of the Jewish diaspora in Mesopotamia and the east. During the subsequent Hellenistic and Roman periods a vast western dispersion appeared in Egypt, North Africa, Syria, Asia Minor, Greece, Italy, Spain, and on the northern frontiers of the Roman empire. Certain of these regions became independently creative in the history of ancient Judaism (the Hellenized Jewry of Alexandria, Babylonian Jewry under the Sassanians). Nevertheless, until the end of the second century C.E. the decisive events and creative religious advances of Jewish history took place mainly in Judea and the Galilee, and until about the fifth century C.E. the land of Israel remained the home of a notable portion of the Jews of the Roman empire.

Post-biblical Judean Judaism went a long way toward fulfilling its universal dimension. Jewish proselytism was a widespread phenomenon, as ancient sources testify. Moreover, the religious institutions of Judaism (synagogue, local community, halakhah, biblical hermeneutics, scholar class, etc.), as they emerged out of the historical cocoon of the Judean priestly theocracy of post-exilic times, proved to be eminently suitable for ensuring diaspora survival in all but the most inhospitable circumstances. The price paid was acceptance of minority status in the lands of the dispersion. Being a minority in countries where the state religion was Christianity or Islam—both so closely related to Judaism and yet so critical of Jewish determination to adhere to its own conception of religious truth—meant being vulnerable to humiliation, persecution, and expulsion. But the Jews found and developed social niches and political relations, different in each land and age, enabling them to cope with minority status. The reality of Jewish settlement in Zion shrunk to a limited number of localities; besides a few surviving Jewish villages in the Galilee, there was a stream of pious diaspora Jews who came to Erets Yisrael, especially to the academies of its holy cities (Jerusalem, Hebron, Tiberias, and so forth) to pray and learn Torah.

Why? Because the anticipation of Zion as the utopian ingathering of the dispersed at the onset of the messianic age, never dimmed. In Second Temple times it was a diaspora practice to bring the remains of the dead to Israel for burial because the final resurrection would occur there. The Mishnah, the central text of early rabbinic Judaism, lovingly records all the commandments that are incumbent on Jews who dwell in the land, including commandments concerning the destroyed Temple, because in the messianic era the centrality of the Jewish presence there is to be restored in all its sacred beauty and splendor. "There are ten degrees of holiness. The Land of Israel is holier than any other land. Wherein lies its holiness? In that from it they may bring the *Omer* [the barley sheaf offered between Passover and Shavuot], the First Fruits [offering], and the Two Loaves [offering], which they may not bring from any other land. The walled cities are still more holy . . . . Within the wall [of Jerusalem] is still more holy . . . . The Temple Mount is still more holy . . . . The Sanctuary is still more holy . . . . The Holy of Holies is still more holy, for none may enter therein save only the high Priest on the Day of Atonement at the time of the [Temple] service" (Mishnah Kelim 1:6–10). Worshipers faced Jerusalem when they prayed, and in the synagogue the holy ark, holding the scrolls of the Torah, is situated in the wall closest to Jerusalem. The eschatological significance of the land in traditional Judaism can be seen most overtly in the prayerbook. The *amidah,* the central sequence of benedictions incumbent on all adult males, contains the appeal: "Sound the great horn for our freedom; lift up the banner to gather our exiles, and gather us from the four corners of earth. Blessed are you, O Lord, who gatherest the dispersed of your people Israel." The grace after meals contains the petition: "Show mercy, O Lord our God, to Israel your people, Jerusalem your city, Zion in which your glory rules, the kingdom of the house of David, and the noble and sacred house that bears your name . . . . We pray that you rebuild Jerusalem, the holy city, soon, in these very days. Blessed are you, O Lord, who in mercy will build Jerusalem anew." The wedding blessings contain the following hope: "May Zion and the land of Israel, so long without children or joy, now become glad and joyful with children living happily in the land. Blessed are you, who makes Zion joyful through her children." The order of prayers for the interment of the dead concludes, "May the Omnipresent comfort you together with all the mourners of Zion and Jerusalem." The Passover seder, the remembrance *par excellence* of collective Jewish liberation, concludes with the formula *ha-*

shanah ha-ba' a biyerushalayim (next year in Jerusalem). In the earthly Jerusalem they sing for the rebuilt—i.e., the eschatological—Jerusalem.

The two levels, the land as homeland and symbol, intersect in the Middle Ages in the concept of *aliyah*. From the verb *la' lot* (to ascend), used to describe travel from low-lying Egypt to mountainous Canaan (see Gen 13.1), was formed the noun *aliyah,* designating pilgrimage to the land of Israel from the diaspora with the connotation of a spiritual ascent. During the first centuries of Muslim rule in the Middle East, when the leading rabbinic institutions were those of Iraq, the revival of Jewish learning in the land of Israel was spurred by a Karaite *aliyah*. (The Karaites were a group of Jewish sects who rejected the talmudic tradition and rabbinic authority.) In the ninth and tenth century, Karaite *avelei Tsiyyon* (mourners for Zion) settled in Jerusalem to devote their lives to prayer and ascetic practice. Daniel al-Kumisi, from northern Persia, penned an appeal to the Karaites of the dispersion: "The Lord himself has commanded the men of the Exile to come to Jerusalem and to stand within it at all times before Him, mourning, fasting, weeping, and wailing, wearing sackcloth and bitterness, all day and all night . . . . Therefore it is incumbent upon you who fear the Lord to come to Jerusalem and to dwell in it, in order to hold vigils before the Lord until the day when Jerusalem shall be restored."[1]

In the twelfth and thirteenth centuries, there was an increasing *aliyah* from the west, even though Crusader rule resulted in a low point in the numbers and condition of the Jews in Palestine. The illustrious Spanish religious philosopher and poet Judah Halevy developed a new genre of Hebrew poetry, the ode to Zion, to express what the land of revelation symbolized to pious diaspora Jews:

> Beautiful heights, joy of the world, city of a great king,
> For you my soul yearns from the lands of the West.
> My pity collects and is roused when I remember the past,
> Your glory in exile, and your temple destroyed.
> Would that I were on the wings of an eagle,
> So that I could water your dust with my mingling tears.
> I have sought you, although your king is away,
> And snakes and scorpions oust Gilead's balm.
> How I shall kiss and cherish your stones.
> Your earth will be sweeter than honey to my taste.[2]

In this vein in the next century was the *aliyah* of Spanish biblical exegete and rabbi Moses ben Nahman (Nahmanides), who sent the following to his children: "I write this letter in Jerusalem, the holy city, to thank and praise the Rock of my salvation. I was privileged to arrive safely there on the ninth of the month of Elul [1267 CE] and to stay there until the day after the Day of

Atonement. But what can I say to you concerning the country? Great is the devastation and, to put it briefly, the more sacred the places, the greater the desolation . . . . May God . . . who thought us worthy to see Jerusalem in her desertion grant us that we may behold her built and restored, and the glory of the Lord shall return to her."[3]

For the medieval Spanish qabbalists (Nahmanides was among them) the land of Israel was a central channel for the flow of grace between the terrestrial and the heavenly realms.[4] The Qabbalah helped spur a new wave of *aliyah* in the sixteenth century following the expulsion of Jews from Spain and Portugal. For almost a century, Sephardic and other qabbalists who settled in the Galilean hillside town of Safed developed prayers and ceremonies to be undertaken at the reputed graves of ancient talmudic and mystical saints in the nearby hills. The messianic hymn *Lekha dodi* by Solomon Halevy Alkabetz has become a regular introit of Sabbath eve worship:

> Come, my beloved, to meet the bride;
> Let us welcome the presence of the Sabbath . . . .
> O sanctuary of our King, O regal city, arise, go forth from your
>   overthrow;
> Long enough have you dwelt in the valley of weeping;
> Truly He will have compassion upon you.
> Shake yourself from the dust, arise;
> Put on the garments of your glory, O my people!
> Through the son of Jesse, the Bethlehemite, draw close to my soul,
>   redeem it . . . .

The communities in and around Ottoman Palestine were the scene of an enthusiastic reception of Shabbatai Tsevi in the 1660s, the central figure of the most important Jewish messianic outburst of the early modern period. The *aliyah* from Poland of Judah Hasid and his followers in 1700 marked yet another wave of return, reinforcing the Old Yishuv (the settlement of pious Jews in the land) that constituted Jewry in the land of Israel until the Jewish national renascence of the 1880s.

This medieval stasis was upset irrevocably by the revolutionary changes forced on the Jewish people in one country after another in the last two hundred years. Between the late eighteenth and the early twentieth centuries, reforming governments undertook to dismantle the internal walls that divided society into distinct corporations and that defined Jewry as a second-class, semi-autonomous entity with only limited rights of residence, occupation, and public expression. One of the mightiest liberations of modernity has been the extension of active participation in the mainstream of society to groups that had been thought of as inherently marginal or of statuses that had been considered inherently subservient. As part of this demolition of anachronistic medieval obstacles to progress, proponents of liberal reform were willing to recognize the Jews as human beings first and foremost, and award them civil and political equality according to the social contract binding all citizens of the enlightened state regardless of their religious preference.

The new conception of an emancipated Jewry was not something imposed on most Jews against their will; it was absorbed by Jewish self-understanding as well. Increasingly, Jews could no longer accept as transient and essentially irrelevant the old isolation and disabilities. The process of political emancipation seemed to acknowledge the legitimacy of unimpeded Jewish integration into the social whole and the full legitimacy of the Jewish religion as an authentic expression of human religiosity. But the promise and disappointments of modernity created a new set of tensions in Jewish history between normalization and uniqueness, that is, between the desire for a life free of the disabling complexes that stemmed from being the object of extraordinary conspicuousness, suspicion, and even fear, together with the determination to reaffirm the transcendent meaning of Jewish identity.

At first the historical fact and theological ideal of Zion seemed irrelevant to the Jew recognized as citizen of the modern polity and as active participant in modern society; there were Jews who felt Judaism could dispense with it altogether, except in the early chapters of Jewish history texts and only as a symbol. However, a major theme of modern Jewish history has been the gradual recovery of the meaning of Erets Yisrael, both practical and religious. The state of Israel has become a powerful presence in contemporary Jewish life partly as the result of contingent circumstances and historical needs, but equally as the result of the dialectic of modern Jewish self-definitions. The Zionist movement emerged in the last quarter of the nineteenth century, at a time of nationalist ferment throughout Europe, especially among long-repressed ethnic groups in Central and Eastern Europe. Zionism has been explained as the Jewish national liberation movement. It is that—and more. Zionism has become a microcosm of the complexities and tensions in modern Judaism. To understand Zionism and, therefore, the State of Israel is to understand the extraordinary vulnerabilities of being Jewish in the twentieth century, the intense longing for redemption from the conditions that exposed the Jews to these vulnerabilities, and the powerful sources of hope within the Jewish tradition.

With the retrospective insight afforded by living in the last decades of the twentieth century, we can appreciate that one of the initial justifications for Zionism was the pragmatic need for a homeland to enable Jews to cope with the destructive impact of anti-Semitism. Actually, arguments for modern Jewish resettlement in the land of Israel by various writers before 1880 paid minimal attention to Jew-hatred, but the upsurge of anti-Semitism converted these individual, isolated proto-Zionist ideas into an ideology with resonance among the Jewish masses. Within two decades Zionism became a major force and political ideal within the Jewish communities of East Europe and elsewhere.

Properly speaking, the term *anti-Semitism* was coined in the 1870s as a translation of old Judeophobic themes (the Jews as Christ killers, ritual murderers of Christian children, allies of Satan) into pseudo-scientific terms (the Jews as an alien, domineering, and parasitic race). Noisy charges of an innate Jewish will-to-power, attribution to malevolent Jewish influence of the social dislocation and disorienting modernism that accompany economic change, the appearance of explicitly anti-Semitic political parties in Central and Western Europe, the pogroms in Russia in 1881–82 and hostility to the Jews shown by the Russian government—these were some of the features of a powerful backlash against the legal emancipation and social integration of the Jews in the modern nation-state. In response and rebuttal of anti-Semitism came the Zionist idea of auto- or self-emancipation.

Self-emancipation involved the creation of a Jewish homeland where the Jewish people, evacuated from the lands where they would never be truly accepted, could establish their own democratic commonwealth. In the decades before World War I, when America was still open to mass Jewish immigration and disemancipation seemed an impossibility, the main argument for political Zionism was, ironically enough, psychological rather than political. The psychic price of being made to feel alien was especially oppressive to Jews who had thought they had attained or were on the verge of attaining in their diaspora homelands fraternity, as well as liberty and equality. Instead of being the recipients of a hypocritical and incomplete emancipation by the ruling groups of Europe, Zionists argued, Jews could only protect themselves adequately against continued discrimination and share equally in the opportunities of modern civilization if they had a land of their own where they were the host and the majority. Most Jews knew this land had to be "the land of the fathers" to which the people was destined eventually to be ingathered.

As mentioned, there were important voices in early Zionism who did not make the problem of anti-Semitism their main point of departure. Within the East European *Hibbat Tsiyyon* (Love of Zion) movement of the 1880s that preceded the establishment of the World Zionist Organization by almost two decades, was the tendency that came to be called spiritual Zionism. For its theoreticians, a return to Zion created the opportunity of building a base for the revival of Hebrew culture in modern forms and responsive to modern ideas. Only in the land of Israel could a Jewish renaissance express itself in all areas of creative life, rather than be confined within the four walls of the contemporary synagogue or Temple only and according to the Procrustean conception of a Western religious denomination. Spiritual Zionism, therefore, was primarily concerned with giving new force and expression to the ethical values of biblical and rabbinic Judaism, rather than adapting modern political nationalism to the needs of the Jewish people.

A third view, whose earliest expression also predated Political Zionism, was that a return to Zion would give the Jews an opportunity to actualize the ideal of a truly just society. Drawing on the various strands of European socialism, the Workers of Zion and other Zionist socialist and labor groupings that were formed in the first years of the twentieth century gave center stage to the theme of social perfectionism. Zionism would enable Jews to escape from the economic abnormality inherent in diaspora existence. According to the Zionist socialists, hypernationalist anti-Semitism had shown itself clearly able to mobilize a following not only among peasants but also in the industrializing cities. The modern Yishuv (Jewish settlement) in the land of Israel could transform Jewry into a normal people, able to participate in the just new world that socialism envisioned. The occupational basis of Jewish life and the class relationships within the Jewish community required a veritable revolution. And, as some labor Zionists argued, in the land of Israel Jews could experience personal redemption through labor, especially in cooperative agricultural communities that eliminated the distortions of human nature inherent in capitalist society.

After World War I, when the rights of the Jews to a homeland in Palestine were endorsed by the British government in the Balfour Declaration and affirmed in the League of Nations mandate, the groundwork for the new Jewish commonwealth took shape. The various ideological streams mentioned above were brought together in a Yishuv dominated by socialist idealism, a secular Hebrew renascence, and Western democratic values. With the closing off of the possibility of mass emigration of Jews almost everywhere and the establishment of regimes that endorsed anti-Semitism in many parts of Europe, especially in Nazi Germany after 1933, the central function of Zionism became saving Jewish lives, not only Jewish civilization and Jewish psyches. Since then the most immediate and urgent reason for the existence of a Jewish state has been its ability to rescue Jews caught in extreme conditions that threatened them with persecution (even with slaughter) primarily because they were Jews. A split emerged in the Zionist movement in the 1930s over the tempo of development and the goals of the Yishuv in relation to the agonies of European Jewry, but what could be done was severely limited by the restrictions imposed by the British on Jewish immigration to Palestine. It is against this background that the accomplishments of the State of Israel, since winning independence and full sovereignty in 1948, are to be measured.

Whatever else have been Israel's achievements and failures, its response to the need for a Jewish refuge where special visas are not required has been demonstrated repeatedly: with Jewish survivors in the displaced persons camps in Europe after World War II, with the Jews of most Arab lands in the late forties and early fifties, with Jews in Eastern Europe and the Soviet Union, Argentina, Ethiopia, and other countries since then. The nations of the world are not prepared to meet this Jewish need without reservations, quotas, and other qualifications that have proven to be disastrous in Jewish history. This is the argument for Israel as the means of Jewish normalization at its most fundamental—that the Jews have the same right as any comparable group to an instrumentality effectively able to defend the people.

Israel's failures since 1948 have been the failures of almost every Western democratic society that does not have a sufficient territory to render it reasonably secure and sufficient national wealth to mute social antagonisms. Israel has gathered in Jews from tens of different countries of many levels of social and economic development; persisting social tensions in Israel reflect the difficulty of welding so many different Jewish cultures together into a harmonious modern nation. This problem is found in almost every heterogeneous society, as is the declining appeal of secularistic ideologies of social perfection. Even Israel has experienced the malaise of post-industrial, technologically advanced, urbanized nations elsewhere in the world. The achievements of Israeli inventiveness in certain branches of the economy are evident, as are the attainments of Israeli literature, including a new Hebrew poetry that reaches the level of the great medieval and biblical poets, and of Jewish scholarship and learning, both traditional and modern. Israel's greatest failure, of course, has been the inability to establish peace with its Arab neighbors, including the Arabs of Palestine. Whatever the tactical mistakes of the government of Israel in this regard, they are overshadowed by the refusal of the Arab governments of the Middle East (except Sadat's Egypt) to accept as legitimate a sovereign Jewish state in their midst. The normalization of having an Israel as a recognized voice in the international order runs up against the abnormality of the Jewish condition once again. Beyond the usual considerations of power politics, an earlier Judeophobic demonology seems to have been transferred to the Jewish state not only by Israel's immediate enemies but by some Third World governments and leftist political tendencies.

In the two decades since Vatican II, the turning point with respect to the meaning of Zion to the Jewish people was the June war of 1967. The silence, even of governments friendly to Israel, during the crisis provoked by Nasser before the war and the ineffectualness of the United Nations gave new applicability to Balaam's definition of Israel as "a people dwelling alone" (Num 23:9). Israel's lightning victory seemed a miraculous salvation that brought Israeli rule and therefore Jewish access to some of the most revered places of ancient Israelite history, such as the tombs of the patriarchs at Hebron and of Rachel near Bethlehem, the sites of Shiloh and Bethel in Samaria, the Jewish Quarter and the Western Wall in old Jerusalem. Despite the travails of the last decade and along with a decline in the idealistic fervor of secular Jewishness, an astonishing revitalization has occurred in Jewish religiosity. Secular Jews have become *baalei teshuvah* (repentant observers of the commandments) and have turned to traditional Jewish studies and practice, a symptom among Jews of the broad movement of searching for God and spiritual wholeness that is evident in the West. And not only in the West, as the upsurge of Shiite fervor indicates. Charismatic renewal, evangelical revivalism, the reawakening of fundamentalist energies have had their Jewish manifestations as well in and through Israel, where some traditionalist and newly traditionalist Jews have been inspired by a messianic zeal for taking possession of the entire land. Very problematic, certainly for a negotiated Jewish-Arab peace in Palestine when that becomes possible, is the apocalyptic spirit and militant initiatives of the *Gush Emunim,* who have been a major force in the founding of new Jewish settlements in the West Bank. This demodernizing militancy raises a challenge for the humanitarian values that have characterized modern Zionism from its inception and for the religious pluralism that has become the Jewish norm in the West. Yet a broad Jewish religious revival is a force which Zionism and the State of Israel has helped to make possible. Another of the surprises of history: that what began as a program of secular autoemancipation, socialist idealism, and cultural nationalism should open the door to a renewal of Jewish faith, the recovery of ancient forces within the heart of the people, and, one hopes, the purgation of their dross toward a new vision of Jewish spiritual fulfillment.

We have mentioned the tension in modern Jewry between the desire for normalization and the experience of uniqueness as evidenced in the unfolding of modern Zionism. Both elements are in the process of being redefined. In the light of modern Jewish history, normalization means not merely acquiring a state "like all the nations" (1 Sam 8:5), but the emphatic rejection of the traditional victimization of the Jews so that the Jewish people can fully participate in the shaping of the conditions of its life and destiny. Zionism, like Reform, Conservative, and Orthodox Judaism and the various secular Jewish movements in Eastern Europe, is one of the several efforts by modern Jews to take control of forces shaping Jewish survival. Zionism, like these other tendencies, has expressed the periodic need of every tradition to reassess the meaning of its primary commitments. (After all, Vatican II came of the same need for reassessment and reformulation in the Catholic Church.) Normalization in this sense can never cancel Jewish uniqueness. A secular State of Israel can never cut the umbilical cord connecting it to the religion of the Jews. The land of Israel is the ancient homeland, the place where Judaism came into its own; it is likewise a crucial element in the complex of meanings and symbols which shape the structure of Jewish faith. That is not the least of the reasons why Israel is presently so vital to many Jews and, one would hope, to our Catholic friends as well.

NOTES

1. Leon Nemoy, editor, *The Karaite Anthology: Excerpts from the Early Literature* (New Haven: Yale University Press, 1952), pp. 36–37.

2. David Goldstein, translator, *The Jewish Poets of Spain* (Baltimore, Maryland: Penguin Books, 1965), p. 129.

3. Franz Kobler, editor, *Letters of the Jews Through the Ages,* volume one (London: East and West Library, 1953), p. 226.

4. "Happy is he whose lot it is during his lifetime to abide in the holy land; for such a one draws down the dew from the heavens above upon the earth, and whoever is attached to this holy land in his lifetime becomes attached afterwards to a supernal holy land. . . . —*The Zohar,* translated by Maurice Simon and Harry Sperling (London: Soncino Press, 1934), vol. 5, p. 72.

Israel, Jerusalem,
and the Middle East

REV. EDWARD H. FLANNERY

Several years ago an Orthodox rabbi, when asked what he expected of Christians today, replied, "Just respect our tie with the State of Israel, nothing else." His pithy remark made clear that for him Israel held a paramount place in his model of interfaith dialogue and his faith-commitment. Allowing for its dramatic terseness and eliding the "nothing else," his position is not far from that of the vast majority of Jews. *Per contra*, today, twenty-five years after the issuance of *Nostra Aetate*, 4, which urged "fraternal dialogue" with Jews upon Christians, the tie that binds the Jewish people and their religious tradition to the land and State of Israel[1] remains a stumbling block for many Christians. Pivotal among Jewish concerns and essential to Judaism itself, both historically and theologically considered, it remains peripheral to Christian interests, suspect in the dialogue, and fraught with many misunderstandings. The disparity of perspectives separating Christians and Jews here forms a gap in the dialogue that has impeded its progress from the start. It is time the gap be closed. What is so sacred to virtually all Jews must be accorded the full acceptance and understanding that it merits, not only for the sake of good relations but in the interest of truth and justice.

In the "Guidelines and Suggestions Implementing the Conciliar Declaration *Nostra Aetate*, 4" issued by the Vatican Commission for Religious Relations with Jews in 1975, Catholics—indeed all Christians—were encouraged to "strive to learn by what essential traits Jews define themselves in the light of their own religious experience"—a cardinal principle of the Jewish-Christian dialogue. On the whole, the principle has been conscientiously put into practice by dialoguing Christians except in discussions on the State of Israel. With the exception of a small group of experienced Christians dialogists, the subject is generally unwelcome, and in some instances taboo.

The Vatican, in effect, pre-empted the implementing of the principle on Jewish self-definition when a year previous to its publication it created a Vatican Commission for *Religious* Relations with Jews. It was made plain by the title and initial meetings of the Commission that Israel was not a fitting subject for its discussions. Such discussion, it was made clear, would be reserved for other curial departments, such as the Secretariat of State, which deal with international political questions. The situation that resulted was an unpromising one. Jews in dialogue, for whom Israel was first among their religious, institutional, and personal concerns, were expected to place that concern in brackets in their discussions or, more precisely, keep it out of the dialogue.

Despite fruitful annual meetings of the International Vatican Liaison Committee with the International Jewish Committee for Interreligious Consultations, the Vatican has continued to maintain a cool neutrality toward Israel and for reasons that appear to many as obsolete has yet formally to recognize that state. On the other hand, it is true, a *de facto* Vatican recognition of Israel has been in operation, with open and frequented doors on both sides of the Israel-Vatican relationship. The relationship appears to improve with the passage of time. Though the Vatican has not as yet relaxed its official stance, some breakthroughs have occurred with national hierarchies. In 1973 a Committee for Relations with Jews of the French episcopate did concede—after much nuancing and balancing—that "the conscience of the world community cannot refuse the Jewish people who had to submit to so many vicissitudes in the course of its history, the right and means for a political existence among the nations."[2] The statement was not wholeheartedly endorsed by the French church. More of a breakthrough came in the statement on Catholic-Jewish Relations of the National Conference of Catholic Bishops in 1975 in these words:

> In dialogue with Christians, Jews have explained that they do not consider themselves as a church, a sect, or a denomination, as is the case among Christian communities, but rather as a peoplehood that is not solely racial, ethnic or religious, but in a sense a composite of all these. It is for such reasons that an overwhelming majority of Jews see themselves bound in one way or another to the land of Israel. Most Jews see this tie to the land as essential to their Jewishness. Whatever difficulties Christians may experience in sharing this view they should strive to understand this link between land and people which Jews have expressed in their writings and worship throughout ten millennia as a longing for the homeland, holy Zion.

This helpful statement was tempered somewhat with a caution:

> Appreciation of this link is not to give assent to any particular religious interpretation of this bond. Nor is this affirmation meant to deny the legitimate rights of other parties in the region, or to adopt

any political stance in the controversies over the Middle East, which lie beyond the purview of this statement.[3]

A fair enough caution were it not that the very existence of Israel has been made moot in the "controversies over the Middle East."

John Paul II has advanced the Catholic perspective in a positive direction. In a homily delivered in 1980 when, apparently adhering to the official Vatican position, referring to the establishment of the State of Israel he commented that "a sad condition was created for the Palestinian people who were excluded from their homeland. These are facts that anyone can see." The Pope here unwittingly gave strong evidence to the effectiveness of Arab propaganda on the subject (see below). In the same homily, however, he linked the establishment of the state to the Holocaust in these words: "The Jewish people, after tragic experiences connected with the extermination of so many sons and daughters, driven by the desire for security, set up the State of Israel." This was the first time that Israel and the Holocaust have been linked together on an official level. Another advance was made in 1984 in the Pope's Apostolic Letter *Redemptionis Anno* in which he wrote:

> For the Jewish people who live in the State of Israel, and who pre-
> serve in that land such previous testimonies to their history and their
> faith, we must ask for the desired security and the due tranquility
> that is the prerogative of every nation and condition of life and of
> progress for every society.[4]

This was an unequivocal affirmation of Israel's right to live in peace and security as a society and a nation.

The World Council of Churches and the National Council of Churches in the United States have insisted on treating Israel as a purely political and polemical subject that is not to benefit from interfaith conversation, but more recently have somewhat emended their positions. In a statement of 1983 the Governing Board of the latter body adopted a resolution urging a new Middle East policy and the United States that would effect substantial reductions in arms transfers to and from the Middle East nations—a recommendation which, if heeded, could have led to the extinction of Israel. Meanwhile a document adopted by the World Council of Churches in 1982 conceded that Israel "constitutes part of the long search for that survival which has always been central to Judaism through the ages."[5]

The most significant advance in Jewish-Christian understanding must be accredited to the scholarly dialogue of Christians and Jews that has been diligently and progressively working in this area for the last several decades.[6] Regrettably, this important pioneering effort has escaped the notice of the

Christian community at large and even of the theological community as a whole, though in recent years a few theologians of international renown have increasingly taken up the discussion of the relationship of Judaism and Christianity—a necessary prelude to any satisfactory theological consideration of Israel. But then, even among seasoned dialogists one can detect betimes an occasional anti-Zionist coloration in their thinking[7] and, moreover, most theologians who enter the Jewish-Christian colloquium give the subject of Israel a fairly wide berth.

The Christian's reluctance to look upon the State of Israel with a full and open heart is disappointing and in a certain sense surprising. Given the magnitude of contempt, degradation, and murder that was visited upon the Jewish people throughout the centuries and the direct involvement of the Christian churches and peoples in this oppression, given the horror of the Holocaust perpetrated in our time, given the continuing prevalence of antisemitism in so many parts of the world today—given all this, one might expect that Christians would welcome, indeed rejoice in the return of the Jewish people to a small sliver of their ancient homeland—if not from compassion and a sense of justice at least from a sense of guilt and repentance. The fact that they do not calls for explanations. From another point of view, there should be no surprise. Given the lingering anti-Judaism of traditional Christian theology, the all but total ignorance of so many Christians of the age-old antisemitic record and its Christian origins, and, more recently, the emergence of a virulent anti-Zionism, both social and political, the reluctance becomes an expectable reaction. The roots of the reluctance, in other words, run deep; and they run in several directions, specifically, into anti-Zionism, antisemitism, and theological anti-Judaism, directions which, if separable, tend to converge and reinforce one another.

The complexity of an adequate discussion of Israel should be faced at the outset. Misunderstandings on the subject generally flow from oversimplifications, and are often reducible to excessive reliance on newspaper or propagandistic accounts. The term "Israel" is a highly over-determined one, and rarely denotes just one of its several possible meanings. It can on occasion signify all at once: an ancient land, nation, or people; the foundational theological matrix and symbol of Judaism, and a modern democratic national state. All of these meanings tend to overlap and intermingle. This intricate complexus of meanings is further complicated by another category which enriches the Israelite and Israeli reality: Zionism. In its comprehensive sense this category can be defined as whatever ideology, cause, or movement that favors or promotes the Jewish possession, retention of, or return to, the ancient Jewish homeland, known today as the State of Israel. Regrettably, antisemitic fictions and political polemics have grossly tarnished this word and the reality it denotes. A sacred word on the lips of most Jews it has become one of opprobrium not only on the lips of members of the PLO and Israel's Arab enemies but often on those of Christians remote from the scene of the Middle East conflict, and even of some dedicated to Christian-Jewish understanding. One may well speculate whether their understanding of the word does not derive more from the sinister aura of conspiracy and domination given it by the infamous "Protocols of the Elders of Zion" (circulated to this day) and more recent distortions of Arab and Soviet propaganda than from the open and honorable history of the Zionist idea and movement. This semantical problem is a serious one because of the toll it takes of Jewish-Christian understanding and dialogue. The sole antidote is obviously a complete and unbiased study of the Zionist phenomenon in all its aspects.

The chief obstacles to an accurate and full comprehension of Israel and its place in the Jewish-Christian interface have been (1) the politicization of what is essentially a religious phenomenon, and (2) the mythologization of that part of the phenomenon that is truly political. The depoliticization of the discussion on Israel and the demythologization of the political opposition to that State are accordingly prime requisites for further progress of the Jewish-Christian dialogue.

The Jewish-Christian dialogue is an interfaith encounter, wherein two fundamentally cognate faith-traditions strive for mutual understanding and—in view of historical realities—reconciliation. Though fundamentally cognate, both faiths are also essentially different. Judaism can best be described as a peoplehood originating in a particularist religious tradition. Christianity is a creedal commitment of a more universalist stamp. It is out of this difference in their basic constitution that the problem of Israel arises. From a Judaic standpoint Israel belongs ultimately in a religious and therefore ecumenical category; from a Christian perspective (insofar as it ignores or excludes Jewish self-definition) Israel is a political matter. It is from this potential but unnecessary dichotomy of views that the reluctance of many Christians in dialogue to accept Israel as a legitimate agendum for the dialogue stems. An odd paradox is evident here. If by Jewish self-definition Israel is endowed with a theological significance and is a central element of Jewish identity, the Christian polemicist's objection to it as an acceptable subject for religious conversations and as a politicization of the subject is itself a politicization of the dialogue. The situation is thus reversed. The objection amounts to a violation of the principle of self-definition to which all entrants to the dialogue lay claim and therefore poses a threat to authentic dialogue. What is said of *objection* to the subject can be extended, if to a lesser degree, to any reluctance or discouragement that might affect placement of the subject on the dialogical agenda.

Is the State of Israel entitled to theological significance independently of Jewish self-definition? Why, in other words, in so many cases of dialogue must the answer to this question come only from Jewish participants? A simple familiarity with the Christian's Hebrew Scriptures, commonly called the Old Testament, and a cursory acquaintance with Jewish history and thought should be enough for Christians to arrive at the Jewish answer unaided. The widespread inability of Christians, even some of the ecumenically aware, to come to this understanding on their own points to two defects on the Christian side that merit further exploration in dialogical discussion: the tendency of Christian "fulfilment" theology to filter all Judaism out of the Hebrew Scriptures by over-spiritualizing and over-allegorizing them and, secondly, the assumption that with the fall of the Second Jewish Commonwealth in 70 C.E. Israel, to all effective religious purposes, came to an end. These theological postures are tantamount to a denial of the Jewish roots of Christianity and, moreover, a contradiction of the Pauline assurance of the perpetuity of Israel's covenant (Rom 9:4). And they render a true knowledge of Judaism, ancient or post-biblical, impossible.

Judaism is essentially Zionist. From its inception the land of Israel (*Eretz Yisrael*), as promised, possessed, or to be repossessed, has been a constant of Jewish history. The promise appears early in the Torah (Gen 12:1), and from that point, possession of or return to the Promised Land became a dominant of Jewish life. Residence outside of Israel for believing Jews was considered exile (*galut*). The God of Israel, the people of Israel, the nation of Israel, the Torah of Israel, were inextricably linked to *Eretz Yisrael*. Only on its soil could the Torah be fully implemented; only with Jewish inhabitation of the land could the Messianic era come about. Throughout the millennia, living in or returning to it became a recurring theme of Jewish writings, religious and secular, ancient, medieval, and modern. Jewish liturgy is replete with references and prayers for return to Israel and rebuilding of Jerusalem. Three times a day throughout the centuries the pious Jew prayed from the *Amidah* for return to Zion. Jewish fastdays, the Passover Seder, the Day of Atonement service, Sabbath and holiday prayers give vent to the yearning of the Jewish soul for the Holy Land—holy Zion. Meanwhile the Talmud, that massive corpus of Jewish law and teachings, includes hundreds of references to the land of Israel. It is no exaggeration to say that Judaism is saturated with Zionism. The political movement launched by Theodore Herzl at the turn of the century is no more than a latter-day political manifestation of the deep Messianic and Zionist core of Judaism itself. To ask loyal Jews to ignore or suppress this Zionist attachment or keep it out of the interreligious dialogue is to ask them to divest themselves of Judaism.

One may wish that Christian anti-Zionists were conversant with the existence and history of Christian Zionism. It is an interesting but little known page in our history that should be reread today. It would help to show that Christian pro-Zionism need not necessarily be only a response to Jewish urging but an impulse that finds energies in Christianity itself—and not necessarily in a fundamentalist context. It is an interesting fact that some of the British inspirers and architects of the Balfour Declaration, which aided so powerfully the political development of the Jewish State, were motivated in considerable part by Christian Zionists. Another root of that State was the antisemitism in Christian countries. Ironically, Christians thus, indirectly, had a double hand, one negative, one positive, in the creation of the State of Israel.

The Middle East (Arab-Israeli) conflict has proven a grave distraction for the Jewish-Christian dialogue and for Jewish-Christian understanding generally. Numerous Christians, unaware of any bias on their part, see the establishment of the State of Israel very simply as a serious injustice inflicted upon the Palestinian Arab population by the Israelis. Through this prism they fail to perceive much significance, historical or theological, in the new state, and direct their attention exclusively to problems of Arab refugees, a Palestinian state, and other socio-political aspects of the problem. The peril in which Israel continuously exists and the problem of its security and survival become in this way secondary considerations, if they are considered at all. The simplicity and one-sidedness of this approach, for one thing, stems in most cases from inadequate information and uncritical acceptance of Arab or anti-Zionist propaganda. The United Nations can serve as a large-scale sample of this way of approaching the Middle East problem. It is imperative, in any case, for the health and survival of the Jewish-Christian embrace that the misinformation and mythologizing that have engulfed the conflict be dispelled.

Affirming or defending the case for Israel need not, and should not, of course, entail any insensitivity to Palestinian Arab rights and aspirations. Criticism of their propaganda is not to be equated with a rejection of these. It is understood, on the other hand, that no affirmation or defense of the Arab case shall admit of any requirements or demands that would impugn the sovereignty or jeopardize the security of the State of Israel.

The root-problem of the Arab-Israeli conflict is the refusal of many of Israel's enemies to accept or respect Israel's right to live in peace and security. The effective resolution of that problem would establish the basis of solution of all other issues and problems involved in the unhappy situation; failure to resolve it renders their solution permanently impossible.

The foundation of the State of Israel rests on solid juridical and moral grounds, more solid indeed than those of many states recognized by the United Nations and the international community. But before inspection of the foundations from a legal or juridical and moral point of view, the question of theological or Scriptural foundations should be asked. Can or should biblical promises be used to found the present state? Obviously not. Biblical or theological validation can, to be sure, be affirmatively discussed in interfaith dialogue, but should not be used to provide a political or legal rationale for this or any other contemporary state. Modern political requirements preclude draw-ing a political conclusion from theological or Scriptural premises.

The juridical or legal basis of the State of Israel involves a lengthy and complex development, but can be very briefly and simply outlined. The Bal-four declaration (1916) won widespread international encouragement for the formation of a Jewish homeland in Palestine, and eventually was one of the dominant influences in having this principle incorporated in all major instru-ments of the peace treaties touching the Middle East (San Remo and Sèvres) in 1920, the British Mandate in Palestine and the Churchill White Paper in 1922. After 1930, in the wake of many Arab-Jewish clashes in Palestine and several British studies of the situation there, Britain in frustration—and perfidy[8]—finally turned the matter over to the United Nations, which after a further study proposed a plan in 1947 for the partitioning of Palestine into two States, Arab and Jewish (excluding Trans-Jordan, the first Palestinian state). In this plan the Jews were given those portions of the land where they consti-tuted a majority—an important but little noted fact. The General Assembly passed the partition plan by a vote of 33 to 13, with Russia and the United States voting for partition. The Arabs rejected the United Nations' decision, while, in May 1948, the Palestinian Jews set up the State of Israel. The portion of territory allotted to Palestinian Arabs was later annexed by Jordan. Mean-while five Arab armies marched against Israel, as many Palestinian Arabs, often with the urging of their leaders, fled the battlefield in the hope of re-turning when Israel was permanently crushed, thus creating the refugee prob-lem. This first of several anti-Israeli wars altered the original borders of the Israeli state, as have others since. In 1949 Israel was accepted as a member of the United Nations. Two attempts were made thereafter in the World Court to invalidate the establishment of Israel, but were voted down. Juridically, no serious question can be placed on the validity of the establishment of the State of Israel.

But, if legal, was it moral? Did one people displace another people to occupy its homeland? A ubiquitous myth, circulated by Arab and pro-Arab propaganda, says yes. The myth usually runs in this way: an alien people (the Jews) expelled the indigenous people (the Arabs) from the homeland they had occupied from time immemorial, forcing them to fester in poverty on the bor-ders of that homeland. A secondary myth often appended to this one tells of excellent relations that existed between Arabs and Jews in Arab countries prior to the settlement and establishment of the State of Israel.

What are the facts of the matter? Recent research tells a different story, indeed turns these myths upside-down.[9] Jews were never fully absent from Palestine following the expulsion of 70 C.E. Throughout the centuries the Holy Land remained a center of Jewish spirituality and a place of pilgrimage, residence, and yearning for national return. Finally, in 1948, it must be repeated, the territory conceded by the United Nations to Palestinian Jews contained a Jewish majority, a majority that had been created by peaceful purchase and international cooperation. Was Palestine, then, an Arab land with a teeming population that had been there from time immemorial now to be displaced by Jewish interlopers? Not at all. Nothing that in accepted terminology could be considered an Arab nation or people existed. Palestine was seen as a part of Southern Syria. Much of the population was nomadic, and a large portion of its population was of recent immigration, much of which had followed Jews into Palestine because of the increased prosperity they would enjoy there—a fact that is true to this day. After the 1947 war the traditional rule of ten years residency to be considered a refugee had to be reduced to two years in order that much of the Arab population that had fled Israeli territory could qualify. Some 500,000 Arabs had left Israel to become refugees, many of them leaving of their own accord simply to vacate the field of battle. On the other hand, approximately five to six hundred thousand Jews had to flee most of the Arab countries of the Middle East shortly thereafter, thus creating what is considered by many observers as an even exchange of refugees. In any event, in no sense can it be said that the Jewish people expelled the Arab Palestinians from their homeland to make room for themselves. As to the treatment of Jews in Arab lands before the establishment of the State of Israel, a cursory knowledge of Arab history would show that the *dhimmis* (non-Islamic residents), including Jews, were treated with contempt and harassment. According to Islamic law and custom, they were always to be kept in a position inferior to Islamic citizens. Many degrading and insulting practices were instituted to implement this policy. This traditional attitude and policy can be seen as one of the chief causes of the enduring Arab resentment of the existence and accomplishments of the Israeli State in the Middle East.

In view of the foregoing myths and facts the question arises: Why have so many non-Arab Christians, even some in dialogue with Jews, accepted *whole* the myths of anti-Israeli propaganda without any serious attempt to check the factuality of any part of them? Which returns us to the already discussed reluctance to admit Israel as a bonafide subject of the agenda of dialogue.

Is theology involved? Is the refusal to allow a theological consideration of Israel or merely the tendency to disfavor it a residue of the deicidal myth, which often included the idea that Israel could never return to its homeland or temple, or again of the theology of supersession which consigned Israel to obsoleteness in the Christian dispensation? Possibly. Certainly the deicide charge is no longer tenable for a Catholic, having been rejected by the Vatican Council statement on the Jewish people (*Nostra Aetate*, 4). But can it not stay on as a species of unconscious theological hangover, taking the form of a vague uneasiness at the prospect of the Holy Land, particularly Jerusalem, in the hands of Jews? We are aware that in the early part of the century, when the Zionists were promoting the idea of a return of the Jews to Palestine, the Papacy, the Vatican, and some theologians manifested a distinct opposition on theological grounds. The question is one for Christians to ponder. It would be wise for us to suspect that some of the old anti-Judaic theses and feelings may still be operative on a subliminal level.

Is antisemitism involved? Otherwise put, is anti-Zionism in its various degrees and forms antisemitic? Not necessarily, but almost always. The distinction here is between the theoretical and the practical. It is possible to be anti-Zionist and not an antisemite. This could be the case of a contemporary Arab, a highly introverted ideologue who can divorce himself from the emotional and the partisan, a person who is free of prejudice but holds a brief in favor of the Arab cause, and so on. On the other hand, it has become more difficult with time to remain anti-Zionist and non-antisemitic, given the mortal threat to Israel's existence by its Arab enemies. Until 1948, to be one or the other was optional; in 1985 the anti-Zionist option veers toward genocide. The practical reason to suspect the anti-Zionist is based on the pervasiveness of antisemitism. Twenty-three centuries old, it lives on today in both virulent and milder widespread forms, so that few are free of its taint—this despite what might be called the conspiracy of silence that affects it: everyone denies that he or she is antisemitic and is supported in his or her denial by almost everybody else. If however it is so widespread, is it possible that the anti-Zionist is by exception bereft of it? Would not it be he or she at whom one would look first for its presence? Be that as it may, close enough observation will generally show that under examination the anti-Zionist will exhibit the usual, if not greater, symptoms of the antisemitic virus. It is on the anti-Zionist front, moreover, that the antisemitic assault is most zealously pressed today.

Virtually all that has been said about the centrality of Zionism and Israel in Jewish life, thought and worship can be said of Jerusalem, if not more so. It is a city that is holy to Jews in ways that it is not to Christians or Muslims. For them its holiness derives not from sacred places or holy personages who lived in it; in Judaism the city itself is holy. A city chosen by God Himself for the people of Israel, Jerusalem was the first capital in the formation of Israel as a nation under King David and ever since has remained as the very center of Jewish aspirations and concerns. Jerusalem and Zion became all but synonymous, and both came to represent both the land and the people of Israel as a whole. In the Prophets and Psalms the Holy City is seen and loved as a mother of all the children of Israel and the site of their ingathering upon which the Messianic era will be built.

The Holy City is sacred to Christians and Muslims too but not to the degree that it is to Jews and Judaism. If one were to hazard a schematization of importance of its relationship to the three great monotheistic religions, one might peg the relationships as primary to Judaism, secondary to Christianity, and tertiary to Islam. To Christians it is hallowed because it was the site of the passion, death and resurrection of Jesus and the birth of the church. Christian exegesis and hermeneutic to a large extent de-territorialized the divine plan of salvation, so that the Holy Land and Jerusalem was assigned the role of reliquary (the supreme one) and fomenter of Christian piety. In time the accent was transferred from the earthly Jerusalem to the celestial Jerusalem of John's Book of Revelation, of which it was considered a pale reflection. For Muslims the city is secondary to Mecca in worship and piety as a reminder of Muhammad's mystical visitation and ascension. Physically, the Prophet never set a foot in Jerusalem, and, moreover, the word does not appear in the Koran.

This Holy City, the "city of peace," host to the devotions of Jews, Christians, and Muslims, could not fail to become embroiled in the Middle East conflict. The three faiths lay claim to it in one way or another, and the United Nations and several countries do the same. In the partition plan of 1947 the United Nations asked for its internationalization, but by the early 1950s ceased entirely to press for it. The Vatican continued to call for internationalization until 1969, when a new formula was adopted requesting some species of international "statute" guaranteeing free access to the holy sites and the rights of Christians in the area. Today only Arab states ask for internationalization. The need of an international statute can be questioned, but also recommended. The Israeli government, it would seem, is not opposed. It is a matter of some countries interested in safeguarding the shrines and pilgrims offering a proposal to Israel. (The question of sovereignty is not involved.) All such an agreement would do is put on paper what has been in operation since 1967 when Israel retook the Old City from the Jordanians. Since then Israel's conduct with respect to the shrines and the Christian and Muslim populations (*qua* Christian and Muslim) has been exemplary. Under Jordanian occupation from 1948 to 1967 no Jew could visit the Old City or the Western Wall; a road was built through the most sacred of Jewish cemeteries; tombstones were desecrated; all synagogues were converted into secular use or razed; and a Hilton-type hotel was built atop the Mount of Olives. And not a single church or government raised a voice of protest or concern. Why now the hue and cry when all religious rights are respected and protected?

One might expect that a Christian could not look upon the State of Israel without certain scriptural and theological reverberations. The people of the Bible back in the land of the Bible is a development that should remind him, however vaguely, of his origins. But this is not often the case. Since many Christians see Israel as a purely political and secular affair they refuse to see any possible connection between it and the Israel of old. This is a break with tradition.

There has always been a "positive theology" that is expected to formulate or revise its conclusion in the light of happenings in the world that may conceal theological implications. These have been called "signs of the times." Israel has always been one of them, but always in a negative reference. The question today is whether, now that in defiance of all expectations—secular as well as theological—the people of Israel are back in their ancient homeland, this sign of the times will be interpreted in a positive light.

The supposed lack of resemblance between the present State of Israel and the Israel of biblical times is a favorite observation of many anti-Zionists. These critics, viewing Israel in a myopic light, fail to see the genuinely religious, even messianic, character that marks even Israel's secular endeavors. Any visitor to a kibbutz will understand this. It is interesting, on the other hand, that when Israel is not viewed as secular it is usually described as a theocracy, a religious establishment as it was in its earliest days. There has, in any case, always been only one Israel, whether it worshiped its One God or at the altars of the Baalim. Moreover, is not expecting a beleaguered state not yet a half century old to fulfill its highest ideals demanding something expected of no other country?

It is, of course, not possible to undertake a theological study of the State of Israel without the benefit of a thorough revision of the traditional Christian theology of Judaism, which as yet has been hardly broached by most theologians. More than a refutation of the deicide charge is required. The Vatican II Declaration (*Nostra Aetate,* 4) has already opened the way by signalizing the spiritual bond that unites the Church and the Synagogue and by summarizing some pertinent parts of St. Paul's Epistle to the Romans. Writing about thirty years within the Christian dispensation, the Apostle makes clear that Jews still "have the covenants . . . and the promises" (Rom 9:4–5); that "God's gifts are irrevocable" (Rom 11:29); that because of our common patrimony Jews are "most dear" (Rom 11:28). Little further proof should be needed of Judaism's continuing election and its special status in the Christian outlook, its special claim to Christian assent. An acknowledgment of Israel's ongoing election in the divine plan invites a review of other assumptions that grew up in that bitter period when the Church and the Synagogue separated so harshly.

If it can be said that the Christian theology of Judaism is far from complete, it can be said that a Christian theology of Israel as a land hardly exists.[10] And presumably it will not greatly progress until the former is well underway. Its creation, further, will probably not make much headway in the present atmosphere, so inflamed by the Arab-Israeli conflict, one side of which would bar the merest consideration that Israel might have a positive religious significance. If we are not entirely to politicize theology, certain questions regarding Israel must nonetheless be posed.

In his *Israel: Echo of Eternity,* Rabbi Abraham Heschel challenged Christian theologians to reconsider their age-old habit of allegorizing everything in the Old Testament while literalizing all in the New.[11] And indeed, in response the Christian can question whether *everything* in the Old Testament was fulfilled in Christ. There are, clearly, things in the First Covenant that were not fulfilled in the Second or New Covenant. Christ did not propose to fulfill *all* messianic expectations of the First Covenant; rather did He ignore some, and even contradict others. Could not some of these expectations be held for fulfillment at a later time?

If Judaism still has the covenants and promises (Rom 9:4–5), and these originally involved the land, on what ground must the land be excluded from them in post-biblical times? The ancient prophecies always spoke in terms of a divine pattern or sequence, involving sin, exile from the land, repentance, and return to the land. Whereupon would Israel's latest exile elude these prophecies? Does the fact that Christianity has de-territorialized its message to a large extent require that it impose this hermeneutic on Judaism too?

Such is one of the questions that seek answers from the Christian theologian. The present state of the Christian theology of Judaism is not sufficiently advanced to render much help in answering it, and the present situation in the Middle East acts as a deterrent. So the theological effort will probably be prolonged. Perhaps what is more necessary than theologizing is a *metanoia,* an authentic repentance for the contribution Christianity has made over the centuries to bring about the tragic rift between Christian and Jew and to some degree also the impasse in the Middle East.

NOTES

1. The words land and state of Israel will be used interchangeably in this essay. Statehood today is an absolute requirement for any landed people, especially the Jews, that would live in security.

2. See H. Croner, *Stepping Stones to Further Jewish-Christian Relations* (New York: Paulist Press, 1980), p. 14.

3. *Ibid.,* p. 34.

4. Quoted in E. Fisher, "The Pope and Israel," in *Commonweal,* January 11, 1985, p. 16.

5. See "Ecumenical Considerations on Jewish-Christian Dialogue" (Pamphlet), World Council of Churches, Geneva, 1983.

6. See J. Pawlikowski, *What Are They Saying About Jewish-Christian Relations* (New York: Paulist Press, 1980), ch. 2.

7. For an example of this see Rosemary Ruether's "Polarization in Israel" (*National Catholic Reporter*, September 14, 1984, p. 14) where Dr. Ruether, a stalwart in the Jewish-Christian enterprise, strongly reproves Zionism as a "form of nationalism that most Americans regard as unacceptable and, ironically, a Fascist state if settlements continue to be established in the West Bank or annexation takes place," and concludes that if Israel is to remain a democratic state it must cease to be a Zionist state. Apparently Ruether sees Israel and Zionism exclusively in a secular and political perspective.

8. In the decades of the British Mandate over Palestine the British administrators and soldiery became increasingly less zealous in implementing the Balfour principle even to a point of open opposition and sabotage.

9. See J. Peters, *From Time Immemorial: The Origins of the Arab-Israeli Conflict in Palestine* (New York: Harper and Row, 1984). This exhaustive work of research (with 1,800 annotations) puts definitively to rest the popular myths touching the conflict.

10. Foundations for a theology of the land in Judaism and Christianity have already been laid by a few pioneers of the subject, notably Walter Brueggemann, *The Land* (Philadelphia: Fortress Press, 1977), W.D. Davies, *The Gospel and the Land* (Berkeley: University of California Press, 1974), and a number of theologians of the "Israel-Study" group in unpublished papers (New York: National Conference of Christians and Jews).

11. See *Israel: Echo of Eternity* (New York: Farrar, Straus and Giroux, 1967), pp. 139–44 and 161–67.

PART II

The Role of Scripture in Catholic-Jewish Relations

I. INTRODUCTION

When shown an early draft of the proposed Vatican Council statement on the Jews in November of 1963, the European director of the American Jewish Committee expressed his pleasure that the document contained "a total rejection of the myth of Jewish guilt for the crucifixion."[1] This confident assertion from a Jewish leader reflects the remarkable nature of the Council's efforts to re-establish a dialogue of respect between Christians and Jews rooted in reconsideration of the sacred Scripture of the two faiths. After two thousand years of animosity between them, and sometimes bitter hatred and persecution by the dominant Christian majority using the death of Christ either as a reason for "punishing" Jews or for explaining why atrocities may have occurred, it was a significant milestone that the Catholic Church dealt with the responsibility for Jesus' death in this new way. Cardinal Bea, who presided over the writing of the Council Statement on the Jews, had forcefully argued to the bishops that the New Testament itself recognized the Jewish leaders of Jesus' time were not formally guilty of Deicide since both the Gospels (Luke 23:34) and the Acts of the Apostles (Acts 3:17, 13:27) said that they had acted without full knowledge of Christ's divinity. Even less, Bea declared, could the Jewish people as a whole at the time of Jesus be held accountable for his death.[2] A year later, the bishops of the Council accepted the final draft of the document with all these points still in central focus.[3]

This vignette points out the importance that biblical reflections have taken in Catholic attempts to reconsider the nature of the Church and its apostolic role in the world. It also points out that such a return to the Bible brings to the fore the question of Christianity's relations with the Jewish people both in biblical times and now. It signals that Scripture studies will have a major role in Catholic-Jewish dialogue for the future. One reason for this, naturally, is that both Judaism and Christianity share a series of sacred texts in the Hebrew Scriptures.

Since both faiths acknowledge that these books are a normative source of divine revelation that is to guide the formulation and understanding of our beliefs and worship of the same God, shared study and discussion of the Bible can be combined with mutual learning about and re-examination of each other's differences in faith in order to deepen the common bonds and become more sympathetic to the value of our diverse development. This means that Christians will have to take the Hebrew Scriptures (Old Testament) much more seriously along with the New, and Jews will have to overcome their reluctance to have anything to do with the New Testament and learn more about its teachings. Emil Fackenheim has expressed another important desideratum: just as Catholics are returning to look at the Scriptures anew, Jews too will have to look at the sacred text fresh and not solely through the eyes of their traditional commentators.[4]

But at the outset of any discussion on the role of the Scriptures in the Dialogue, it must be made clear that both faiths remain different faiths at this time and will continue to develop in separate directions. Dialogue demands that the two parties acknowledge the other as a completely valid and separate religious faith in its own right. No matter what one might want to say of the historical, social and religious situation of the communities that put together the Jewish and Christian Scriptures, it remains a fact that the present-day communities are quite distinct and the products of nearly two thousand years of non-biblical differentiation since the first century C.E. matrix of the latest books of the Scriptures.[5] This means that each faith has developed a quite different manner of interpreting and handling the Hebrew Scriptures through the centuries. Thus those engaged in dialogue, and especially the biblical scholars, will need to do much more than seek out the original senses of biblical texts. To contribute toward the Dialogue they will need to know about the history of interpretation in both Jewish and Christian traditions. It also means that both sides will have to address the delicate question of the relationship of the Christian Scriptures to the Hebrew Scriptures on a new footing without the apologetics of each faith asserting itself as the first and last point to be made.

Despite these caveats, the future of the Dialogue looks very promising from the perspective of renewed examination of Scripture as a basis. Certainly, as Tommaso Federici pointed out in a very perceptive article on "Catholic-Jewish Relations Today,"[6] for the Catholic Church the biblical movement is the first and most important aspect of a renewal that sees the living out of the Scriptures as the necessary condition for the life of the Church in the world. There have been four areas in which this renewal has largely taken place in this century, and these four will also be the main arena for the continued impact of the Scripture study on the dialogue between Jews and Christians. They are (1) the modern shift in religious perspective from the narrow circles of one's own faith to a larger worldview; (2) the development of new hermeneutical methods and approaches to reading the Bible; (3) vastly increased historical knowledge of the ancient world and especially the first century of the common era; (4) theological developments based upon a fuller exegesis of the texts. I shall try to outline some of the more significant accomplishments as well as the future challenges in each of these four areas in the following paragraphs.

II. THE SHIFT IN RELIGIOUS PERSPECTIVE

It is a sad fact of Christian history that anti-semitism has played a large role in several different periods.[7] Not all persecution of the Jews has been due to religious Anti-Judaism, of course, for often cultural and political suspicions played a far larger role. Nevertheless, important writers such as Ambrose, Augustine and John Chrysostom used the New Testament as a basis for condemning Jews to isolation and quarantine from Christian groups, and often vented alarmingly violent language against the "evils" of Jewish teaching.[8] Much of the teaching of the Old Testament in Christian settings has also contained a very negative attitude toward Judaism as a legalistic, sterile and ritualistic religion.[9] Fortunately, however, there have emerged several factors of note that are changing the adversary relationship to one of mutual cooperation:

(a) The Holocaust and the founding of the state of Israel have forced Christians to confront the horrifying results of anti-semitism run rampant and the shock of seeing a Jewish state again in a land out of which many Christians believed they had been driven as divine punishment.[10] These two events have also forced Jews to look again at the bases of their faith in God and his promises to them. Both sides realize that many of our past assumptions don't hold up anymore, including several for which we had appealed to the Scriptures for support.

(b) The ecumenical movement among the Christian churches has been active for over fifty years.[11] This has forced a return to the Scriptures in order to explore the bases for unity and diversity among the Christian denominations themselves, and to test the claims of the Reformation against those of Roman Catholicism and Orthodoxy. It has certainly made the Christian exegetes more sensitive to the diversity within the biblical books of both Testaments, but especially the New, upon which different understandings of the churches have been based.

(c) The Catholic Church itself has undergone a remarkable revival of interest in the Scriptures. This can be generally traced to the encouragement given professional biblical exegetes within the Church by Pope Pius XII's encyclical on Biblical Studies, *Divino Afflante Spiritu,* issued in 1943.[12] In it he invited Catholic scholars to use the tools and means necessary to unlock the secrets of the Scriptures and present them in modern terms to the understanding of the Church.

(d) The Second Vatican Council itself initiated new steps toward both the expansion of biblical study within the Church and fuller dialogue with Judaism. The Council prepared the *Dogmatic Constitution on the Church* (*Lumen Gentium*) as a fundamental statement upon which all other documents would be based. It stands out for its appeal, not to canonical or philosophical concepts of the Church, but to biblical.[13] Many of these, such as the "people of God," are rooted in the Hebrew Scriptures (see paragraphs 6 and 9). Beyond this, the *Dogmatic Constitution on Divine Revelation* (*Dei Verbum*) and the section on the Jews in the *Declaration of the Relationship of the Church to Non-Christian Religions* (*Nostra Aetate*) explicitly confirm the permanent revelatory value of the Hebrew Scriptures and the enduring nature of the divine promises to Israel (*Dei Verbum*, par. 14; *Nostra Aetate*, par. 4). Such firm commitments to the place of Israel in God's plan have led to a renewed concern for teaching the Old Testament course in a non-polemical manner. These documents have also given birth to a widespread consideration of the roles of Christians toward Jews among official church bodies in local communities. Already, there are two full volumes of various church statements on Jewish-Christian relations from the twenty-year period 1965–84 gathered by Helga Croner.[14]

(e) The proliferation of Religious Studies departments in the major universities which include specialists in all major world religions has brought into the picture viewpoints and beliefs from beyond the Judaeo-Christian tradition. It will no longer be possible to study the nature of sacred texts without including the claims of other religious groups to sacred books of their own.[15] While it may seem to relativize the value of the Bible as *the* sacred book, it certainly presents the Jewish and Christian biblical student with the realization of our common sources over against all others. Indeed, there are even further attempts to initiate a "trialogue" among the great monotheistic faiths of Judaism, Christianity and Islam.[16]

(f) At the same time that Religious Studies departments are developing programs in world religions, many have instituted specific programs in Judaic Studies to help western students reclaim their religious heritage. These programs make accessible to numerous Christian students who enroll for one or more courses in aspects of Judaism a fuller and more accurate knowledge of Jewish belief and tradition than has generally been available in centuries past. But recently Richard Hecht warned his fellow scholars that "a specialist in the religious traditions of ancient Israel or in the religion of the Jews is not always among the highest priorities in departments of religion."[17]

(g) A major danger of Jewish-Christian dialogue is that many Christians think they know what Judaism is *by* reading the Hebrew Scriptures, and many Jews think they know what Christians are all about despite *not* reading the New Testament![18] The points that have been made in the paragraphs above have to do largely with educating ourselves to rejecting old stereotypes and seeing each other in a different light. There is need for kindness and respect and interest in the faith of the other.[19] Dialogue implies that each side accept the self-definition of the other side and seek to understand it both as it is understood by the definer and as it relates to one's own religious self-definition.[20] This leads naturally to our next point of concern: *hermeneutics*.

III. HERMENEUTICS AND CHANGES IN BIBLICAL INTERPRETATION

Pope Pius XII's encyclical on Biblical Studies, *Divino Afflante Spiritu*, was a milestone in many ways for Catholic Scripture scholars. But by far the most important was that it actively encouraged the scholar to go beyond traditional Church uses of the Bible to employ historical and linguistic means to discover the mind of the ancient writers:

> Let [the biblical scholar] diligently apply himself so as to acquire daily a greater facility in biblical as well as in other oriental languages and to support his interpretation by the aids which all branches of philology supply . . . . Aided by the context and by comparison with similar passages, let [such scholars] therefore by means of their knowledge of languages search out with all diligence the literal meaning of the words . . . so that the mind of the author may be made abundantly clear.[21]

The results have been spectacular. Forty years have passed, and Catholic scholars employ the same tools and methods used in the best critical scholarship done by their Protestant and Jewish colleagues.[22] This in turn has led to specialization among Catholic biblicists at the university level. The need for mastery of ancient languages and an adequate comprehension of the historical and archaeological data has ruled out the older possibility of competence in both Testaments. At the same time, the rise of specialists in the Hebrew Bible also provides the churches with a needed core of professional educators who love these Scriptures and work to prevent misunderstanding or distortion of their message.

Christians are also discovering the Talmud and Midrashim. Rosemary Ruether noted that one of Christianity's weakest points has been its lack of familiarity with the Jewish interpretive tradition of the Scriptures that could balance its own heritage from the Fathers of the Church and the medieval theologians who largely viewed the relation of the two Testaments from a promise-fulfillment perspective.[23] Although the observation of Paul van Buren will remain true that Christians generally never invest the energy to engage the Torah with the same seriousness of the Jewish people, specialization has stimulated a deeper Christian study of the Talmud and Jewish tradition.[24] This will make some of the rich reflection of Judaism on the Torah and Scripture more easily available to Christian students.

The task of addressing the proper evaluation of the New Testament teaching of Jesus in the light of first century Judaism has also begun in earnest. It is a formidable puzzle that will take the combined efforts of Jewish and Christian scholars working collaboratively. It will present a unique challenge to Jews in the Dialogue, who have rarely considered the New Testament as significant for understanding their faith.[25] However, this cannot continue to be the situation. First century developments that brought Christianity into being and also separated it from Judaism are just as crucial to what modern Judaism has become as they are to Christianity's self-definition as a separate faith.

One area of mutual cooperation that has developed between Christian and Jewish scholars is the field of textual criticism of the Bible. The rise of divergent textual traditions and the investigation of expansions and variant readings have been explored by both in depth. Another area has been the translation of the Scriptures into English. The *Revised Standard Version*, the *New American Bible* and even the *Jewish Publication Society Bible* have all included experts and consultants from the other faith in their editorial process. The same is true for the larger commentary and dictionary projects. The *Anchor Bible* has a broad mix of Christian and Jewish scholars, and a glance at the credits' page for the Supplement volume of the *Interpreter's Dictionary of the Bible* reveals a veritable who's who of biblical teachers from both faiths.[26]

On another level, many Jewish and Christian theologians have independently come to the conclusion that it is time to look at the texts of the Bible with fresh eyes, and not simply through the thick lens of our separate exegetical traditions.[27] Michael Fishbane pointed out that, in this regard, the Bible as the matrix of the sacred is gone for the Jew, and the problem of interpreting scriptural texts has become very complex indeed.[28] At the same meeting, David Tracy, a Catholic, insisted that a theological interpretation of Scripture cannot overlook the impact of current events. Scholars must employ a "hermeneutics of suspicion" (that is, a critical method) to spot the delusions and distortions in each of our traditions.[29] Clearly for these scholars, it has become essential for Jewish and Christian biblical interpreters to generate multiple new levels of appropriation for the modern reader.

All of these concerns reflect the importance of hermeneutical methods to reach an ecumenical understanding of the biblical text. It also suggests that as Jews and Christians learn to know and respect the approaches taken by the other, dialogue will lead to better communication and shared insight about the Bible in general. It may also mean real advances as a result and joint study in certain areas. These include the following:

(a) The tanakh must be studied in its own right by both Jews and Christians before it is related by Christians to the New Testament.[30] As the French bishops noted carefully in their statement on Jewish-Christian relations, "A true Christian catechesis ought to affirm the present value of the whole Bible."[31]

(b) A new language needs to be developed to express the interrelations between the two Testaments. Christians above all will need to reject the formulation of that relationship as an *Old* Testament superseded by a *New*. The teaching of the *Dogmatic Constitution on Divine Revelation (Dei Verbum)*, par. #14, will have to be applied more widely, namely that the integrity of the Hebrew Scriptures must be respected. It is no longer possible to maintain that the Old Testament is a Christian book to be interpreted solely in reference to Christ, the hermeneutical style so beloved in the Middle Ages, nor even to accept Luther's dictum, *Was Christum treibet* ("What promotes Christ"), as a basis for evaluating different parts of the Hebrew Bible.[32] The traditional Christian principles of interpretation such as typology, allegory and promise-fulfillment should not be given exclusive stress. Rather, factors of continuity between the Testaments, such as the Jewishness of Jesus, the common tension in eschatology found in the first century, and the new approaches of hermeneutics, should be given greater place.

This point applies to the study of Paul in a special way. Statements on what he did and did not oppose in the "Law," and just what his opponents did and did not hold, require more careful research.[33] Often it has not so much been Paul as his patristic interpreters that are problematical. The same caution holds true for interpretation of John's Gospel. For example, the polemical thrust of the Johannine writings relative to the special concerns and needs of his church has come to the fore in recent studies on the Gospel.[34]

(c) It will become possible for Christians to retrieve the Jewish dimension of their faith more fully. More emphasis needs to be placed on the Jewish origins and roots for such New Testament conceptions as the kingdom of God and salvation. Looking at the eschatological aspects of both what has been fulfilled and what has not in the divine plan will prove of great value for the dialogue. Both Judaism and Christianity can profit from seeing what is not yet fully realized in the revelation that has been spoken through both faiths.[35]

(d) The discussion of what Christians mean by the idea of "mission" relative to Jewish understanding of "witness" needs further clarification and discussion in the Dialogue.[36] The Second Vatican Council rejects any concept of mission that involves undue proselytism. Tommaso Federici has offered a promising example of rethinking the concept of Christian mission in a larger context that incorporates the message of the Hebrew Scriptures as well as of the Gospel. He suggests that the command to sanctify God's name throughout the world (*qiddush ha-shem*) links the mission of both Christians and Jews together: see Ex 9:16; Num 20:12; Is 8:13; 29:23; Ez 20:41; 36:23, Mal 1:11, 14.[37]

(e) A shift away from a purely historical-critical method of exegesis toward a more reader-center hermeneutic and toward a "canonical criticism" should prove valuable.[38] It involves placing less emphasis on what the ancient authors wanted to say in their own language and more on how a contemporary reading can come to grips with the Bible as a sacred word for today. It will open up a better insight into how texts have come to their present accepted meaning relative to the changing social and historical developments of the communities that have preserved and interpreted these texts over the centuries. The Bible has a long history of reinterpretation through the centuries that influences and often narrows our present ability to read the message fresh. Readers who use historical-critical approaches will find this an easy step to make, but it should prove a special challenge to many in Judaism and among Fundamentalist Christians who tend to see the Bible as a timeless word of God, as clear in its singular message now as when it was written. The insight of Roman Catholic theology that revelation in Scripture is basically God's revelation of Himself, and not primarily a series of doctrines or logical truth, proves beneficial in this regard. The Bible is the Spirit-guided community of faith's response to this self-revealing God, and the articulation of that response is in the historically-conditioned and inadequate manner of human communication. These words of Scripture need to be understood anew by the faith communities in ways that reflect the speech and language of each succeeding age. Both faiths need to examine how much their present interpretation of Scripture can be reappropriated in better understanding through the Dialogue.

IV. THE GROWTH IN OUR HISTORICAL KNOWLEDGE
OF THE BIBLICAL PERIOD

The twentieth century has seen an explosion in the number of historical records made available for the study of the ancient world. No reputable scholar today would approach any interpretation of a biblical text without reference to the archaeological, historical, and literary remains pertinent to the particular subject matter or time period in which it was composed. This is particularly true for the last century before Christianity and the first century of the Common Era. The brief survey that follows will suffice to indicate some of the key elements affected by new historical information or a new understanding of that period.

(a) *The Post-Exilic Development of Judaism.* Many standard introductions to the Old Testament treat the post-exilic period from Ezra to the time of Jesus in a bare outline fashion, content to note a few key developments.[39] One such development would be the flowering of wisdom literature, generally attributed to a new school learning stimulated by the canonization of the Torah and the consequent shift of Israelite religion toward study by a "People of the Book." Another development is apocalyptic, which arose as a response to the loss of prophecy. Christian commentators often see a strong connection between this and the rise of early Christian expectations. Beyond these, there is little said on the centuries after 500 B.C.E. Two significant Old Testament theologians, Claus Westermann and Walther Zimmerli, are almost silent on the value of the post-exilic period as a whole.[40] They avoid any condemnation of the Judaism that arises in this time as a negative movement, but one still gains the impression that such Christian scholars generally view Judaism as a definite decline from the dynamism and vitality of the earlier Israelite faith. Introductions to the Hebrew Scriptures written by Christians need to remedy this by concentrating on the changes wrought in the Exile and after as the most formative stage of the Biblical tradition.

(b) *First Century Judaism.* One of the most promising areas for common agreement in the Dialogue has turned out to be the nature of Judaism in the period from 50 B.C.E. The discovery of the Qumran scrolls and other documents in the vicinity of the Dead Sea have added enormously to our fund of knowledge about this era.[41] Above all, they have revealed a wide diversity in Palestinian Judaism. Both Christian and Jewish scholars have re-evaluated the Pharisees and their beliefs in this light and generally agree on their importance for the succeeding development both of normative Judaism and also of Christianity.[42] Jesus himself must be seen as basically supportive of the Pharisaic movement. An excellent summary of the current consensus about first century developments can be found in Martin Cohen's article in *The Bible and Modern Scholarship*.[43] Church statements have picked up on this aspect and accented the Jewish soil of the teaching of Jesus: "Most essential concepts in the Christian creed grew at first in Judaic soil."[44]

(c) *Jesus the Jew.* The contribution of Jewish scholars to the foundations of Dialogue can be seen most clearly in the studies of Jesus and his teaching from the viewpoint of Judaic tradition.[45] In many cases, this is able to highlight the teaching methods of Jesus and the content of his message in the light of traditional rabbinic principles found in the Talmud and Midrashim. When Christians listen carefully, they realize that the standard Christian sourcebooks for Jewish thought of the period, such as Strack-Billerbeck, *Kommentar zum Neuen Testament aus Talmud und Midrasch*,[46] are totally inadequate because of their one-sided selection of material and negative evaluation of Jewish religion.[47]

Recognition of the Jewish thought-world behind many of the Gospel passages sharpens the challenge to critical scholarship to distinguish carefully among the original teaching of Jesus, its development in early Jewish-Christian communities, and further adaptation to the Gentile mission. One ecumenical advance that has resulted from this bears on the death of Jesus. There has been widespread recognition that the sentence of execution cannot be blamed on the Jewish people as a whole, and that Roman policy and Roman politics are likely to have played a more important part in the death of Jesus than the Gospels present.[48]

(d) *The Early Christian Communities and the Gospels.* One question that has to be addressed constantly by those involved in the Dialogue is just how anti-Jewish is the New Testament.[49] The focus on historical forces in the first century brings more and more of the tensions and polemical concerns of different groups to light. Judaism was certainly not a unified movement but showed several sectarian trends for whom polemical attacks on other groups was a way of life. The disciples of Jesus should not be exempted from this high-spirited defense of their beliefs nor should their foundational documents be exempted from possible polemical intent.

The question of Christianity's continuity with Judaism and of its separation from it requires complex answers. Already this has been the subject of many fine studies, and its continuing importance will see more to come.[50] One thing can be asserted at the outset. The polemics are least in the early Gospel of Mark and greatest in the latest Gospel of John. This suggests that the strains became much greater after the Jewish Revolt of 66 to 70 C.E. At that time, even the Jewish-Christian communities in Palestine publicly broke with their fellow Jews over the war.

Current study of the Talmudic sources indicates that such animosity was not a one-way street. The institution of a daily prayer against the *Minim* ("Sectarians") by the rabbis after 70 C.E. would seem to have included Jewish Christians among the "Minim."[51] The lesson to be learned is that both faiths must be willing to re-examine their own sources, the New Testament for Christians, and the Talmud for Jews, with the "hermeneutics of suspicion" noted in Section III above. Only by discovering the rich dynamics at work in the first century will we gain a clearer idea why the two faiths split in such different directions.[52]

(e) *Paul as a Jew.* The publication of E.P. Sanders' *Paul and Palestinian Judaism* established a landmark for future studies of Paul.[53] It provides a firm basis on which to consider the major trends of Judaism that Paul knew in his day, and it questions the all-too-common Christian conceptions of Paul's opposition to that Judaism. Needless to say, Paul emerges as one much more sympathetic to the Judaism of his own past than most Christian commentators have allowed. Indeed it now confirms that Krister Stendahl's remark that Paul did not preach about "how I could be saved, but about how Gentiles could enter the Jewish covenant" was right on target.[54] The position of Paul cannot be described as placing the teaching of Jesus in opposition to Judaism, but in showing how Christ fulfilled the Torah. Paul saw Christianity continuing its link to Israel as one people of God who had a non-revocable place in God's plan.[55]

Christians have led the way in this re-evaluation of Paul,[56] but much credit must also go to Jewish scholarship which has prepared the way.[57] Much of their work was done long before the renewed call of *Nostra Aetate* itself in 1965, but there is still a particular need for Jewish scholars to study Paul and give their insights into his teaching.

(f) *The Talmud and Midrash*. It barely needs reinforcement from previous sections that the study of the Jewish sources by competent Christian scholars has only begun. More attention will certainly be paid to this in the future. From the Jewish side, Jacob Neusner's extensive writings have brought the concerns of the historical-critical method to bear on these difficult texts and has prepared the way for others to follow.[58]

V. THEOLOGICAL AND EXEGETICAL CONCERNS IN THE DIALOGUE

What has been noted so far about changing attitudes, shifts in critical method, and the growing historical re-evaluation of the first century assures us that a solid foundation is being laid for serious dialogue between Jews and Christians concerning the basics of the Scriptures. Fruitful areas of dialogue have taken place regularly on questions of public policy, the lessons of the Holocaust, the significance of the state of Israel, and many other issues. But no issue is more vital for future mutual support than wrestling with the questions about our biblical faith so that each side can accept the other as truly faithful to God's will for it. All the good will and social contacts in the world cannot overcome the negative influence of a faith-conviction that the two faiths are fundamentally incompatible and in stark opposition to one another.

On the level of the Dialogue itself, this will mean a willingness for Jews and Christians to explore such topics as the kingdom of God, the messiah, and other crucial differences in a neutral manner, listening carefully as well as explaining to each other.[59] On the level of theological stance, it will mean a conviction that continuity unites the two Testaments and not disjunctiveness. For the Christian exegete this involves the recovery of the value of the Hebrew Scriptures for the Church, and at the same time serious reflection on Paul's thought in Romans 9–11 and Ephesians 2:11–13. For Roman Catholics specifically, it is noteworthy that the Vatican Council's *Dogmatic Constitution on the Church* (*Lumen Gentium*), par. 16, uses Romans 9–11 to speak of the Jews as the people remaining dear to a God who does not repent of his gifts or his call to them. For the Jews, theological dialogue will mean breaking new ground in exploring New Testament theology that has never been part of their religious horizon. Many Jewish scholars have already entered into this arena with helpful contributions: Jacob Petuchowski, Pinchas Lapide, David Flusser, and Eugene Borowitz.[60]

A small number of topics have vital importance for the Dialogue and are generating considerable discussion.

(a) *Monotheism and the Common Worship of the Same God.* Mark 12:28–30 and Matthew 22:34–38 report that Jesus accepted the *Shema* of Deuteronomy 6 as the greatest commandment of the Law, thus confirming that he saw his message as continuing the revelation of God's saving actions to Israel. Deeper reflection by Jews and Christians together on our obedience to, and worship of, the same self-revealing God should lead to greater gains in shared understanding than any other approach.[61] It will prepare the way for the next and most serious step—exploring the implications of belief in a God whose universal rule and will extends to all peoples and all faiths, and how that belief affects the exclusive claims of Judaism and Christianity alike.

(b) *Revelation.* Dialogue will be needed to explore the nature of God's revealing word in the Scriptures. Jews tend to see the absolute validity of the interpretation of revelation that has developed within their faith, while Christians speak of the finality of Christ over any further or different interpretation. New outlooks on both sides will continue to stress the pluralistic dimensions of revelation and its expressions.[62] Jacob Agus refers to this task as a quest for insight in which the two faiths will enrich each other in the process of mutual exploration.[63]

(c) *Covenant.* Historically, the widest gulf between Christians and Jews has been fostered by the use of ''Old'' versus ''New'' in speaking of the covenant (Latin *testamentum*). From the Christian side this has often implied that the earlier covenant with Israel was abrogated or superseded by Christ and his teaching.

The search for continuity between the Testaments now centers on the question of an ongoing covenant that links the two. Paul van Buren expresses the outlook succinctly when he says that the New Testament was never intended to be a new will, but a codicil to an existing will.[64] Generally, solutions fall along one of two lines of development. The first sees a single covenant in which both Jews and Christians have a place, although it takes different forms for each. The second recognizes two separate covenants willed by God, one for Jews and the other for Gentiles. Either model seems possible to me if we keep in mind that both must be treated equally in any covenantal will of God.[65] From a Christian side, a one-covenant model looks the best, but from a Jewish view, perhaps the two covenants might better protect their traditional understanding of the faith.

Christians have done the most thinking on this question. Much of this has been enshrined in church statements over the last few years. In comparison, Jewish thinkers have produced little on covenant until now.[66] Some hard questions must be asked of them for this to be a mutual enterprise. Can Jews recognize a place for Christianity as a legitimate extension of the first covenant? Is the development of Judaism as it has actually taken place historically in the tradition of the Talmud and beyond the only legitimate development? Is the unity of the community of faith so central that no offshoots may be allowed to develop along separate paths? Was the end of the diversity represented by the Jewish "sects" of the first century the authoritative end of all permissible diversity in the expression of covenant community? Still ahead lies intensive discussion of the Noahide commandments in Jewish tradition as a way for the Gentiles. Currently they are treated only peripherally, or even excluded from most Jewish consciousness as a source of reflection on the nature of the covenant. Finally, it may be remarked that much of the work on covenant bonds between Jews and Christians remains to be done.

(d) *Christology and Messianic Hopes.* The key question for the Christian believer is what stance he or she takes about Jesus as the Christ. This means more than "messiah," including a whole vision of God's saving will for the world. For the vast majority of Jews, of course, the claim that Jesus can be identified in any way with the hopes for a messiah, or with the figure of the Son of Man in Daniel, is what sets the Christians definitely apart from Judaism.[67] Christian theology in time has emphasized a catechetical language that speaks of Christ's life, death and resurrection as the fulfillment or epitome of divine revelation and salvation in such a way as to leave little room for Judaism's continued role as the Chosen People. There can be little doubt that Christian pogroms and other persecutions of the Jews over the centuries have had roots in a popular teaching which suggested divine rejection of the Jews for their blindness toward Christ's teaching and a divine "punishment" for allowing him to be put to death. Although official statements have forcefully rejected such teaching, many believers still hold to it. Moreover, popular Christology also allows little room for Judaism within the divine plan, since salvation demands explicit faith in Jesus.

Christology is certainly a central problem for the Dialogue. But it should not be totally separated from the historical situation of Christians gradually abandoning the practice of the *halakah* as they turned more and more to Gentile membership. This, too, must be recognized as the cause of major difference between Jew and Christian.

Any discussion of Christology will be a very sensitive topic requiring a great deal of theological reflection on both sides. Some important Christian studies have already addressed the formulations of traditional Christological theses and examined them for both their strengths and their weaknesses.[68]

A fine Jewish response is also available from Eugene Borowitz in his *Contemporary Christologies: A Jewish Response.*[69] Christian theologians will have to give special attention to the role of Christ vis-à-vis Judaism and other world religions so that these, too, can have a place in God's plan of salvation without explicit knowledge of Christ. Jews will have to reassess whether their restrictions on when the messiah can or cannot come are the products of anti-Christian polemics, and whether Jesus as a *rabbi among rabbis* may not have a normative place for Gentiles.[70] In any case, Christology must be placed inside a radically theocentric framework which will allow honest dialogue on how each group views its place in the single universal plan of God.[71]

(e) *Other Biblical Issues.* Topics such as the promise of the land, and its loss,[72] the value of the theology of creation in Scripture as a common basis for recognizing the divine plan,[73] and the concepts of mission and witness all have a role to play in future discussion,[74] although the four treated above must never be brushed aside, for they are fundamental.

VI. CONCLUSION

The preceding discussion ranges over a considerable variety of topics and reflections on the Dialogue because the Scriptures themselves invite a wide range of responses, and all of these issues can be found central to both the Hebrew Scriptures and the New Testament. This is, of course, a very positive aspect of biblical study for the Dialogue. As both faiths study the Scriptures and their own history of interpretation more fully, the more the common elements of our faiths will emerge, and the less serious will seem our past history of antagonism.

Not unnaturally, Christian re-examination of the biblical foundations has progressed more broadly, probably because Christians have a commitment to both the New Testament and the Hebrew Scriptures as sacred texts. Jews have less interest in this theological and biblical side of the Dialogue since the New Testament stands outside their faith commitment. But Jewish scholars must not neglect the invitation to Dialogue through exploration of the Bible. In an increasingly pluralistic and secularistic world, the work of proclaiming and witnessing to the work of the one God through his word of revelation in the Bible is claimed by both faiths. The credibility of that revelation will be severely hampered if church and synagogue cannot even agree on what they read and where they disagree, nor respect one another's testimony to the same God. To paraphrase the warning of the great American Revolutionary War statesman and wit, Benjamin Franklin, "Gentlemen, if we do not all hang together, we shall all hang separately."

NOTES

1. Quoted in Ralph Wiltgen, S.V.D., *The Rhine Flows into the Tiber: A History of Vatican II* (Hawthorne Books, 1967) 168–69.

2. Ibid. p. 172. This speech was delivered on September 25, 1964.

3. The entire *Declaration on the Relation of the Church to Non-Christian Religions* is available in A. Flannery (ed.), *Vatican Council II: The Conciliar and Post-Conciliar Documents* (Costello Publishing Co., 1975) 738–742. See also Msgr. Jorge Mejia, "Survey of Issues in Catholic-Jewish Relations," *Origins* 7, #47 (May 11, 1978) 744–48, for a fuller list of important guidelines that followed from the Council statement.

4. This remark was delivered in a talk at a conference titled *Sacred Texts: The Hermeneutics of Religious Literatures in a Post-Holocaust Age,* held at Indiana University on October 17–19, 1982.

5. See Jacob Petuchowski, "Christian-Jewish Dialogue," *The Jewish Spectator* 47 (Winter 1982) 22–25.

6. *Origins* 8, #18 (October 19, 1978) 273–83, esp. p. 273.

7. See such studies as Malcolm Hay, *The Roots of Christian Anti-Semitism* (Freedom Library Press, 1981); Charlotte Klein, *Anti-Judaism and Christian Theology* (Fortress Press, 1978); Edward Flannery, *The Anguish of the Jews* (revised edition; Paulist Press, 1985); Eugene Fisher, *Faith without Prejudice* (Paulist Press, 1977).

8. Rosemary Ruether, *Faith and Fratricide* (Seabury Press, 1974) 117–82 (chapter 3).

9. See Joseph Blenkinsopp, "Judaism and Teaching the Old Testament," *The Living Light* 13 (1976) 360–73.

10. For recent studies on the Holocaust and Christian-Jewish relations, see Eugene Fisher, "A New Maturity in Christian-Jewish Dialogue: An Annotated Bibliography 1973–1983," *Face to Face: An Interreligious Bulletin* XI (Spring 1984) 29–43, esp. pp. 41–43.

11. For an overview of the history of the ecumenical movement, consult Jacques Desseaux, *Twenty Centuries of Ecumenism* (Paulist Press, 1983).

12. Originally printed in *Acta Apostolicae Sedis* 35 (1943) 297–326. Translated and published in English in *Rome and the Study of Scripture* (Grail Publications, 1962) 80–107.

13. Avery Dulles, S.J., "Introduction: The Church," in *The Documents of Vatican II,* edited by Walter M. Abbott, S.J. (Guild/America Press, 1966) 9–13.

14. Helga Croner, *Stepping Stones to Further Jewish-Christian Relations: An Unabridged Collection of Christian Documents* (Stimulus Foundation/Paulist Press, 1977); and *More Stepping Stones to Jewish-Christian*

Relations: An Unabridged Collection of Christian Documents 1975–1983 (Paulist Press, 1985).

15. This was the major theme addressed by all the speakers at conference held at Indiana University on October 17–19, 1982, entitled, *Sacred Texts: The Hermeneutics of Religious Literatures in a Post-Holocaust Age.*

16. See Fisher, "A New Maturity in Christian-Jewish Dialogue: An Annotated Bibliography 1973–1983," *Face to Face* XI (Spring 1984) 43.

17. Richard D. Hecht, "Research Needs in the Study of the Hebrew Bible and the Study of Judaism," *Council on the Study of Religion Bulletin* 11, #5 (December 1980) 137–45, esp. p. 137.

18. Rolf Rendtorff, "Toward a New Christian Reading of the Hebrew Bible," *Immanuel* 15 (Winter 1982–1983) 13–21.

19. At this point, I would like to make a practical suggestion. Since both American Jews and Christians are often barely aware of the tradition of Jewish life and belief through the last two thousand years, there is a need for a Museum of the Diaspora in the United States like the fine example in Tel Aviv. A visit to the museum in Tel Aviv leaves one with an overwhelming impression of the rich cultural life and the strong faith of the Jewish communities in every part of the world.

20. See Eugene Fisher and Leon Klenicki, "Basic Jewish and Christian Beliefs in Dialogue: The Presentation of the Other," *PACE* 13 (May 1983) 1–5 for practical suggestions. See also the series of essays in E.P. Sanders, *Jewish and Christian Self-Definition,* vols. 1, 2, and 3 (Fortress Press, 1980, 1981, 1982).

21. *Divino Afflante Spiritu,* pars. 16 and 23.

22. See Moshe Greenberg, "Can a Modern Critical Bible Scholarship have a Jewish Character?" *Immanuel* 15 (Winter, 1982–1983) 7–12. [Editor's Note: Lawrence Boadt's own recent volume, *Reading the Old Testament: An Introduction* (Paulist Press, 1984) provides an excellent synthesis of contemporary Catholic scholarship.]

23. "Toward a New Covenantal Theology," in Frank Talmage, ed., *Disputation and Dialogue* (ADL-Ktav, 1975) 320–29.

24. Paul van Buren, *Discerning the Way: A Theology of the Jewish-Christian Reality* (Seabury Press, 1980) 120–65.

25. Michael Cook, "Jesus and the Pharisees—The Problem as It Stands Today," *JES* 15 (1978) 441–460.

26. The *Supplement* volume is edited by Keith Crim and others, published by Abingdon Press, 1976.

27. See the remark of Emil Fackenheim quoted above in section I and note 4.

28. Given orally at the Indiana University conference cited in note 15 above.

29. See note 28, and Tracy's earlier article, "Religious Values after the Holocaust: A Catholic View," in A. Peck, editor, *Jews and Christians after the Holocaust* (Fortress Press, 1982) 87–107.

30. See Joseph Blenkinsopp, "Tanakh and the New Testament: A Christian Perspective," in L. Boadt, et al., editors, *Bible Studies: Meeting Ground of Jews and Christians* (Paulist Press, 1980) 96–119.

31. The Statement by the French Bishops' Committee for Relations with the Jews was issued in April 1973; found in Helga Croner, *Stepping Stones to Further Jewish-Christian Relations* (Paulist Press/Stimulus, 1977) #Va, p. 60.

32. Rolf Rendtorff, "Toward a New Christian Reading of the Hebrew Bible," *Immanuel* 15 (Winter 1982–1983) 13–21.

33. See especially the new views expressed by E.P. Sanders, *Paul and Palestinian Judaism: A Comparison of Patterns of Religion* (Fortress Press, 1977).

34. Recent studies include those of J.L. Martyn, *History and Theology in the Fourth Gospel* (Abingdon, 1968); J.L. Martyn, *The Gospel of John in Christian History* (Paulist Press, 1978); Raymond E. Brown, *The Community of the Beloved Disciple* (Paulist Press, 1979); John Meier and Raymond Brown, *Antioch and Rome* (Paulist Press, 1983).

35. See the article of David Tracy, cited in note 29 above.

36. See especially the volumes in the Stimulus series that deal with this issue: Helga Croner and Leon Klenicki, editors, *Issues in the Jewish-Christian Dialogue: Jewish Perspectives on Covenant, Mission and Witness* (Paulist Press, 1979), and Martin Cohen and Helga Croner, *Christian Mission—Jewish Mission* (Paulist Press, 1982).

37. Federici, "Catholic-Jewish Relations Today," *Origins* 8, #18 (October 19, 1978) 273–83, esp. pp. 277–79.

38. For discussion of a "reader-centered hermeneutic," consult Paul Ricoeur, *Essays on Biblical Interpretation,* edited by Lewis Mudge (Fortress Press, 1980); for the latest treatment of "Canonical Criticism," see James Sanders, *Canon and Community: A Guide to Canonical Criticism* (Fortress Press, 1984).

39. This is true even of one of the finest and most widely-used introductions, Bernhard Anderson's *Understanding the Old Testament* (Prentice-Hall; 3rd edition, 1975). A welcome exception is W. Lee Humphreys' *Crisis and Story* (Mayfield Publishing, 1979). My own introductory textbook, *Reading the Old Testament* (Paulist Press, 1984) consciously places the greater emphasis on the formative stages of the Bible in the post-exilic period.

40. A point made by Rendtorff in his article cited above in note 32.

41. See the new volume by Neil Fujita, *A Crack in the Jar: The Signif-*

icance of the Dead Sea Scrolls and Other First Century Literary Finds for the New Testament (Paulist Press, 1985).

42. See Ellis Rivkin, *The Hidden Revolution: The Pharisee's Search for the Kingdom Within* (Abingdon Press, 1978), and John T. Pawlikowski, *Christ in the Light of the Christian-Jewish Dialogue* (Paulist Press, 1982) 76–107.

43. Martin Cohen, "The First Christian Century as Jewish History," *The Bible in Modern Scholarship*, edited by Philip A. Hyatt (Abingdon Press, 1965). 227–51.

44. Statement on Catholic-Jewish Relations by the U.S. National Conference of Catholic Bishops, November 1975; collected in Croner, *Stepping Stones to Further Jewish-Christian Relations* (Stimulus/Paulist Press, 1977) 32.

45. See Samuel Sandmel, *We Jews and Jesus* (Oxford University Press, 1965); Geza Vermes, *Jesus the Jew: A Historian's Reading of the Gospels* (Collins Press, 1971); David Flusser, *Jesus* (Herder and Herder, 1969); Harvey Falk, *Jesus the Pharisee* (Paulist Press, 1985).

46. Issued in four volumes from 1922–28 in Munich.

47. Eugene Fisher discusses this well in his article, "The Impact of the Christian-Jewish Dialogue on Biblical Studies," *Christianity and Judaism: The Deepening Dialogue*, edited by Richard Rousseau, S.J. (Ridge Row Press, 1983) 117–138, esp. p. 122. Also see the remarks of Samuel Sandmel, "Parallelomania," *JBL* 81 (1962) 1–13.

48. A number of excellent studies have been published in the last few years. See a listing in Eugene Fisher, "A New Maturity in Christian-Jewish Dialogue: An Annotated Bibliography 1973–1983," *Face to Face* XI (Spring 1984) 34, and the summary treatment in John Pawlikowski, *What Are They Saying About Christian-Jewish Relations?* (Paulist Press 1980) 1–32.

49. A listing of recent treatments can be found in Fisher's bibliography cited in the preceding note. Perhaps the most widely known treatment is Rosemary Ruether's *The Theological Roots of Anti-Semitism* (Seabury Press, 1974). A more balanced treatment can be found in Alan Davies, editor, *Antisemitism and the Foundations of Christianity* (Paulist Press, 1979).

50. Consult David Flusser, "Theses on the Emergence of Christianity from Judaism," *Face to Face* X (Fall 1983) 19–22.

51. Ben Zion Bokser, "Religious Polemics in Biblical and Talmudic Exegesis," *JES* 16 (1979) 705–26. Some scholars have concluded that the inclusion of Christians among the "Minim" did not take place until later centuries, when the *nosrim* ("Nazarenes") were explicitly added to the prayer. Cf. A. Finkel, "Yavneh's Liturgy and Early Christianity," *JES* 18 (1981) 231–250; R. Kimelman, "*Birkat Ha-minim* and the Lack of Evidence for an Anti-Christian Prayer in Late Antiquity," in E.P. Sanders, ed., *Jewish and Christian*

Self-Definition (Fortress, 1981) vol. 2 pp. 226–244; S.T. Katz, "Issues in the Separation of Judaism and Christianity," *JBL* 103 (1984) 43–76.

52. Alan Davies deals with this in his introduction to the volume cited above in note 49, pp. xiii–xvii.

53. See note 33 for credits.

54. Stendahl, *Paul among Jews and Gentiles* (Fortress Press, 1976); cited by Nancy Fuchs-Kreimer, "Christian Old Testament Theology: A Time for New Beginnings," *JES* 18 (Winter 1981) 76–93, esp. p. 89.

55. This is explicitly stated by the Council document *Nostra Aetate*, par. #4.

56. See, for example, the older work of H.J. Schoeps, *Paul: The Theology of the Apostle in the Light of Jewish Religious History* (Westminster, 1961), and the more recent study of W.D. Davies, "Paul and the People of Israel," *NTS* 24 (1978) 4–39, and Krister Stendahl, *Paul among Jews and Gentiles* (Fortress Press, 1976).

57. Scholars such as Samuel Sandmel and David Daube have offered numerous studies and background reports over the years on questions of diaspora Judaism and first century practices that provide a background to the thought of Paul. They are too numerous to cite here.

58. Jacob Neusner's critical studies of the tractates of the Babylonian Talmud have been issued over the last twenty years from Brill and Company, Leiden, Holland. They now amount to more than twenty volumes. See his *Method and Meaning in Ancient Judaism* (Brown Judaic Studies 10; Scholar's Press, 1979).

59. See Eugene Fisher, "Whither Christian-Jewish Relations?" *Doctrine and Life* 33 (April 1983) 226–38.

60. Jacob Petuchowski, "Messianic Hope in Judaism," *Concilium 98: Christians and Jews* (Crossroad, Seabury Press, 1975) 56ff; Pinchas Lapide and Jurgen Moltmann, *Jewish Monotheism and Christian Trinitarian Doctrine* (Fortress Press, 1981); David Flusser, "Theses on the Emergence of Christianity from Judaism," *Face to Face* X (Fall 1983) 19–22; Eugene Borowitz, *Contemporary Christologies: A Jewish Response* (Paulist Press, 1980).

61. See J. Coert Rylaarsdam, "Judaism: The Christian Problem," *Face to Face* XI (Spring 1984) 4–8; also the statement of the Vatican Commission for Religious Relations with the Jews, *Guidelines and Suggestions for Implementing the Conciliar Declaration "Nostra Aetate,"* as cited by Msgr. Mejia in *Origins* 7, #47 (May 11, 1978) 747.

62. Irving Greenberg, "New Revelations and New Patterns in the Relationship of Judaism and Christianity," *JES* 16 (1979) 249–67.

63. Jacob Agus, "Revelation as Quest—A Contribution to Ecumenical Thought," *JES* 9 (1972) 521–43.

64. Paul van Buren, *Discerning the Way: A Theology of the Jewish-Christian Reality* (Seabury Press, 1980) 159–61.

65. See earlier studies by Michael McGarry, *Christology After Auschwitz* (Paulist Press, 1977); John Pawlikowski, *Christ in the Light of the Christian-Jewish Dialogue* (Paulist Press, 1982); Monika Hellwig, "Bible Interpretation: Has Anything Changed?" in *Bible Studies: Meeting Ground of Jews and Christians;* edited by L. Boadt et al. (Paulist Press, 1980).

66. See, for a quick overview on this issue, Leon Klenicki and Eugene Fisher, "Basic Jewish and Christian Beliefs in Dialogue: Covenant," *PACE* 13 (January 1983) 1–4.

67. On a brief overview of the messianic debate, Gerard Sloyan and Pinchas Lapide exchange views in *Face to Face* IX (Winter and Spring 1982), "From Messiah to Christ: A Religious Transition" (Sloyan), and "Mashiah and Christos: Two Hopes Personified" (Lapide), 29–37.

68. See, for example, the works of Pawlikowski cited in note 65 above, and the article of David Tracy, cited in note 29.

69. Paulist Press, 1980.

70. A comprehensive introduction to the problem is found in Lucien Richard, *What Are They Saying About Christ in World Religions?* (Paulist Press, 1981).

71. See the comments of Rylaarsdam, cited above in note 61.

72. Walter Bruggemann, *The Land* (Fortress Press, 1977).

73. See Leon Klenicki and Eugene Fisher, "Basic Jewish and Christian Beliefs in Dialogue: Creation," *PACE* 13 (December 1982) 1–4.

74. See the works cited above in note 36, and the bibliography provided by Eugene Fisher in his *Annotated Bibliography,* cited in note 10.

The Bible
and Catholic-Jewish Relations

MICHAEL J. COOK

Now is the time for new direction in applying Scriptural study to Catholic-Jewish relations. The salutary results of the last two decades of scholarly dialogue on the Bible must now be effectively channeled into the *lay* arena, and requisite pedagogical techniques must now be devised. In view of my special emphasis on the importance of lay understanding, my approach to the theme of the Bible and Catholic–Jewish relations will pose a sharp contrast to many other treatments of this subject.

I believe breakthroughs to our laities are warranted because, for relations between Roman Catholics and Jews to improve substantively, we require interchange on more levels than merely religious leadership alone. Throughout our trouble-ridden history, it has been within the wider lay social contexts (neighborhood living, business interaction, public and private school education as well as education in houses of worship) that bias, suspicion, stereotyping, and misunderstanding have assumed deep rootage, becoming virtually independent from whatever shifts in attitude or policy may have eventuated within theological, clerical, or academic circles. Reinforcing this entrenchment has been this circumstance: most laypersons simply lack opportunity for sustained and informed Bible study, not to mention for absorption of innovative and progressive trends in exegesis. Accordingly, it is especially among our lay constituents that we still commonly encounter those uncritical and literalist comprehensions of the Biblical message which for centuries have fueled divisiveness and ill-will between Catholic and Jew.

I am indeed as interested in lay attitudes among Jews as among Roman Catholics. Differing circumstances attendant to each group, however, engender an asymmetry in my concern, occasioning my separation of this discussion into two segments. I first address the problem as it seems to me to involve the Roman Catholic laity.

Some may readily protest: the importance of envisioning Bible study in relation to the needs and contexts of the Roman Catholic laity was recognized

109

and addressed years ago. *Nostra Aetate* and the guidelines for its implementation were formulated with the laity explicitly in mind, and delineated specific dimensions of Bible study requiring revision for lay understanding, often with the particular end in view of enhancing Catholic-Jewish relations. Catholics were now urged to recognize the Jewish ancestry of Jesus, his mother, the apostles, and many of the disciples who proclaimed the gospel to the world; to understand Christian faith in terms of continuity with that of the "Old" Testament rather than as radically replacing it; to construe Jesus' teachings as consistent with Jewish exegesis of his day; to realize that Jesus' death as recorded in the Gospels should not be blamed upon all Jews then living, without distinction (nor upon Jews of today); to view Jewish Scripture in such a way that it seem not to espouse only a religion of legalism, fear, and justice, devoid of love of God and humanity; to recognize the theological significance to Jews of the Biblical bond between the Israelites and the Holy Land; and generally to achieve familiarity with how Jews themselves understand the Bible and their own religion.

Problematic, however, is whether these directives were ever in and of themselves commensurate with the enormity of the obstacles to be overcome. The prospects of their actually producing *substantive* revisions in Catholic lay attitudes toward Jews and Judaism were, I submit, limited from the start. In my frequent experience and interchange with Catholic lay audiences over the last decade, I certainly have sensed their greater openness toward Jews and Judaism. But I have also sensed what I, respectfully, would deem only a superficial grasp on their part of the ramifications of Biblically-related issues for Catholic-Jewish relations, not to mention a severe underestimation by Roman Catholic clergy of the extent of pedagogic innovation required to confront and resolve our problems.

The obstacles I consider so formative can be suggested, in part, by the following series of ten anti-Jewish impressions, demonstrably inherent in centuries of Christian Biblical exegesis and constituting therefore the most determinative of influences on Catholic-Jewish relations:

1. The Jews are responsible for crucifying Jesus; they are guilty of deicide.

2. The tribulations of the Jewish people constitute God's punishment of the Jews for killing Jesus.

3. Jesus originally came to preach only to the Jews; when they rejected him, he abandoned them for the Gentiles instead.

4. The children of Israel were God's original chosen people by vir-

tue of an ancient covenant. But by rejecting Jesus, the Jews forfeited their chosenness. Now, by virtue of a new covenant,
Christians have replaced the Jews as God's chosen people.

5. The Jewish Bible ("Old" Testament) repeatedly portrays the
   opaqueness and stubbornness of the Jewish people and their
   faithlessness to God.

6. The Jewish Bible is filled with predictions of the coming of Jesus as the Messiah (or "Christ"), yet the Jews are blind to the
   meaning of their own Scripture.

7. By the time of Jesus' ministry, Judaism had ceased to be a living
   faith.

8. The essence of Judaism is a restrictive and burdensome legalism.

9. The New Testament religion—Christianity—emphasizes love;
   the Jewish Bible emphasizes legalism, justice, and a God of
   wrath.

10. The oppressive legalism of Judaism reflects the disposition of
    Jesus' opponents called "Pharisees" (forerunners of the "rab-
    bis"); in their teachings as well as their behavior, the Pharisees
    were hypocrites.

Our progress in bringing these focal issues into the lay arena has been
stymied, it seems to me, by three factors in particular:

First, the discussion of the focal issues has itself become sidetracked by
a tangential debate over whether anti-Judaism resides in the New Testament
itself or is instead a derivative of patristic exegesis of these texts. To be sure,
the spirited nature of this debate, together with the extensive volume of ensuing
publications,[1] evinces how integral the problem of confronting anti-Judaism
in the New Testament has become within current Christian-Jewish dialogue.
Yet whichever conclusion emerges as the more viable, preoccupation with this
problem has had the effect of eclipsing or at least preempting consideration of
whether and, if so, how to alert the laity to the ramifications of this discussion
and how to deepen their comprehension of the ways in which anti-Jewish exegesis of the New Testament has determined the nature of much Catholic-Jewish interrelational history.

Second, most often religious leaders have preferred keeping this discussion among themselves rather than encouraging its exploration in conjunction with their laity. When I have inquired of Catholic clergy (i.e., those who have been consistently involved in Catholic-Jewish dialogue) how many have actually sponsored any programs in their specific churches designed to convey the subjects explored in Catholic-Jewish symposia to their lay constituents, the response has been disappointing, indeed disconcertingly so.[2] Remaining unanswered, meanwhile, are questions concerning how they would present and communicate such subjects and how effective such presentations would be.

Possibly most critical of all, therefore, is the difficulty of creating pedagogical techniques for conveying the results of Biblical dialogue. To be sure, as long as Catholic-Jewish symposia on the Bible have featured as discussants *clergy* and *educators,* their relative sophistication in Biblical training has contributed materially to the success of the venture. Facilitating productive analysis and mutual comprehension has been their growing consensus that indeed historical conditioning did play a profound role in the development of New Testament writings, a recognition enabling us not only to explain but also to explain *away* the bases of virulent anti-Judaism suggested by many New Testament texts.[3] This shared awareness of literary, form, and redaction criticism (regardless of possible disagreement as to their respectability) has expanded our language of discourse, rendered possible more refined subtleties of expression, and assisted all of us in understanding where we differ and what we may share in common.

Lay constituents, however, are generally far less conversant with scholarly theories concerning the development of Biblical traditions. On the contrary, in most cases they automatically incline toward acceptance of texts at face value and usually assume the same of their clergy and educators. And indeed, since for them the wording of the New Testament texts remains a constant (in terms both of literal translation and apparent surface meaning), how can lay constituents be expected to comprehend *why* anti-Jewish tendencies, a constant throughout the history of New Testament exegesis, should now so suddenly be dismissed as merely the by-product of first century interreligious rancor? In retrospect, therefore, official directives that the Catholic laity achieve a more sympathetic understanding of Jews and Judaism actually portended but little likelihood of realization since they were unaccompanied by pedagogical techniques *commensurate* with the problem. And the present hesitancy to pursue the question of whether and how to instruct the laity of course only further stymies progress in developing the necessary approaches.

In view of the above criticisms, I propose what some might consider a startling change of course. But I have described our current impasse at such length so as to demonstrate why innovation is warranted. Stating the matter succinctly, I would ask Roman Catholic educators to expose their laity to how the *New* Testament is understood by Jews and how Jews understand the Jewish Bible in relation to *Christianity*. I anticipate that this exposure will facilitate lay comprehension of critical issues in Catholic-Jewish dialogue. Before attempting to demonstrate the "why" and the "how," I offer a justification of this proposal.

Vatican II and its guidelines urged Roman Catholics to learn how Jews understand their own religion. For Jews, such *self*-understanding entails a confrontation with what Judaism both does and does *not* espouse. In this sense, a Jewish understanding of Judaism encompasses as well a comprehension of how Christianity differs and how Judaism assesses claims advanced by the New Testament. At issue herein is a matter of *reciprocity* which I feel Vatican II failed to address: The Jewish lay community is well-versed concerning Christianity's views of Judaism, especially because the Gospels are punctuated by value judgments concerning Jews and their religion; given the Christian-oriented society in which Jews perceive themselves as living, these assessments seem *to Jews* part and parcel of the general religious milieu. The *converse*, however, is hardly the case: the Catholic laity generally have no informed awareness of Judaism's evaluation of Christianity or of Judaism's responses to Christian theological propositions—even those which directly impinge upon Judaism! Circumstances are such not only because Jewish Scripture (available for Christian readership) contains no mention of Christianity but also because, where Jewish Scripture is construed by some Christians as predictive of the coming of Jesus, such interpretation is distinctly at variance with Jewish exposition of the same texts. I am convinced that the cause of mutual understanding would be materially advanced were Jewish reactions to the ten anti-Jewish impressions incorporated into the dialogical process as it involves Catholic lay education. Indeed, I cannot be sanguine about prospects for productive dialogue in the future unless this is accomplished. Of course, I am speaking here only about exposure to Jewish perspectives, with no correlative expectation that these perspectives be accepted.

It would hardly be sufficient for me merely to relinquish the matter at this juncture. Definitely in order are some preliminary illustrations of what I have in mind—examples which will have direct application to the list of anti-Jewish impressions presented earlier. Inherent in each of these impressions is the question of anti-Judaism in the New Testament. Earlier, I characterized this topic as tangential because it has diverted our attention from the need to move these focal issues into the lay arena. Once they *are* transferred into the lay arena, however, the subject of anti-Judaism in the New Testament emerges as curricularly central! I propose the following as a means of facilitating presentation of the problem:

A number of Gospel passages which to Jews seemingly manifest an anti-

Jewish orientation should be selected and studied by Catholic laypersons *in the light of their Gospel parallels*. Subsequent to analysis of their content, inferences should be drawn from the evidence.

Example #1—"Jesus Before the Sanhedrin"

MARK 14:55–56
⁵⁵Now the chief priests and the whole council sought testimony against Jesus to put him to death; but they found none. ⁵⁶For many bore false witness against him, and their witness did not agree.

→

MATT. 26:59–60
⁵⁹Now the chief priests and the whole council sought *false* testimony against Jesus that they might put him to death, ⁶⁰but they found none, though many false witnesses came forward.

Here the lay student is to be helped to observe that, by virtue of a single word, the Matthaean account differs significantly from the Markan rendition. In verse 59 of Matthew, there appears the word "false." While in Mark the Jewish officials sought (true) testimony against Jesus, in Matthew they set about finding *false* testimony ab initio. This means that, in Mark's understanding, the Jewish authorities honestly believed Jesus *guilty* and sought witnesses to confirm their belief; yet in Matthew the Jewish authorities believed him *innocent* and sought *false* witnesses to condemn him.

Example #2—"The Question Concerning Tribute to Caesar"

MARK 12:13–17
¹³And they sent to him some of the Pharisees and some of the Herodians, to entrap him in his talk. ¹⁴And they came and

said to him, "Teacher, we know that you are true, and care for no man; for you do not regard the position of men, but truly teach the way of God.

Is it lawful to pay taxes to Caesar, or not? ¹⁵Should we pay them, or should we not?" But knowing their *hypocrisy,* he said to them, "Why put me to the test? Bring me a coin, and let me look at it."

→

MATT. 22:15–22
¹⁵Then *the Pharisees* went and took counsel how to entangle him in his talk. ¹⁶And they sent their disciples to him, along with the Herodians,

saying, "Teacher, we know that you are true, and teach the way of God truthfully, and care for no man; for you do not regard the position of men. ¹⁷Tell us, then, what you think. Is it lawful to pay taxes to Caesar, or not?"

¹⁸But Jesus, aware of their *malice,* said,

"Why put me to the test, you *hypocrites,* ¹⁹Show me the money for the tax."

Here the lay student is to observe that in Mark Jesus' Jewish opponents are deemed hypocritical, but in Matthew *malicious* as well as hypocritical. Even though the two accounts are virtually identical, in Matthew the Jewish leaders appear one shade the more disreputable; moreover, they are disparaged now by Jesus' own words (i.e., in a quotation ascribed to him personally rather than in a detached evaluative judgment attributable to the redactor).

Example #3—"The Great Commandment"

THE GREAT COMMANDMENT

MARK 12:28–34

[28]And one of the scribes came up and heard them disputing with one another, and seeing that he answered them well, asked him, "Which commandment is the first of all?" [29]Jesus answered, "The first is, 'Hear, O Israel: The Lord our God, the Lord is one; [30]and you shall love the Lord your God with all your heart, and with all your soul, and with all your mind, and with all your strength.'

[31]The second is this, 'You shall love your neighbor as yourself.' There is no other commandment greater than these." [32]And the scribe said to him, "*You are right, Teacher;* you have *truly* said that he is one, and there is no other but he; [33] and to love him with all the heart, and with all the understanding, and with all the strength, and to love one's neighbor as oneself, is much more than all whole burnt offerings and sacrifices." [34]And when Jesus saw that he answered *wisely,* he said to him, "*You are not far from the kingdom of God.*"

MATT. 22:34–40

[34]But when the Pharisees heard that he had silenced the Sadducees, they came together. [35]And one of them, a lawyer, asked him a question, to test him. [36]"Teacher, which is the great commandment in the law?" [37]And he said to him,

"You shall love the Lord your God with all your heart, and with all your soul, and with all your mind. [38]This is the great and first commandment. [39]And a second is like it, You shall love your neighbor as yourself. [40]On these two commandments depend all the law and the prophets."

Here the lay student should be apprised that this pericope constitutes the single Markan representation of camaraderie between Jesus and a Jewish leader. In the parallel tradition in Matthew, meanwhile, the camaraderie is nowhere evident. The pleasant conversation in Mark becomes a *confrontation* in Matthew: Matthew alleges that the intent of the Jewish leader was hardly to engage Jesus in amicable discussion but rather "to test him." Meanwhile, the paragraph expressing mutual admiration in Mark (12:32–34a) is curiously absent in Matthew. Also missing in Matthew is the most important sentence of Jesus' Great Commandment: "Hear, O Israel: the Lord our God, the Lord is one." That is to say, in Matthew, Jesus' Great Commandment is no longer addressed preeminently to the Jewish people.

Example #4—"The Sentence of Death"

MARK 15:12–15	MATT. 27:22–26	LUKE 23:21–25
"Then what shall I do with the man whom you call the King of the Jews?" [13]And they cried out again, "Crucify him." [14]And Pilate said to them. *"Why, what evil has he done?"*	them, "Then what shall I do with Jesus who is called Christ?" They all said, "Let him be crucified." [23]And he said, *"Why, what evil has he done?"*	[21]but they shouted out, "Crucify, crucify him!" [22] *A third time he said to them, "Why, what evil has he done? I have found in him no crime deserving death; I will therefore chastise him and release him."* [23]But
But they shouted all the more, "Crucify him."	But they shouted all the more. "Let him be crucified."	they were urgent, demanding with loud cries that he should be crucified. *And their voices prevailed.*
→		→

MARK 15:12–15	MATT. 27:22–26	LUKE 23:21–25
	[24]So when Pilate saw that he was gaining nothing, but rather that a riot was beginning, he took water and washed his hands before the crowd, saying, "I am innocent of this man's blood, see to it yourselves." [25]And all the people answered, His blood be on us and on our children!"	
[15]So Pilate, wishing to satisfy the crowd, released for them Barabbas;	[26]Then he released for them Barabbas, and having scourged Jesus,	[24]So Pilate gave sentence that their demand should be granted. [25]He released the man who had been thrown into prison for insurrection and murder, whom they asked for; but Jesus he delivered up *to their will.*
and having scourged Jesus, he delivered him to be crucified.	delivered him to be crucified.	

In Mark, the Roman governor, Pontius Pilate, acquits Jesus once, and it is the Jewish mob who call for Jesus' crucifixion. In Matthew, the incorporation of vv. 24–25 maximizes the Jews' responsibility for Jesus' death even as it further downplays Pilate's own involvement. In Luke, meanwhile, the Jewish responsibility is dramatically intensified ("they were urgent, demanding with loud cries," "their voices prevailed," "that their demand should be granted," "the man . . . whom they asked for," "delivered up to their will") even as Pilate acquits Jesus *three* times rather than merely once.

The methodology of studying these and scores of other Gospel parallels is hardly new, yet relatively few are the Catholic laypersons who are even remotely aware of it. Undeniably, fundamentally critical theological dilemmas surface when this methodology is employed. But if we are serious about analyzing the dynamics of Scripture's role in Catholic-Jewish relations and in translating this analysis into terms meaningful for lay comprehension, then the scrutiny of Gospel parallels is a primary launching point.

What conclusions are laypersons to draw from such an exposure? Clearly, the inferences are not to be prejudged. I personally aver that a correlation may often be observed in Gospel texts between lateness of date and intensification of anti-Jewish sentiment. A consensus of New Testament scholarship not only identifies Matthew and Luke as later than Mark, but specifies Mark as their major source. Accordingly, the cited variations of Matthew and Luke from Mark could actually be conscious *departures*—reflecting not simply dependence on additional (though unidentifiable) sources but possibly intentional anti-Jewish alteration of the Markan tradition, expressive therefore of the editors' own inclinations and conditioned by the tense climate of Christian-Jewish discourse pervading their day and suffusing their locales.[4] One could also posit that, over history, the more intensely anti-Jewish versions have also tended to become the more popularly accepted by the lay element, this being especially the case with the Fourth Gospel, the favorite of many. John, which characteristically designates Jesus' enemies collectively as "the Jews," has been far more instrumental in conditioning lay identification of Jesus' enemies than have the Synoptics which generally denote Jesus' opponents merely by the names of leadership groups (e.g., "scribes," "Pharisees," "Sadducees," "chief priests," "elders," "Herodians").[5]

Anti-Jewish sentiment in the New Testament, therefore, emerges as a function of developing church theology, such that passages productive of ill-will by Christian toward Jew (with inevitable reciprocation) emerge as in no necessary respect a function of Jesus' personal preachment. All these concerns strike me as vital in helping the Catholic (and Jewish!) laity to comprehend Gospel traditions as more than an undifferentiated mass, and to experience the revelation that traditions long generating impediments to our mutual welfare may never have been grounded in historical facticity! It is of course not necessary, in my judgment, that Catholic laypersons agree that sections of the New Testament are anti-Jewish—only that they come to understand how *Jews* can see the matter that way.[6]

This problem is illustrative of many issues wherein exposure to Jewish perspectives concerning Christianity would at least serve to deepen lay Catholic awareness of the ramifications of Catholic-Jewish dialogue on the Bible. As this is true of Jewish perspectives on the New Testament, so is it true of Jewish perspectives on Christianity's relation to the Jewish Scriptures.[7] The Gospels repeatedly cite the Jewish Bible as being predictive of the coming of Jesus such that lay readers are naturally puzzled that Jews do not accept Jesus. After all, in the Jews' own Bible (!) Isaiah predicts the Virgin Birth and envisions a "suffering servant" uncannily resembling Jesus and no one else; Leviticus in particular stresses the vital soteriological role of blood in the sacrificial cult; Psalm 22 generates imagery corresponding exactly to the scene of Jesus on the cross; and so forth.[8] Does not this bewilderment inexorably occasion value judgments concerning the intelligence and clearsightedness of Jews who mysteriously and stubbornly defy the intuitively obvious? The directives of Vatican II do not address this more complex syndrome—they simply are not commensurate with the obstacles to be overcome.

There surfaces here the same problem of inequity: Jews know full well what many a Catholic layperson believes about Jews, Judaism, and the Bible, yet Jewish perspectives on the Bible, together with the reasoning underpinning them, fail of inclusion in the Roman Catholic learning process. Jews have long posed a fourfold response to this phenomenon of Christian citation of Jewish Scripture which, whether correct or not, at least furnishes a rational basis for the Jewish stance: first, that many of the prooftexts advanced simply do not mean what the New Testament exegesis of them alleges;[9] second, that the uncanny correlation between Jewish Scriptural texts and the image of Jesus derives from the Christian tradition's conforming of Jesus' image to Jewish Scriptural motifs;[10] third, that fundamentally central Scriptural predictions concerning the Messiah yet *not* fulfilled by Jesus' ministry either fail of inclusion in Christian exegesis or are postponed to the Second Coming (an eventuality not normative for Jewish Messianic thought);[11] fourth, that the essence of theology should be founded and presented in terms of categories transcending mere prooftexting. Persuasion one way or the other is not my intent or the issue—I assert only that the cause of dialogue would be better furthered were the Jewish position conveyed and recognized by the Catholic laity as possessing cogency rather than seen by them as nebulously and inexplicably running counter to what is deemed to be logical and self-evident.

Also unfamiliar to much of the Catholic laity are Jewish views concerning the historical Jesus (especially concerning the nature of his attitude toward the Law and his relations with Jews and Gentiles,[12] the nature of his alleged controversies with the Pharisees,[13] and the nature of his trial[14]), and Jewish responsès to so many of the stereotypes still commonly accepted by some. Thus, for example, the *lex talionis* ("eye for an eye," etc.), often cited to characterize the "Old" Testament, could be construed as a revolutionary progressive measure for its day (placing limitations on the extent of permissible retaliation)—and, in any event, was understood in Rabbinic Judaism as mandating only monetary compensation, not literal retaliation at all;[15] the dispersion of the Jews throughout the Mediterranean world, sometimes interpreted as a punishment for the Jews' non-acceptance of Jesus, actually preceded Jesus' birth by centuries (such that more Jews lived outside Palestine than within by the time of Jesus' birth); the Temple's destruction in the year 70, understood by some as retribution for the Jews' rejection of Christianity,[16] is traceable on the most elementary level to Rome's military superiority and the inevitability of her brutal retaliation for the Jewish revolt. Indeed, with regard to each of the ten anti-Jewish impressions cited earlier, what we are essentially dealing with is a stereotype of one sort or another—and each would become cast in a significantly different light were Jewish perspectives only incorporated into Catholic pedagogical discussion of Judaism. The way to counteract these impressions lies not only in an issuing of directives to cease accepting them but more productively in a process of learning how Jews themselves have reacted to them and how Jewish perspectives can be brought to bear in an analysis of their cogency.

What, then, should be said concerning the Jewish side of the ledger—that is, lay attitudes among *Jews* with respect to the Bible and Catholic-Jewish relations? The challenge in this case is no less imposing, for here, too, progress has been disappointingly slow—though for quite dissimilar reasons.

To begin with, since Roman Catholicism extends the Bible's message far beyond the termination point identified by Judaism, inevitably Jews will feel less of an impetus to discuss the New Testament (a corpus which is not theirs) than Catholics will to discuss the Jewish Bible (which is part and parcel of theirs). And with further respect to the Hebrew Scriptures. Jews do not perceive the Bible as in any fashion directed toward the coming of Jesus. Accordingly, fundamental disagreements surface not only concerning what is encompassed by the term "Bible" but also concerning how the import of its content is to be construed. Of course, the existence of such disagreements might render dialogue that much more attractive, exciting, and fruitful. Yet more often the practical effect has been to engender among Jews discomfort with the very idea of the Bible serving as a focus of dialogue in the first place.

Transcending these contrasting perceptions is an overarching consideration: for early Catholicism, a need developed to define Christianity's relationship to Judaism in a way in which Judaism has never felt the need to define its relationship toward Christianity. Early Christians had to explain to themselves as well as to others in what way they were the heirs of the promises of the God of Scripture, and what factors had occasioned their having supplanted the Jews as God's Chosen. They also had to justify their departures from Judaism—both their non-observance of practices Judaism had long enjoined and their introduction of observances of which Judaism had come to express disapproval. Jews, by contrast, did not feel any analogous need to define themselves in relation to Christianity, primarily because Judaism was the mother religion and had long existed without Christianity's presence on the scene. For many Jews to this day, this fundamental distinction renders the very need for dialogue puzzling.

Further, the problem of anti-Judaism resurfaces in yet another guise. Since the early Christian concerns had come to be couched in the language of anti-Judaism, the New Testament itself has ironically been a major impediment to Jews' discerning, distilling, and appreciating the import and relevance of

Jesus' message for those of his own day as well as those of still later generations. This dynamic itself erodes enthusiasm for dialogue. Because Jews have felt victimized throughout history by what Christians recognize as a significant component of their Bible, because in their self-perception they are the injured party, it turns out that, if dialogue is to be seen by Jews as serving a purpose, that purpose usually emerges as quite other than learning about the Bible and Catholic understandings thereof. Instead they are summoned by a more practical motive, indeed one which is twofold—to redress grievances derivative of a history of seemingly relentless Christian oppression, and to extract from Catholics today assurances of support for Jewish survival and for the achievement of practical Jewish concerns. Chief among the latter would be: combating anti-Semitism; rallying support for the State of Israel; explaining Jewish views on the separation of Church and State; fostering sensitivity to Jewish feelings during and around Christian holiday periods; resolving calendrical conflicts between public school and Jewish calendars; altering churchgoers' stereotypes of Jews; stimulating revisions in Catholic textbooks on substantive themes involving Jews and Judaism (e.g., blame of the Jews for the execution of Jesus; the alleged dispersion of the Jews as a divine punishment; the "overagainstness" of Jesus vis-à-vis Judaism; the denigration of the Pharisees; the Catholic role in unsavory periods of Jewish history—such as the Crusades, the Spanish Inquisition, expulsions of Jews, pogroms, the Holocaust). Accordingly, there is a profound and undeniable asymmetry in the Catholic and Jewish agendas for dialogue, and at present prospects for change seem potentially more likely (and thus depend more heavily on movement) within the Catholic lay arena.

What would definitely stimulate dramatic progress would be a realization by Jews of extensive breakthroughs in the sensitivity of Catholic laypersons to Jewish concerns. Yet this in turn can hardly be even envisioned without the fundamental intensification of Biblical education for the Catholic lay sector, along the lines suggested earlier. Over the centuries, interpreters of the New Testament actually did have the authority and the ability and the opportunity to advance modes of interpretation which would have been productive of more harmonious Catholic-Jewish relations (regardless and in spite of the antipathy toward Jews and Judaism resident within the New Testament texts themselves). This was possible, to be sure, because the meaning of Biblical texts inheres not only in the texts themselves but also in the nuances accorded them by educated interpreters. Nevertheless, that authority, that ability, and that opportunity were generally not availed of. Fortunately, however, the opportunity for such constructive reinterpretation and for its implementation on the *lay* level still does remain available. The twentieth anniversary of Vatican II is assuredly an appropriate occasion to rethink where we currently are in relation to where we have been, and to forge new avenues out of the pathways first carved out two decades ago.

NOTES

1. I present my own views on this problem in "Anti-Judaism in the New Testament," *Union Seminary Quarterly Review,* XXXVIII, #2 (1983), pp. 125–137, where I allude as well to G. Baum, *Is the New Testament Anti-Semitic?* (New York: Paulist, 1965); R. Ruether, *Faith and Fratricide* (New York: Seabury, 1974). Cf. also Baum's "Introduction," revising his earlier opinion; Ch. Klein, *Anti-Judaism in Christian Theology,* trans. E. Quinn (Philadelphia: Fortress, 1978); S. Sandmel, *Anti-Semitism in the New Testament?* (Philadelphia: Fortress, 1978); J. Koenig, *Jews and Christians in Dialogue* (Philadelphia: Westminister, 1979); C. Williamson, *Has God Rejected His People?* (Nashville: Abingdon, 1982).

2. The program they most frequently cite is a Passover seder conducted in church. This kind of program, however, really serves educational and experiential needs other than the goals envisioned by Catholic-Jewish dialogue. Often, such seders have been productive of good will. In some regrettable instances, however, haggadahs (the liturgy accompanying seders) as produced by various Roman Catholic churches have interpolated into the traditional text non-Jewish material foreign, of course, to what would have been Jesus' own experience. In such cases, interreligious understanding among the laity has, in my view, actually been impeded.

3. Texts preeminently cited include Mt 8:10–12; 19:28; 21:33–43; 22:1–10; 23:1–36; and Jn 8:19, 24, 44–47, among many others. Cf. works listed in note 1.

4. This consideration occasions the question: Do anti-Jewish departures by Matthew and Luke from Mark suggest the likelihood of Mark's similar departures from *his* sources? A detailed treatment of this problem is found in my book, *Mark's Treatment of the Jewish Leaders* (Leiden: Brill, 1978).

5. See E.J. Epp, "Anti-Semitism and the Popularity of the Fourth Gospel in Christianity," *Central Conference of American Rabbis Journal* 22 (1975), pp. 35–57. On the term "the Jews," see especially T.L. Schram, *The Use of "Ioudaios" in the Fourth Gospel* (Utrecht, 1973). For a more comprehensive treatment of Jews and Judaism in John, see R. Brown, *The Gospel According to John,* The Anchor Bible, Vol. 29 (Garden City: Doubleday, 1966), pp. lxx–lxxv, 229, 368, 674–675, 692, 702, 792, 895; *idem, The Community of the Beloved Disciple* (New York: Paulist, 1979), pp. 40–43, 66–69. Note especially Brown's observation: "Most Gentile readers of today do not notice the strangeness of John's having Jesus and the Jews around him refer to other Jews simply as 'the Jews' . . . (and often they think of Jesus more as a Christian than as a Jew!)" (*Community,* pp. 40–41).

6. The 1975 Statement of the National Conference of Catholic Bishops

declares that the question is also a properly Catholic one, stating: "Correctly viewed, the disappearance of the charge of collective guilt of Jews pertains as much to the purity of the Catholic faith as it does to the defense of Judaism."

7. Among the many books treating Christianity's relation to the Jewish Scriptures, the following represent a wide diversity of well-articulated viewpoints: B. Lindars, *New Testament Apologetic: the Doctrinal Significance of the Old Testament Quotations* (London: SCM, 1961); J. Daniélou, *From Shadows to Reality: Studies in the Biblical Typology of the Fathers* (London: Burns & Oates, 1960); C.H. Dodd, *According to Scriptures: The Substructure of New Testament Theology* (London: Nisbet & Co., 1953); E.E. Ellis, *Paul's Use of the Old Testament* (Edinburgh: Oliver & Boyd, 1957); R.T. France, *Jesus and the Old Testament: His Application of Old Testament Passages to Himself and His Mission* (London: Tyndale, 1971); R.H. Gundry, *The Use of the Old Testament in St. Matthew's Gospel* (Leiden: Brill, 1967); A.T. Hanson, *Jesus Christ in the Old Testament* (London: SPCK, 1965); and G.W.H. Lampe, "The Reasonableness of Typology," and K.J. Woolcombe, "The Biblical Origins and Patristic Development of Typology," *Essays on Typology* (Naperville, Ill.: Allenson, 1957), pp. 9–38, 39–75.

8. In my experience, the "suffering servant" motif is the most frequently cited of these and the countless other such examples; cf. especially J. Gartenhaus, "The Suffering Servant of Jehovah," *The Mediator* 18 (January-March 1945), pp. 2ff.; France, *op. cit.*, pp. 110–135; R.A. Rosenberg, "Jesus, Isaac, and the "Suffering Servant,' " *Journal of Biblical Literature* 84 (1965), pp. 381–388; H.M. Orlinsky, *The So-Called "Suffering Servant" in Isaiah 53* (The Goldenson Lecture, 1964; Cincinnati: Hebrew Union College Press, 1964); H.H. Rowley, *The Servant of the Lord* (London: 1952); A. Neubauer and S.R. Driver, *The Fifty-Third Chapter of Isaiah According to the Jewish Interpreters*, 2 vols. (New York: KTAV, 1969).

9. See especially Isaac Troki, *Faith Strengthened*, repr. (New York: KTAV, 1970); D. Berger and M. Wyschogrod, *Jews and "Jewish Christianity"* (New York: KTAV, 1978); G. Sigal, *The Jew and the Christian Missionary: A Jewish Response to Missionary Christianity* (New York: KTAV, 1981); D. Lasker, *Jewish Philosophical Polemics against Christianity in the Middle Ages* (New York: KTAV & Anti-Defamation League, 1977).

10. Illustrative of this process, in the views of some, would be: the plural animals in Mt 21:1–7 (conforming Jesus to Matthew's misunderstanding of Zec 9:9); the imagery of Jesus on the cross in Mk 15 (conforming Jesus to Ps 22:1, 7, 18); the "gall" and "vinegar" in Mt 27 (conforming to Ps 69:21); the naked young man in Mk 14:51 (conforming to Am 2:16); the solar eclipse in Lk 23:44–45 (conforming to Jl 2:31 and Am 8:9); "suffering servant" imagery in Mt 8:14–17 (conforming to Is 53:40), Lk 22:35–37 (conforming to Is

53:12), Mt 27:57–60 (conforming to Is 53:9), and so forth. Cf. my article, "The Betrayal by Judas Iscariot—An Example of Christian Typological Exegesis," *Association for Jewish Studies Bulletin* 22 (1978), pp. 9ff.

11. E.g., Is 2:2–4; Zec 8:23; Jer 3:17; Jl 4:18; Zec 14:9; etc.

12. See my essay, "Interpreting 'Pro-Jewish' Passages in Matthew," *Hebrew Union College Annual* 54 (1983), pp. 135–146.

13. For bibliography and an analysis of the problem, cf. my article, "Jesus and the Pharisees: The Problem as It Stands Today," *Journal of Ecumenical Studies* 15 (1978), pp. 441–460.

14. Cf. D.R. Catchpole, *The Trial of Jesus: A Study in . . . Jewish Historiography from 1770 to the Present Day* (Leiden, 1971); P Winter, *On the Trial of Jesus* (Berlin: Walter de Gruyter, 1961); E. Rivkin, "Beth Din, Boulé, Sanhedrin: A Tragedy of Errors," *Hebrew Union College Annual* 46 (1975), pp. 181–199; *idem,* review of Haim Cohn's *The Trial and Death of Jesus of Nazareth,* in *Saturday Review* (June 19, 1971), pp. 22, 61–62; S. Sandmel, "The Trial of Jesus: Reservations," *Judaism* 20 (1971), pp. 69–74.

15. See *locus classicus* discussion, in Babylonian Talmud, Baba Kamma 83b.

16. Cf. the Parable of the Marriage Feast, Mt 22:1–14, esp. v. 7.

)

Religious Education Before
and After Vatican II

JUDITH HERSHCOPF BANKI

One can only appreciate the dramatic changes in Roman Catholic teaching about Jews and Judaism initiated by Vatican Council II by contrasting educational materials published since the Council with textbooks and teachers' manuals in common use well into the 1960s.

What we know about the earlier teaching materials derives from a series of textbook self-studies stimulated by the American Jewish Committee at Roman Catholic academic institutions in the United States and Europe.[1] Each of these studies revealed teachings of hostility and contempt for Jews and Judaism that lent credence to Jewish concerns about Christian polemical traditions as a continuing source of anti-Semitism.

In the United States, the Catholic textbook self-study project was carried out at St. Louis University under the supervision of Trafford Maher, and summarized in book form by John Pawlikowski in *Catechetics and Prejudice*.[2]

In light of the progress toward Christian understanding of Jews and Judaism in recent years, it is somewhat shocking to look back on some of the excerpts found in Catholic textbooks most widely used at the time of the St. Louis University research. Accusations of collective guilt and assertions that Jews are a people accursed and rejected by God found frequent expression in these texts, as did the charge that the Jews willfully and culpably blinded themselves to Jesus' significance. Pawlikowski noted that statements stressing the universal theological significance of the Crucifixion were not infrequent in the materials. The difficulty was that this universal viewpoint got lost when the lessons focused on the Crucifixion and the events leading up to it. Thus, the Catholic student might be informed in other lessons that the "sins of all men" were responsible, but "in the representative excerpts from the religion materials, it is Jewish culpability for the suffering and death of Christ that is stressed, rather than the sins of all mankind." A single example will suffice:

However, when the mob saw this, the chief priests took up a cry that put a curse on themselves and on the Jews for all time: "His blood be upon us and our children."

As for references to the Pharisees—described by Pawlikowski as among the most negative encountered in the textbooks—some were so distorted "that the student would find it virtually impossible to sense any human identification with them or to believe that they acted out of human motivation."

The findings of the St. Louis University research provided the basis for a memorandum submitted by the American Jewish Committee to Augustine Cardinal Bea, at his request, over a year before Vatican Council II convened. Cardinal Bea, head of the commission charged with drafting the declaration eventually issued as *Nostra Aetate,* welcomed the documentation, which helped convince him of the need for an authoritative repudiation of anti-Semitism and the rejection of the "deicide" charge at the highest level of the Church.

The European studies, covering Catholic teaching materials in a variety of languages, showed that teachings of contempt were widespread throughout the religious culture. One was conducted at the International University of Social Studies, Pro Deo, in Rome, an institution under papal patronage; the other at the Catholic University of Louvain, Belgium, with the personal endorsement of the Archbishop of Malines and Brussels, Leo Jozef Cardinal Suenens.

The Pro Deo study dealt with textbooks for Catholic religious teaching that were published for use in Italian and Spanish schools, from the elementary to the senior or college level, between 1940 and 1964. A brief supplementary study covered texts issued after Vatican II. The survey focused mainly on Jews and Judaism but also dealt with references to other religious, ethnic, political, and cultural groups outside the Roman Catholic Church.

The Louvain research consisted of two distinct phases. The first was an analysis of religious textbooks from French-speaking countries—France, Belgium, Switzerland, and Canada—published between 1949 and 1964, and used in both public and Catholic secondary schools. The second was an opinion survey exploring what ideas about Jews and Judaism were held by persons who had been exposed to Catholic teaching.

The Pro Deo and Louvain studies were summarized by Claire Huchet Bishop in *How Catholics Look at Jews.* Once again, negative generalizations and accusations against Jews were triggered most by lessons dealing with such conflict themes as the Crucifixion and the Jewish rejection of Jesus as the awaited messiah. According to Bishop, many young Catholics in Italy, Spain, and the French-speaking countries were still being taught into the 1960s— *twenty years after the Holocaust:*

1. That the Jews are collectively responsible for the Crucifixion and that they are a "deicide people."
2. That the Diaspora is the Jews' punishment for the Crucifixion and for their cry "His blood be upon us and upon our children."
3. That Jesus predicted the punishment of his people; that the Jews were and remained cursed by him and by God; that Jerusalem, as a city, is particularly guilty.
4. That the Jewish people as a whole rejected Jesus during his lifetime because of their materialism.
5. That the Jewish people have put themselves beyond salvation and are consigned to eternal damnation.
6. That the Jewish people have been unfaithful to their mission and are guilty of apostasy.
7. That Judaism was once the best religion, but then became ossified and ceased to exist with the coming of Jesus.
8. That the Jews are no longer the Chosen People, but have been superseded as such by the Christians.

The studies provide an abundance of excerpts illustrating these themes. Just a few will demonstrate the extent of the animus. From an Italian textbook:

This people will be torn from their land . . . . scattered through the world . . . . under the burden of a divine curse which will accompany them through the course of their history.

From a Spanish textbook:

The wretched Jews could not imagine the accumulation of calamities that would befall them and their descendants for having taken upon themselves the responsibility for the blood of the Just One, the Son of God.

The French textbooks were relatively freer of the "deicide" charge and of the notion of the "blood curse," but the single such reference projected it onto the Jews of today:

The Jews remain those who reject Christ, and the people whose ancestors solemnly asked that his blood fall upon them.

Bishop further notes that charges against the Jewish people were accompanied by a rhetoric of invective, which attributed the most vicious motives to them—for example:

The first persecutors were the Jews, who were consumed with rage
when they saw the rise of the wonderful Holy Church of Jesus Christ
whom they, out of envy and hatred, had condemned to the cross.

Or the Jews were described in pejorative terms—for example:

. . . . the Sanhedrin, which consisted of 71 bearded, miserly
Jews. . . .

Or, occasionally, they were accused of being Masons or Bolsheviks. In some
Spanish texts, the ritual murder accusation found expression. Even some of
the simplest descriptions betrayed either an intended or an unconscious mali-
ciousness.

The first eleven [of the Apostles] were born in Galilee; the last, Judas, was a Jew.

The Pro Deo researchers, assessing their survey findings as a whole, were
struck by the amount of hostility they uncovered toward Jews and other groups
in both the Italian and the Spanish materials.

Vatican II set in motion a new, more positive attitude toward Jews and
Judaism. Since the promulgation of *Nostra Aetate,* statements by national bishops' conferences (United States, Dutch, Belgian, French, Swiss, German and
Brazilian), guidelines issued by the Vatican's Commission for Religious Relations with the Jews and various papal statements have gone far beyond the
Declaration itself. Such authoritative documents have called for ''a frank and
honest treatment of Christian anti-Semitism in our history books, courses and
curricula'' and ''an acknowledgement of the living and complex reality of Judaism after Christ and the permanent election of Israel'' (Guidelines for Catholic-Jewish Relations, National Conference of Catholic Bishops'
Subcommittee for Catholic-Jewish Relations, 1967); have stressed that ''the
points on which Jesus took issue with the Judaism of his time are fewer than
those in which He found himself in agreement with it'' (Vatican study paper,
1969); have stated that ''The Jewish people is the true relative of the Church,
not her rival or a minority to be assimilated'' (study paper, National Catholic
Commission for Relations with the Jews, Belgium, 1973); have called it ''most
urgent that Christians cease to represent the Jews according to clichés forged
by the hostility of centuries'' (French Bishops' Committee for Relations with
Jews, 1973); have regretted ''that an often faulty and hard-hearted presentation
of Judaism led to a wrong attitude of Christians toward Jews. Hence great care
must be taken in religious instruction, liturgical services, adult education and
theological training, to offer a correct interpretation of Jewish self-understand-

ing" (Swiss Bishops' statement, 1974); have urged Christians "to strive to learn by what essential traits the Jews define themselves in the light of their own religious experience" and emphasized that information regarding the Jewishness of Jesus, the similarity of his teaching methods to those employed by the rabbis of his time, the repudiation of Jewish collective guilt for the trial and death of Jesus and the continuing development of Judaism after the emergence of Christianity "is important at all levels of Christian instruction and education" including "the thorough formation of instructors and educators in training schools, seminaries and universities" (Vatican Commission for Religious Relations with the Jews, 1975).

The question is: How thoroughly have these exemplary guidelines and suggestions been implemented at the parish level, and to what extent has the Church's new policy of respect and friendship for Jews and Judaism been reflected in textbooks, classroom teaching and religious formation?

Here there is much good news and some bad news. Both the Louvain and the Pro Deo studies reported a sharp drop in negative statements in books issued after the Council. Bishop observed: "It seems reasonable to assume that these figures reflect the Church's adoption of a new, positive policy toward Jews and Judaism at the Second Vatican Council." A much more comprehensive survey, Eugene Fisher's study of post-Vatican II Catholic textbooks used in the United States, bears out the expectation that they would be more sympathetic to Jews and Judaism. Fisher's study covered sixteen major religion series currently in use on the grade and high school levels. The 161 student texts and 113 teachers' manuals were published between 1967 and 1975. The findings of that study—along with general observations and recommendations, guidelines for the evaluation of the treatment of Jews and Judaism in catechetical materials, and authoritative Church documents—were published in 1977 under the title *Faith Without Prejudice.*

Focusing on specific themes which are critical to Christian-Jewish relations today, Fisher found great improvement in the treatment of many of them. For example, he found clear references to the Jewishness of Jesus. (In contrast, some of the earlier materials appeared to go to great lengths to avoid identifying the Jews as Jesus' people.) He found the notion of Jewish suffering as an expression of divine retribution completely eliminated from the textbooks. (The only references to this notion clearly condemned it.) He found that references to the Holocaust were handled with great sensitivity. While not negative or hostile, he found that references to violence against Jews occasioned by the Crusades and the Inquisition and references to the modern State of Israel were "inadequate." Despite overwhelmingly positive references to Judaism in general terms, however, textbook treatment of the events of Jesus' passion trigger some of the old negative generalizations, and, throughout all the textbooks, the Pharisees "are painted in dark, evil colors."

Fisher noted: "Because of the impact of Vatican II's declaration and more recent episcopal statements, it was expected that textbooks today would be more positive toward Judaism than those written before the Council. This proved to be true for the high school texts. . . . But the elementary texts . . . actually went down . . . reflecting a higher percentage of negative statements than in 1961. What can account for this?" His answer pointed to the depth of the remaining problems:

> The critical area for Jewish-Christian relations as revealed in the study lies in our treatment of New Testament themes and events. . . . Since the elementary-level textbooks use the New Testament much more now than before the Council, these key problem areas come up more frequently. Almost all of the negative references to Jews and Judaism occur in statements dealing with New Testament themes. . . . Vestiges of the old polemics still remain, and, in view of the author, the teachers' manuals fail to give an adequate background for the correct interpretation of difficult New Testament passages, such as those in Matthew and John.

Fisher also found some instances of lingering triumphalism—including the tactic of taking basic Jewish tenets from the Hebrew Scriptures, subsuming them into Christianity, and then using them to "prove" that Christianity is superior to the Judaism which gave birth to these ideas. A particularly rich illustration of this process of appropriating Jewish values for Christian polemical purposes comes from a recent religious education text:

> For a certain person in a certain place, in a certain time, Judaism may be the best religion. . . . However, Christianity remains the best objectively for three reasons:
>
> 1. Christianity is built on love, not fear;
> 2. Christianity teaches that the whole person is good, both the body and the spirit;
> 3. Christianity teaches that each person is free to be uniquely him or herself.

Needless to say, each of these three precepts is essential Jewish teaching, and all are rooted in the Hebrew Scriptures. The above example, which, according to Fisher, appears in more sophisticated form in many graduate-level texts, is not maliciously intended. But the tendency—or temptation—to make Christianity look good by making Judaism look bad is very deeply ingrained in Christian thinking. It still finds frequent expression in systematic and artificial dichotomies such as law vs. grace, justice vs. mercy, wrath vs. love, flesh vs. spirit, "before" vs. "after," old vs. new, promise vs. fulfillment. Basic Christian teaching and preaching across the ages has drawn from these simplistic oppositional categories. Undoubtedly they have served Christian apologetic defenses, and there are profound psychological barriers to replacing them.[3]

In a recent article in the *Journal of Ecumenical Studies* (Summer 1984) John Carmody quotes the anguished reply of a Christian respondent to a questionnaire as follows:

> If I hear another sermon about the bondage of the law in the OT and the legalistic Jews vs the gospel, I will leave, even if it is my husband's boss. High level people who should know better still use Judaism as a dark foil for the gospel. Is the gospel so shabby that we need to do this? These priests, albeit unwittingly, increase anti-Semitism.

(In this case, the respondent was an Anglican, but the same complaint has come from sensitized Catholics on numerous occasions.)

Despite an abundance of good will and the new openness to Christian-Jewish dialogue, habits of thinking are hard to change. The self-definition-by-denigration model has been criticized by numerous scholars, but not yet fully replaced on the pedagogical level. Current scholarship which sets the conflict events described in the New Testament (particularly the Passion narratives) into historical perspective should be reflected in textbooks and teachers' manuals to a much greater extent than at present. There is a strong need for teacher training in areas related to Jewish-Christian understanding. And the need to reach the future generation of religious leadership—the students in seminaries—is urgent. Not only future teachers but future homilists need help in addressing the themes most vulnerable to the facile and uncritical repetition of anti-Judaic formulas. The kinds of sermons heard in churches, particularly during the Lenten period, can make a great difference in the attitudes of parishioners toward Jews and Judaism. Informed and sensitive preaching can offset the anti-Jewish impact of the Good Friday readings, but in the absence of that information and sensitivity among the clergy, it is very easy to slide into the old categories of rejection and displacement.

Changes in seminary curricula are not easy to come by, and, as has been variously noted, even some of the basic reference materials reflect an apologetic bias. In this area, Eugene Fisher's *Seminary Education and Christian-Jewish Relations* is an invaluable resource. Intended to enrich, rather than replace, existing courses, it provides important perspectives on such areas as Sacred Scripture, liturgy and homiletics, Church history, catechetics, systematic and moral theology, spiritual formation and field education. The American Jewish Committee's program in seminary education, which brings together faculty and students from Christian seminaries with Jewish scholars and rabbinical students in a conference/dialogue setting, is another creative approach to dissipating stereotypes and misinformation on both sides. A Christian seminarian at one of these conferences said, with some exasperation, "Everything I learned about Judaism in seminary was second-hand, through Christian eyes and Christian judgments. This is the first opportunity I have had to learn about Judaism from Jews."

JEWISH EDUCATION

In the area of Jewish education, the problems are of a different order. While Judaism has been influenced in its development by interaction with Christianity more than is generally acknowledged, it does not establish its own credentials in contrast to or comparison with Christianity. The Jewish-Christian encounter, as described in Jewish high school textbooks, is social and historical, not doctrinal or theological. On the one hand, this avoids the whole question of polemical approaches to Christianity; on the other hand, recounting the episodes of persecution, expulsion, and massacre which Jews suffered at the hands of Christians for centuries, and which are among the realities of Jewish history, tends to leave a negative image, not so much of Christian faith, but of the Church as temporal power. In fairness, it must be said that this negative image is somewhat offset by attention paid to righteous Christians who shielded and protected Jews across the years, and to the high value assigned in Jewish textbooks to religious and cultural pluralism and human kinship. Still, many Jews—like many Catholics—are not aware of the momentous changes in Catholic thinking about Jews and Judaism that have issued from the highest levels of the Church since Vatican Council II. Jewish students should be informed of these developments, both in supplementary educational materials and through teacher education.

There are very few textbooks which approach Christianity in a "comparative religions" context. While these materials are self-consciously intended to be fair and balanced, and contain nothing comparable to the systematic teachings of contempt which characterized earlier generations of Christian teaching, one review of Jewish textbooks noted "a leaning toward the simplistic, especially in statements about what doctrines and beliefs separate Jews from Christians."

On the seminary level, Christianity and Jewish-Christian relations are taken seriously, and there are a number of courses dealing with the origins of Christianity, the intertestamental period, medieval and contemporary relations. (There are also a number of extra-curricular interreligious colloquia, weekend retreats and formal or informal programs which bring Jewish seminarians together with their Christian counterparts for study and dialogue. Many of these developments would have been unthinkable a generation ago.) However, most of the courses are offered on an elective basis, and they tend to focus on particular aspects of Jewish-Christian relations and particular time periods. Very few provide a longer view of the development of Christian thought and history. Thus, many rabbinical students graduate with little knowledge about Christian beliefs, history or present communities, and are inexperienced in sharing their own identity and traditions with others. In this, of course, they are not alone.

One does not expect an adversarial tradition of almost two millennia, marred by persecution of Jewry and mutual hostility, to be overturned in two decades. The progress that has been made since Vatican II is remarkable against the background of estrangement that preceded it. But we have much work to do together.

NOTES

1. Parallel self-studies of Protestant and Jewish textbooks were also undertaken.
2. See *Suggested Readings* for annotations.
3. See Ruth Kastning-Olmesdahl's article in the *Journal of Ecumenical Studies,* annotated in *Suggested Readings.*

SUGGESTED READINGS

John T. Pawlikowski, *Catechetic and Prejudice: How Catholic Teaching Materials View Jews, Protestants, and Racial Minorities* (New York: Paulist Press, 1973).

Claire Huchet Bishop, *How Catholics Look at Jews: Inquiries into Italian, Spanish and French Teaching Materials* (New York: Paulist Press, 1973).

Eugene Fisher, *Faith Without Prejudice: Rebuilding Christian Attitudes Toward Judaism* (New York: Paulist Press, 1977).

————, *Seminary Education and Christian-Jewish Relations: A Curriculum and Resource Handbook* (Washington, D.C.: National Catholic Education Association, 1983).

Journal of Ecumenical Studies (Vol. 21, No. 3, Summer 1984) The entire issue of the Journal is devoted to a symposium on the subject of Jews and Judaism in Christian Education. Articles:

"Research on Christian Teaching Concerning Jews and Judaism:
Past Research and Present Needs,"
by Eugene J. Fisher;

"The Image of Jews in Christian Teaching,"
by Judith H. Banki;

"Theological and Psychological Barriers to Changing the Image
of Jews and Judaism in Education,"
by Ruth Kastning-Olmesdahl;

"Categories for a Correct Presentation of Jews and Judaism in Catholic
Religious Training,"
by Peter Fiedler;

Theological Education for the Church's Relationship to the Jewish People,"
by Paul M. van Buren;

"Judaism Vis-à-Vis Christianity: How To Make Changes,"
By John Carmody.
Introduction by Marc H. Tanenbaum.
Editorial, "Teaching the Holocaust and Its Lessons," by Franklin H. Littell.
The articles themselves contain additional helpful bibliographical references.

The Roman Liturgy and Catholic-Jewish Relations Since the Second Vatican Council[1]

EUGENE J. FISHER

The Constitution on the Liturgy, *Sacrosanctum Concilium*, was the first promulgated by the Second Vatican Council.[2] In announcing it, Pope Paul VI commented that "the liturgy was the first subject to be examined (by the Council) and the first too, in a sense, in intrinsic worth and importance for the life of the Church."[3] In calling for the reform of the liturgy, the Church Fathers knew quite well that the Liturgy document would establish the work of the Council as an effort to reform the whole of Church life, both internally and externally.[4] *Sacrosanctum Concilium*, therefore, emphasized not only the renewal of the rites of the liturgy, but also the liturgy's didactic function, "for in the liturgy God speaks to His people and Christ is still proclaiming His gospel."[5]

The Declaration on the Relationship of the Church to Non-Christian Religions, *Nostra Aetate*, proclaimed on October 28, 1965, was one of the final (and most heavily debated) statements of the Council. In "repudiating" and "deploring" all "hatred, persecutions and displays of anti-Semitism directed against the Jews at any time and from any source,"[6] *Nostra Aetate* necessarily repudiated any source of hatred of Jews issuing from the Church's own teaching or practice, such as the oppressive canonical legislation of the Fourth Lateran Council (1215 C.E.) or even the liturgy itself. Indeed, this statement follows immediately the declaration's specific reference to religious education and liturgical preaching: "All should take pains, then, lest in catechetical instruction and in the preaching of God's Word they teach anything out of harmony with the truth of the gospel and the spirit of Christ," which would appear by its wording to be a specific reference back to *Sacrosanctum Concilium*.

1. CONTEXT AND INTENT OF THE CALL TO RENEW CATHOLIC LITURGIES

The historical context of *Nostra Aetate*'s mandate will help clarify the depth and breadth of the liturgical reform regarding Jews and Judaism envisioned in *Nostra Aetate*. *Sacrosanctum Concilium* itself reflected the fruition of the work of several generations of biblical and liturgical scholars. As Tommaso Federici has noted,[7] these same movements also resulted in a renewed appreciation by the Church of the Jewish origins of central aspects of the Church's institutional structure, belief and worship, a point emphasized more formally by Pope John Paul II in a recent address in Rome to representatives of bishops' conferences from around the world:

> Authentic, fruitful and lasting relationships with the Jewish people . . . can and ought to help enrich the knowledge of our own (Christian) roots and to shed more light on certain aspects of this identity we have. Our common spiritual heritage (with Jews) is considerable. Help in better understanding certain aspects of the Church's life can be gained by taking an inventory of that heritage, and also by taking into account the faith and religious life of the Jewish people as professed and lived now as well. This is the case with the liturgy. Its roots have still to be better known and appreciated by the faithful. This is true at the level of our institutions, for they have been inspired ever since the beginning of the Church by certain aspects of the synagogue's community organization. Finally, our common spiritual patrimony is above all important at the level of our faith in one sole and unique God . . . who is our Father and who chose Israel, 'that good olive tree unto which have been grafted the wild branches of the gentiles.'[8]

This papal statement is cited at length because of its many implications for contemporary liturgical renewal. Its final reference to the commonality today (not just in biblical times!) of Christian and Jewish faith-life and to the covenant theology of the Pauline image of the olive tree is an explicit comment on *Nostra Aetate* and a frame with many implications for contemporary and future Catholic liturgical renewal. The latter portion of this paper will attempt to draw out some of these implications for the tasks ahead.

By the time of the Council in the 1960's, to return to the context of *Nostra Aetate*'s liturgical reflection, much work had already been done on the relationship between Christian and Jewish liturgy, for example the classic studies of W.O. Oesterly, *The Jewish Background of the Christian Liturgy*, and Eric Werner, *The Sacred Bridge: Liturgical Parallels in the Synagogue and the*

Early Church. These and later studies[9] have shown the remarkable conformance in the way Jews and Christians orient themselves to God in worship, an insight remarkable only to those who would wish to so overstate the uniqueness of Christianity that all sense of continuity (the "spiritual bond" to use the Conciliar phrase) between Jews and Christians as "peoples of God" is to be suppressed. *Nostra Aetate* definitively rejected that sort of thinking and the "replacement theology" upon which it was based. Even today, however, as we shall see, further work is necessary on the liturgy to fulfill this major mandate of the Council.[10]

On the other hand, by the time of the Council, certain steps had already been taken to begin to remove some of the more blatant forms of the "teaching of contempt" against Jews and Judaism that had, over the centuries, become encrusted on the Roman rite. Most dramatic, of course, was Pope John XXIII's deletion of the phrase "perfidious Jews" from the Good Friday prayer for Jews. In the immediate wake of the Council, Pope Paul VI extensively revised the prayer, which became one "For the Jews" rather than "For the Conversion of the Jews" and now refers positively and supportively to Jewish faith and peoplehood.[11]

Interestingly, on the same day that *Nostra Aetate* was promulgated, the Congregation of Rites issued a decree banning "further veneration" of Simon of Trent. Simon was a child found murdered in 1475. Allegations arose that he had been murdered by Jews so that his "Christian blood" might be used in the synagogue for the Passover seder. This allegation was one of the more infamous of the medieval "blood libel" charges against Jews that have cropped up over the centuries in various areas, from medieval England to late Czarist Russia in our own century. The irony of the continuation of the cult of Simon of Trent is that numerous popes had quite explicitly condemned the blood libel charges over the same centuries, at times in great detail and after lengthy investigations.[12]

Since the Council, further work has been done to remove the anti-Jewish possibilities of the Good Friday liturgy. One such issue has been that of alternates for the "Reproaches" (*Improperia*,) which have often been read by Christians as an attack on Jews and Judaism, with its refrain: "Oh my people, what have I done to you . . ."). In the United States, the Roman Catholic Bishops' Committee on the Liturgy (BCL) has been deliberating various approaches to this problem. In Catholic churches today, the "Reproaches" are optional. In 1977, the BCL joined with the Committee for Ecumenical and Interreligious Affairs in suggesting that other suitable hymns be used instead. More recently, the BCL commissioned the Reverend Lawrence Heiman, C.PP.S., to adapt the verses of Psalm 22 ("My God, My God, why have you forsaken me?") to the original Gregorian chant melodies of the *Improperia*, thus combining the solemn beauty of the music with a most appropriate text to be used, as its rubric notes, "for Christian meditation at this point in the Good Friday liturgy." Copies are available from the Publications Office of the United States Catholic Conference (1312 Massachusetts Avenue, N.W., Washington, D.C. 20005).[13]

While significant work has been done by the Church in implementing the liturgical mandate of *Nostra Aetate,* then, further efforts still need to be undertaken. The following sections of this paper will look in some detail at two areas deserving the major attention of biblical scholars and liturgists alike. These, suggested by the 1974 Vatican Guidelines, are far more complex and sensitive, and less susceptible of straightforward solution than is the case with liturgical phrases, such as "perfidious Jews" or hymns, such as the Reproaches, for they involve, on the one hand, a confrontation with biblical texts that cannot *not* be read during Holy Week, and, on the other, the central question of the relationship between the Scriptures which dominates the selection of texts in the lectionary.

II. HOLY WEEK AND THE PASSION NARRATIVES

Lent, particularly Holy Week with its dramatic Passion narratives, has traditionally been the worst time of the year for Jewish-Christian relations. It is ironic that although the Christian liturgy aims at inculcating in Christians a sense of inner repentance and turning back (*teshuvah*) to God, the intensification of the old "deicide" charge has often induced renewed feelings of hate and violence toward Jews in all too many Christians. In the past, pogroms and other atrocities became favorite "Christian" ways of "celebrating" the Paschal Mystery!

The 1974 Vatican Guidelines for Catholic-Jewish Relations suggest that all those who are involved in preparing homilies, prayers of the faithful, commentaries, and even translations of the Scriptures "destined for liturgical use" should have "an overriding preoccupation" to ensure that nothing in the liturgy will distort a true understanding of the Jews and Judaism, "especially when it is a question of passages which seem to show the Jewish people in an unfavorable light."

In this context, the Guidelines refer explicitly to the formula "the Jews" in John and pejorative uses of the terms "pharisee" and "pharisaism" (a problem that appears especially in Matthew). Concerning the former, it can be noted that John's Gospel seldom makes distinctions among "the Jews," leaving the impression that all Jews "then and now" are implicated in the actions of only a few Jews "then." Read in the context of the Good Friday liturgy of Holy Week, the Passion Narrative of John's Gospel can undo in a single stroke even the most careful catechesis that would seek to implement the Council's repudiation of collective Jewish guilt for Jesus' death.

The problem, of course, is not limited solely to Good Friday or to Holy Week, though it crests at that vital point in the liturgical cycle. The New Testament throughout contains various strata of polemics against Judaism and the Jews who remained faithful to it. These realities cannot be glossed over any more than can the New Testament's acceptance without challenge of slavery as a social reality of the world in which it was written. Biblical scholar Raymond Brown, S.S., urges a direct homiletic confrontation with the text as one way to ensure that negative attitudes toward Jews and Judaism will not be, as they all too often have been and tragically continue to be, the "chief lesson" carried away by the faithful from the proclamation of the Gospel in the liturgy:

> The context of mutual hostility between the Johannine community and the Synagogue must be taken into account when reflecting on the Johannine passion narration. Today Christians are embarrassed by such hostility . . . . An initial response is one of 'Speak no evil; see no evil; hear no evil' namely, to omit the anti-Jewish sections from the public reading of the passion narrative. In my opinion, a truer response is to continue to read the whole passion; not subjecting it to excisions that seem wise to us; but once having read it, then to preach forcefully that such hostility between Christian and Jew cannot be continued today and is against our fundamental understanding of Christianity. Sooner or later Christian believers must wrestle with the limitations imposed on the Scriptures by the circumstances in which they were written. They must be brought to see that some attitudes found in the Scriptures, however explicable in the times in which they originated, may be wrong attitudes if repeated today. They must reckon with the implications inherent in the fact the word of God has come to us in the words of men. To excise dubious attitudes from the readings of the Scripture is to perpetuate the fallacy that what one hears in the Bible is always to be limited because it is 'revealed' by God, the fallacy that every position taken by an author of scripture is inerrant.[14]

Such an approach, of course, presumes a much more thorough catechetical instruction, especially during Lent, regarding Catholic-Jewish relations than is now the general practice, and more thorough preparation of homilists in the dynamics especially of the development of the Passion Narratives.

Systematic theologian David Tracy, working along lines similar to those of Brown, poses the challenge this way:

> The painful, repressed memories of Christian antisemitism have also been aided by the anti-Judaic statements of the New Testament, es-

pecially, but not solely in the Gospel of John. If these scriptural statements cannot be excised, then minimally, they should always be commented upon whenever used in liturgical settings and noted critically in every Christian commentary on the Scriptures. The history of the effects of those New Testament anti-Judaic outbursts should signal the need for Christians, singly and communally, to reflect upon ways to banish forever this bad side of the good news of the New Testament. Those anti-Judaic statements of the New Testament have no authoritative status for Christianity. Even the most "fulfillment" oriented Christology has no real theological need for them. The heart of the New Testament message—the love who is God—should release the demythologizing power of its own prophetic meaning to rid the New Testament and Christianity once and for all of these statements.[15]

Neither Tracy nor Brown would accept any "bowdlerizing" of the New Testament text, but rather, in Tracy's words, urge a "hermeneutics of suspicion" toward it, for the sake of better bringing out the central Gospel message of love and reconciliation. While agreeing with this entirely, it may be suggested that in certain cases a more careful selection of passages for inclusion in the lectionary may be appropriate in a renewed liturgy. The pastoral problem of the Holy Week readings (Good Friday's is, but need not be, always from John's Gospel!), for example, is compounded by the fact that the length of the Passion Narratives, even in the "short form," makes it difficult to present to the congregation the full background necessary for understanding.

Likewise, a look at translations destined for use in liturgical proclamation may be in order today. Recent scholarship,[16] for example, has shown that, as Gerard Sloyan concludes, " 'Jews' is probably a correct translation (of *hoi ioudaioi*) at John 4:9 and 4:22 and 18:20 . . . . In every other case it should be 'Judeans.' " Sloyan comes to this conclusion, it should be noted, not out of a concern for Jewish-Christian relations, but solely on the basis of "the evangelists' terminological intent . . . . Present trends in scholarship incline toward the view that John's concern with the community of his day is uppermost and the events of Jesus' life secondary."[17]

Clearly, any solution will demand a thorough catechesis in parishes throughout the Lenten season to prepare people adequately for receiving the Word of God during Holy Week's highly intense "peak" moments in the reading of the Passion narratives. Several dioceses in this country have been quite creative in meeting this need. In 1976, the Archdiocese of Detroit launched an education program for priests to assist them in integrating the insights of biblical scholarship relating to Catholic-Jewish relations into their Lenten homilies. In 1977, the Archdiocese of Los Angeles prepared a sixteen-page booklet addressed to the Lenten readings for "Cycle C." The booklet contains brief "suggested comments to be included in the bulletin and to be read prior to the first reading at Sunday liturgies during Lent." In 1978 and 1979, comments for Cycles A and B were added. The entire set has been published in *SIDIC* (Vol. 17, no. 2, 1984).

In 1978, the Diocese of Memphis initiated a major adult education program on the Gospel of Matthew which was implemented in nearly every parish of the diocese. It was followed in 1979 by a similar program on the Gospel of John. The Commentary on Matthew, which contains excellent material for proper Christian-Jewish understanding, has been published by Paulist Press. Also in 1978, the Diocese of Memphis produced an excellent eight-page background bulletin on the gospels which should be in the hands of every Christian for Lenten meditation. Outlining the origins of the tragic rift between Judaism and Christianity as it influenced the writing of the Gospels, the background material responds to the question: "Why Did Jesus Die?"

Many other helpful approaches are possible. One excellent resource is John T. Townsend's *A Liturgical Interpretation of Our Lord's Passion in Narrative Form* (NCCJ, 71 Fifth Avenue, Suite 1100, New York, NY 10003), which gives an eminently readable version of the Passion based on the latest biblical scholarship. My own book *Faith Without Prejudice* includes a number of suggestions, such as a sample para-liturgical celebration, "Thy Kingdom Come," and a "Way of the Cross" which emphasizes positive Christian-Jewish themes. Finally, a beautifully simple, yet quite effective idea has come from the congregation of Luther Place Church in Washington, D.C., and it deserves to be spread widely. Their idea is for a Christian congregation to invite a Jew to address the congregation within the context of its Holy Week services. At Luther Place Church, the rabbi invited to speak on a recent Passion Sunday (Palm Sunday) was also a survivor of the Holocaust. Although such an address would not officially constitute the homily for the day, the deeply spiritual witness of a Jew addressing the congregation would, I believe, go far toward breaking down the tendency which tragically still perdures in many Christians, namely, to attach blame to all Jews of all times for the events surrounding the passion and death of Jesus.

Perhaps most significantly, preachers of the gospel must be better trained. They must understand such passages and learn to gear their homilies toward bringing out the central message of the text, the message of the Christ-event, and thus guide their people away from the misunderstandings of Jews and Judaism that will occur without such conscious effort. It must be remembered that we deal not with a "neutral" tradition but one which for two millennia has been sadly skewed toward the negative in its approach to all such questions involving Jews. Truth, and the integrity of the liturgy itself, demand no less than what the 1974 Vatican Guidelines called an "overriding preoccupation" to ensure that negative attitudes are not fostered in this holiest time of the year.

III. CONTINUITY AND DISCONTINUITY IN THE LECTIONARY SELECTIONS

The liturgy is a medium of education at least as important as, if not more so than, the classroom. In the selection of readings in the lectionary, their translation, introduction and interpretation, a theological statement is made not only concerning the nature of the community assembled for worship (the Church) but about its relationship to and with that "other" community whom we know to be in covenant with God, and to whose covenant ours inheres even as it extends it.[18]

On one level, this problem is vividly seen in the selection of texts, in the very juxtaposition of readings from the Hebrew Scriptures with readings from the New Testament. The basis for that selection is as much a statement about that relationship as it is about the "content" of the message consciously proclaimed. Here are raised, in the most dramatic fashion, all of the ancient questions surrounding the relationship between the testaments and between the peoples whose own historical continuity gives witness to them.

Pope John Paul II in his 1980 address in Germany pointed to the mutual interdependence between this classic biblical question and the question of Jewish-Christian relations:

> The first dimension of this dialogue, that is the meeting between the people of God of the old covenant never retracted by God (Rom 11:29), on the one hand, and the people of the new covenant on the other, is at the same time a dialogue within our own Church, so to speak, a dialogue between the first and second part of its Bible (*Origins,* Dec. 4, 1980).

In the liturgy, this internal/external dialogue comes to a head. Unfortunately, the present lectionary, I believe it can be safely said, has been developed almost entirely without conscious reference to either of these issues. Equally unfortunately, little work has been done by our scholars to analyze the impact that the present selections have on Christian attitudes toward the Hebrew Scriptures and the Jews.[19]

To what extent, it must be asked today, do the selections embody a sense of continuity between the Testaments, and to what extent a discontinuity? That is, do the selections juxtapose the one *over against* the other, to the detriment of the "old"? Or do the selections mutually reinforce and illumine each other as do the revelations which they represent?[20] Are "old" and "new" categories of equal esteem, as they function to guide the selection process? Or do they tend, in practice in the liturgy, to take on a "Marcionite" tinge in which the "old" is at best preparatory to and exhausted in the new?

Marcion, the reader may recall, was a second century Christian influenced by Gnostic dualism. He taught that the "Old Testament" taught a different God than the "New," a "Jewish" God of law and fear as opposed to the "new" God of love and mercy taught by Jesus. While Marcion's teaching was condemned as heresy, his dichotomized view of "old" versus "new" testaments has had lasting, if subtle influence on Christian preaching and liturgy over the centuries.

In the period prior to the Second Vatican Council, for example, readings from the Hebrew Scriptures had virtually disappeared from the lectionary, so that their reinstitution became a chief feature of conciliar reform. Likewise, the 1974 Vatican Guidelines still discerned sufficient Marcionite attitudes in the Church to warrant a specific rebuttal: "The Old Testament and the Jewish tradition founded upon it must not be set against the New Testament in such a way that the former seems to constitute a religion of only justice, fear and legalism, with no appeal to the love of God and neighbor (cf. Deut 6:5; Lev 19:18; Mt 22)."

This issue, the question of the relationship between the scriptures, has been one of the great perennial issues of Christian history. (See, for example, R.M. Grant, *A Short History of the Interpretation of the Bible,* Macmillan, 1972). One theory after another has been brought forth in different periods, none totally successfully. In various ways, each of these has tried to hold onto the Old Testament for Christians, mainly by viewing it as a Christian work: For example:

- Typology—in which Old Testament figures and events are seen as "types" or foreshadowings of New Testament episodes, such as in the sacrifice of Isaac by Abraham being seen as a type of Christ on the cross.
- Allegory—in which passages in the Old Testament are said to have hidden meanings apparent only to Christians, e.g. viewing the exodus as being really the story of the passage of the individual soul from slavery to sin into the freedom of grace.
- Proof texts—in which the Hebrew Scriptures are combed for passages which, when taken out of context, could be said to validate Christian doctrines such as the Trinity.

More recent approaches just prior to the Council, such as "spiritual exegesis" (e.g. Henri de Lubac, *Histoire et Espirit,* 1950) and "fuller meaning"
(Raymond E. Brown, *The Sensus Plenior of Sacred Scripture,* 1955), were
often variations, though more sophisticated, of such earlier methods.

These theories all had a common purpose. They sought to avoid Marcion's conclusion and preserve the Hebrew Scriptures as meaningful to the
Christian. They also shared a common flaw—the inability to allow the Hebrew
Bible to speak to the reader with the immediacy of the word of God addressed
directly to him or her. All presumed that the Hebrew Scriptures, without a
theological "filter," are inadequate as revelation in themselves.

Modern biblical scholarship, which has succeeded in recapturing the original message of the biblical authors as addressed to audiences of their own
times, has rendered most of these views unacceptable today. Likewise, the
current dialogue between Jews and Christians, as exemplified by the 1975 Vatican Guidelines, has raised new doubts about the underlying rationale of the
whole endeavor to retain the Hebrew Scriptures by Christianizing them.

The dilemma is an acute one among biblical theologians. The debate
among the various contributors to Bernard W. Anderson's *The Old Testament
and Christian Faith* (Herder and Herder, 1969), for example, is quite heated.
Catholic biblical scholar Joseph Blenkinsopp has raised the issue in a different
context in a remarkable essay for the recent collection, *Biblical Studies: Meeting Ground Between Jews and Christians* (Paulist, Stimulus, 1980), edited by
L. Boadt, H. Croner and L. Klenicki. In it, Blenkinsopp notes that the question
of the relationship between the testaments remains a major stumbling block in
most Christian attempts to formulate an adequate "theology of the Old Testament." The Hebrew Scriptures, viewed entirely through the prism of the
New Testament (or, rather, what we discern of the New Testament message
when viewing it in its turn through the prism of later, often anti-Judaic Christian thought), is not allowed to speak for itself. Christian questions are posed
to a text which often does not recognize the necessity for such questions. Christians' categories and interests are used to organize its contents and message in
a way its authors might well never have expected.

In a sense the problem has even greater urgency for homilists, since the
relationship between the scriptures is so central both to the selection of the
readings and the structure of the liturgy. To take a single (and pregnant) example: Jeremiah 31:31–34, read on the Fifth Sunday of Lent (Cycle B), quite
early came to have a formative influence on Christian liturgy (1 Corinthians
11:23–26) and soteriology (1 Corinthians 3; Hebrews 8:8–12; 10:16–17). In
this passage Jeremiah speaks of a "new covenant . . . written on the heart."
It may thus have been the original inspiration for our very terminology of
"Old" and New" Testaments (see Galatians 4:21–28). Anderson goes so far
as to ascribe to this passage the ultimate rationale for the inclusion of the He-

brew Bible in the canon and the liturgical readings in general (*op. cit.*, pp. 2 and 226). But is the paradigm of "Old v. New" adequate to explain fully the meaning which the Hebrew Bible as God's word must have for the Christian today? Given the fact that we now know that passages such as Jeremiah 31 have profound significance quite apart from their Christological application, can we be justified in reducing their full meaning solely to such use? How, in short, does the homilist approach this perennial and as yet unsolved question? Can we preach the Hebrew Bible as the word of God on its own terms, or must we continue to imply that it has been rendered "superfluous" by the apostolic writings?

The Tridentine Missal of 1570 resolved the problem by virtually ignoring the Hebrew Bible on Sundays, favoring instead readings from epistles and gospels alone. The new Lectionary has wisely rectified this omission, though at the same time raising the issue anew.

In approaching it, users of The Liturgical Conference's *Homily Service* are perhaps more fortunate than most. Gerard Sloyan's commentaries consistently illustrate that the gospel determines the selection of the first reading in such a way as to make apparent the "organic relation" which exists between the two.

The 1974 Vatican Guidelines for Catholic-Jewish relations likewise urge homilists to emphasize "the continuity of our faith with that of the earlier covenant." The term "earlier," here, has particular significance since it avoids the pejorative connotations of the word "Old" which, as John Sheerin pointed out in *Homily Service* ("Serving the Word," Vol. 9, No. 4), is the equivalent for us of "obsolete, dead, decadent."

The Guidelines likewise state—and here is where the issue becomes less clear—that "an effort will be made (by homilists) to acquire a better understanding of whatever in the Old Testament retains its own perpetual value, since that has not been cancelled by the later interpretation of the New Testament" (cf. *Dei Verbum* 14–16).

The question remains: What constitutes "whatever"? How do we draw a balance between continuity (the unity of the Bible, both testaments taken as a whole) and discontinuity (the uniqueness of the Christ-event)?

Overemphasis on discontinuity leads, of course, to Marcionism, a path already rejected by the Church. It can also lead to the process of de-Judaization of Christianity which the American bishops deplored in their Statement on Catholic-Jewish Relations of November 1975. It leads to dualism, as found in Marcion's preaching and in many homilies today (law v. gospel, justice v. love, flesh v. spirit, etc.).

A false approach to continuity, on the other hand, can vitiate the integrity of the Hebrew Bible by subsuming it into Christian doctrines. This in turn means a loss of the authentic fullness of the word of God as originally inspired, and a reduction of the Hebrew Bible into a mere propaedeutic to the Christian faith. Such triumphalism, many would argue, is no longer appropriate in an age of dialogue.

Perhaps it is time to strike a new balance between the two. We know today that the "old" covenant of Judaism was in no way abrogated by our own in Christ. On the contrary, as St. Paul reminds us in Romans 9–11, our covenant depends on and is nourished by a living Judaism that has retained its own perpetual validity: "Remember that you do not support the root. It is the root which supports you" (Romans 11:18). Given this renewed vision of ourselves and Judaism, it becomes necessary for us to rethink critically some of the more popular approaches of the past, so that we can begin to construct a more positive liturgical view of both testaments.

One such approach, important in liturgical tradition, has been the typological. But, it must be asked, is typology truly adequate as a criterion for choosing one text from the Hebrew Scriptures over another? Will the spiritual riches of the Hebrew text in the long run be impoverished by over-reliance on typology in establishing the liturgy of the Word? I do not claim to have all the answers here, but the question remains a nagging one which I believe those competent in liturgical studies within the Church need very much to address from the point of view of the dialogue.

An even more nagging question raised directly by the Vatican Guidelines is that of the promise/fulfillment theme, which is so predominant in the choice made from the prophetic writings, especially during Advent and Lent. Do these selections, as included in the present lectionary, focus the congregation's hopes on the Kingdom which Jesus preached, which Jesus called us to prepare for and which is the primary underlying vision of the prophets themselves? Or do they exhaust the prophetic vision entirely in a set of "proof-texts" which would imply that the Kingdom is wholly "fulfilled" already here and now in Jesus? Here, of course, is a tension basic to the structure of the New Testament itself: the tension between the "already here" of the eschatological hope, and the "not yet" of the realization that we still must pray, as Jesus taught us, "Thy Kingdom Come."

The Kingdom, God's Will being done "on earth as it is in heaven," has certainly not yet "come" in any normal sense of the term. Liturgy as educational praxis should reflex this tension that lies at the heart of Christianity. Both poles, the fulfillment-in-one-sense-in-Jesus and the Jesus-calls-us-to-be-part-of-the-fulfillment, I believe, need to be evoked in our congregation if liturgy is to do its proper task. At present, only the former is adequately presented in the liturgical selections.

At this point it becomes clear that our theological terminology needs to be renewed to be adequate to the tasks before us. That is the theory of Jewish-Christian dialogue, with the result that the praxis of liturgy, which should embody the insights of the dialogue, has difficulty formulating adequate criteria. The 1974 Vatican Guidelines raise this point quite carefully in their section on the liturgy, and in doing so illustrate, I believe, the need for fuller theological clarification:

> When commenting on Biblical texts, emphasis will be laid on the continuity of our faith with that of the earlier covenant, in the perspective of the promises, without minimizing those elements of Christianity which are original. We believe that those promises were fulfilled with the first coming of Christ. But it is nonetheless true that we still await their perfect fulfillment in His glorious return at the end of time.

"Fulfillment vs. perfect fulfillment," I would with all due deference submit, is a distinction that will need to be made more clearly if it is to be communicated to our people whether in our catechetical texts or from the pulpit. Yet it is one of the most significant advances of the dialogue to have taken us to the point where such a distinction can for the first time be discerned. Failure to make it turned many of the medieval "disputations" into classic examples of non-communication, leading to entirely unnecessary bitterness and even violence between our two religious communities.

In 1263, for example, the great Spanish thinker, Rabbi Nahmanides, was called by the King of Aragon to respond to a series of proof texts offered by Christian scholars. How could the Jews not see that all of these biblical prophecies were fulfilled in the person of Jesus?

Nahmanides responded on an entirely different level than his questioners anticipated. Referring to the biblical prophecies that the coming of the messianic age would be marked by universal peace and justice in the world (e.g. Is 2:4; Mic 4:3, etc.), Nahmanides pointed out the wars, plagues, oppressions and other evils rampant in the world he knew. The Christians, in short, were focusing on the *person* of the Messiah, the Jews on the messianic *age* that the Messiah would inaugurate. Each was a *non sequitur* so far as the other was concerned. Yet to focus on the Kingdom (the Messianic Age) not only allows theological space for the acknowledgment of the validity of the Jewish response, it can also add a sense of realism, and deeper spiritual hope and longing to the Christian liturgy that is quite authentic on Christian terms. Indeed, it can help to restore the sense of tension spoken of earlier that is all too easily lost when focusing solely on the Jesus we "have" and failing to respond to the Jesus who calls us to surpass our best efforts in building up God's Kingdom. True dialogue thus enables us not only to know the "other" better, but also to know ourselves better, to see in our tradition spiritual depths we might otherwise have missed.

IV. DIALOGUE THROUGH LITURGY

Despite the unresolved nature of certain of the liturgical problems still facing us in theory and practice two decades after the close of the Vatican Council, many Catholics have begun to develop local practices capable of celebrating our efforts at reconciliation between the Church and the Jewish people, and also educating the Catholic faithful in a positive way on the "common spiritual heritage" stressed by recent papal teaching. Such practices, if approached with a sensitiveness to the authenticity and integrity of both Jewish and Christian liturgical traditions and avoiding carefully any sense of syncretism, can provide moments of that deeper spiritual dialogue, *panim al panim* with Jews, toward which the Council oriented the Church as a whole. Here, I will mention two of these possibilities as they have been worked out in local practice in this country.

1. Easter and Passover

Over the years, the Christian Church's solar calendar and Judaism's lunar calendar have spiraled around one another in a stately liturgical dance of the seasons. Often Easter Sunday coincides with the Passover. This coincidence should make the season of Lent a particularly appropriate time for Christian meditation on the liturgical relationship between Christianity and its parent spiritual tradition. The relationship between Easter and Pesach (Passover) lies much deeper in the nature of our liturgical traditions than the mere fact (disputed by some scholars) that Jesus happened to institute the Eucharist while celebrating a Seder. The adoption of the Exodus experience is central to Christian interpretation of the Christ Event and thus of the Eucharist as the celebration in mystery of that event. Just as Passover celebrates freedom from bondage and freedom for joyful observance of the happy gift of Torah, so Easter (and consequently every Mass, because every Mass is a reflection of Easter) celebrates the Christian sense of freedom from slavery to sin and the happy gift of participation in Jesus Christ's death and resurrection. The striking parallels between the Seder (which means "order") and the Order of the Mass powerfully reflect this central liturgical rootage of Christian sacraments in Jewish ritual.[21]

It is encouraging that Christian congregations are turning more and more to the Seder during Holy Week as a "para-liturgical" exercise of great educational and spiritual value. Caution, however, must be observed, since it happens all too often that Christians cannot resist the urge to "baptize" the Seder by ending it with New Testament readings about the Last Supper or, worse, by reducing it to a mere prologue to the Eucharist itself. Such thoughtless mergings represent a distortion of both religious traditions, because the Seder is, after all, an integral part of Jewish family piety binding Jews into one religious people. The *Newsletter* of the Catholic Bishops' Committee on the Liturgy (Lent, 1980) offers the following suggestion:

> When Christians celebrate this sacred feast among themselves, the rites of the haggadah for the seder should be respected in all their integrity. The seder . . . should be celebrated in a dignified manner and with sensitivity to those to whom the seder truly belongs. The primary reason why Christians may celebrate the Passover festival should be to acknowledge common roots in the history of salvation. Any sense of "re-staging" the Last Supper should be avoided . . . . The rites of the Triduum are the (Church's) annual memorial of the events of Jesus' dying and rising.

In 1979, the Roman Catholic Archdiocese of Louisville issued guidelines, with background notes, which can serve as a model for other Catholic dioceses as well. The Louisville guidelines, issued jointly by the ecumenical and liturgical offices, note that combining the Seder with the Eucharist can give the unfortunate implication that "the Seder finds its fullness in Jesus," thus subtly reducing Judaism to a mere propaedeutic for Christianity. The guidelines further advise that a study of contemporary Judaism should be undertaken during Lent and that a Jewish couple or family might appropriately be invited to conduct the ritual in a correct way. In this regard, an excellent edition of *The Passover Celebration: A Haggadah for The Seder,* by Leon Klenicki, has been jointly published by the Anti-Defamation League of B'nai B'rith and the Liturgy Training Program of the Archdiocese of Chicago.

2. Yom HaShoah and Yom HaAtzmauth

Yom HaShoah (Holocaust Memorial Day) and Yom HaAtzmauth (Israel Independence Day, May 9) are both new festivals in the Jewish liturgical calendar, reflecting two central events of Jewish history which have taken place in this century. Their dates are tied to that of Pesach, and in a real sense they together form a dynamic commentary on the ancient message of the Passover. Like the High Holy Days of Rosh Hashanah (New Year) and Yom Kippur (Day of Atonement), which occur in the Autumn each year, Yom HaShoah and Yom HaAtzmauth can be properly understood only if they are seen as constituents of a larger liturgical unity. The reason for this is that the two events which are commemorated, namely Nazism's nearly successful campaign of genocide and the reestablishment of the Jewish state of Israel after two millennia, are inextricably connected in Jewish consciousness. As Auschwitz represented the death of a large portion of the Jewish people and its intellectual and spiritual center, so the ingathering into *Eretz Israel* represents a dramatic rebirth. Rabbi Irving Greenberg, in a passage filled with allusions to Ezekiel and Isaiah, makes this theme of Jewish resurrection quite explicit:

> The real point (of Israel's rebirth) is that, after Auschwitz, the existence of the Jew is a great affirmation and act of faith. The re-creation of the body of the people, Israel, is renewed testimony to Exodus as ultimate reality, to God's continuing presence in history proven by the fact that His people, despite the attempt to annihilate them, still exist. [22]

The dynamic of past tragedy and future hope characterizes our precise point in liturgical reform as it does the relationship between our peoples. Reconciliation can come only through continued renewal not only of our Catholic liturgy but more importantly, as Jeremiah would remind us, of our hearts. [23]

V. SUGGESTED GUIDELINES FOR HOMILISTS

By way of summary, I would like to suggest a few basic principles that can serve as parameters for preaching on the relationship between the first reading and the gospel during the Sunday homily. From these general principles, some immediate and concrete guidelines can be drawn.

A. *Contra Marcion*

1. Affirm the value of the whole Bible. The Hebrew Scriptures are the word of God and have validity in and of themselves. Allow the word to be spoken directly to the congregation without posing later doctrines as filters between them and the text.

2. Place the typology inherent in the Lectionary selections in its proper historical setting, neither overemphasizing or avoiding it. Always seek to draw out the original meaning that the Hebrew scriptural portion had for its original audience. Show that this meaning is in no way vitiated or diminished by New Testament applications or understandings. (See Gerard Sloyan, *Commentary on the New Lectionary,* Paulist, 1975.)

3. Avoid "Salvation History" or developmental approaches which would demean the Hebrew Bible by implying that it was merely a crude or unfinished propaedeutic for the New Testament, or otherwise insufficient as revelation. It is the same God who speaks in both.

4. Avoid dualism. The 1975 Vatican Guidelines state that the Hebrew Bible "and the Jewish tradition founded upon it must not be set against the New Testament in such a way that the former seems to constitute a religion of

only justice, fear and legalism, with no appeal to the love of God and neighbors (čf. Dt 6:5; Lev 19:18; Mt 22:34–40).''

B. Anti-Triumphalism

1. Preserve a humility of vision in respect of the promises. This is especially important when dealing with the readings from the prophets (e.g. Isaiah and Jeremiah) during Advent and Lent. While Jesus, in a mysterious way, ''fulfilled'' these promises, the Vatican Guidelines caution that ''it is nonetheless true that we still await their perfect fulfillment in his glorious return at the end of time.''

2. Stress the continuity between the scriptures as a living relationship between root and branch (Romans 9–11). Judaism and Christianity stand in partnership, not in opposition, in witnessing to the Name of the one God to whom Jesus prayed and in the mission to build the kingdom of God on earth. The Vatican Guidelines note, ''With the prophets and the apostle Paul, the Church awaits the day, known to God alone, on which 'all peoples will address the Lord in a single voice and serve him with one accord' (Soph 3:9).''

3. Explain the profound Jewishness of Jesus and his teaching, and its parallels to the teaching of the Pharisees, with whom Jesus had in common almost every point of his own teaching. It is this that gives the Hebrew Bible its relevancy for the Christian: that Jesus and the apostles accepted it as the word of God for them; that Jesus' message presumes in his hearers people imbued with the divine message of the Torah; that Jesus' prayer to and his relationship with the Father is to and with the one God revealed in the Hebrew Scriptures.

4. Exploit the positive elements of readings such as Romans 9–11, which the American bishops in their 1975 statement called ''long-neglected passages which help us to construct a new and positive attitude toward the Jewish people.''

5. Use Jewish sources in expounding the meaning of the Hebrew Scriptures, and as background for the apostolic writings. They are Jewish works and can only be properly understood from within the framework of that richly complex and vital tradition. Rabbinic sayings often parallel and shed light on those of Jesus. (A good source for homiletic sayings from the Talmud can be found in Montefiore and Loewe, *A Rabbinic Anthology,* Schocken, 1974). Both the Vatican Guidelines and the 1975 Statement of the American Bishops stress that ''the history of Judaism did not end with the destruction of Jerusalem, but went on to develop a religious tradition . . . rich in religious values.'' Since we share a common scripture, and a common understanding of God as embodied in that scripture, we can learn much about prayer and religious practice from the living Judaism of today.

C. *Terminology and Style*

1. Avoid the use of the term "Old Testament." It is not "old" but a living reality addressed to us today. Preferable are terms such as "the Hebrew Scriptures" and "the apostolic writings."

2. Avoid or explain fully stereotypical uses of words such as "the Jews" in John and "the Pharisees" in Matthew. The Vatican Guidelines mandate this even for liturgical translations, noting that "Judaism in the time of Christ and the apostles was a complex reality, embracing many different trends." This reality cannot be adequately presented in simplistic categories, but must be explained in detail—or not used at all.

3. "With respect to liturgical readings, care will be taken to see that homilies based on them will not distort their meaning, especially when it is a question of passages that seem to show the Jewish people as such in an unfavorable light" (1975 Vatican Guidelines).

4. The Hebrew Scriptures and Judaism should not be characterized as "superseded," "abrogated," or "merely preparatory" to the apostolic writings. Rather they should be seen as having "perpetual value" and "continuing validity."

5. Stress the links between the Christian liturgy and the Jewish liturgy from which it sprang. Note the common elements without diminishing the uniqueness of either tradition. Use the short versions of the Passion narratives during holy week so that adequate time can be devoted to explaining the historical background.

6. If the long versions of the Passion are used, allow time during Lent and in catechetical programming for presentation of the background of the biblical text confrontation with possible anti-Jewish implications, and most importantly, actual dialogues with Jews.

7. Use a suitable psalm or other song in place of the *Improperia* (Reproaches) on Good Friday (e.g. Psalm 22).

8. Evaluate the stations of the cross used in the parish and omit or change any anti-Jewish references or implications. (An alternate form of the stations can be found in *Faith Without Prejudice,* pp. 115–118.)

NOTES

1. Portions of this essay are excerpted or modified from articles by the author originally appearing in the journals: *Ecumenical Trends* (March 1981, published by the Graymoor Ecumenical Institute, Garrison, NY), *Liturgy* (May 1978; published by the Liturgical Conference, 810 Rhode Island Ave., N.E., Washington, D.C. 20008); and *SIDIC* (Vol. 15:2, 1982, published by the Sisters of Sion, Rome).

2. Dec. 4, 1963. On the same day, the Council also issued its lesser "Decree on the Instruments of Social Communication." For texts and initial commentaries see *The Documents of Vatican II*, ed. Walter M. Abbott, S.J. (New York: Guild, America, Association Presses, 1966).

3. *L'Osservatore Romano*, December 5, 1963.

4. The Latin title of the Constitution taken from its first words, "This most Sacred Council," clearly indicates this interest.

5. *Sacrosanctum Concilium*, no. 33, Abbott edition, p. 149.

6. Because of Pope John XXIII's original mandate in calling the Council that it not engage in condemnations (anathemas) of any sort, but rather be marked by the positive orientation of its teaching, the Latin phrase meaning "and condemns" was dropped from this sentence of the declaration. That the Church did not intend any weakening of its attack on antisemitism with this decision was shown in the reaffirmation of this very line in the "implementing" document for *Nostra Aetate*, no. 4, issued by the Vatican's Commission for Religious Relations with the Jews almost a decade later. The 1974 Vatican Guidelines use the word "condemn" not once but twice in "restating" the Council's intent: "While referring the reader back to this document (*Nostra Aetate,*) we may simply restate here that the spiritual bonds and historical links binding the Church to Judaism *condemn*, as opposed to the very spirit of Christianity, all forms of antisemitism and discrimination, which in any case the dignity of the human person would alone suffice to *condemn*." (Italics added)

7. Tommaso Federici, "Study Outline on the Mission and Witness of the Church," *SIDIC* (Vol. 11:3, 1978) 25–34.

8. *L'Osservatore Romano*, March 6, 1982. Eng. transl. in E. Fisher, *Seminary Education and Christian-Jewish Relations* (National Catholic Education Association, 1983, 90–92). Note the pope's emphasis on the fact that this liturgical heritage is not just biblical, but equally based on rabbinic and contemporary Jewish life as well.

9. Sofia Cavalleti, "Christian Liturgy: Its Roots in Judaism," *SIDIC* (Rome: Vol. 6:1, 1973, 10–28); see Eugene Fisher, "The Influence of Jewish Liturgical Spirituality on Christian Traditions: Some Observations," in L. Klenicki and G. Huck, eds., *Spirituality and Prayer: Jewish and Christian Understandings* (N.Y.: Paulist Press Stimulus Books, 1983, 139–147); C.A. Rijk, "The Importance of Jewish-Christian Relations for Christian Liturgy," *SIDIC* (Rome: Vol. 6:1, 1973); A. Nocent, "The Contribution of Judaism to the Christian Liturgy of Marriage," *SIDIC* (Rome: Vol. 14:1, 1981, 11–19); D. Flusser, "Notes on Easter and the Passover Haggadah," *Immanuel* (Jerusalem: No. 7, 1977, 52–61); F. Gavin, *The Jewish Antecedents of the Christian Sacraments* (London: SPCK, 1982); L. Bouyer, "Jewish and Christian Liturgies" in L. Sheppard, ed., *True Worship* (Baltimore: Helicon Press, 1963, 29–44); A. Baumstark, *Comparative Liturgy* (London, 1958); M. Brocke and J.

Petuchowski, *The Lord's Prayer and Jewish Liturgy* (N.Y.: Seabury, 1978); A. Finkel, "The Passover Story and the Last Supper" in M. Zeig and M. Siegel, eds., *Root and Branch* (Roth, 1973, 19–46); and E. Fisher and D. Polish, eds., *Liturgical Foundations for Social Policy in the Catholic and Jewish Traditions* (Univ. of Notre Dame Press, 1983).

10. Pope John Paul II's March 6, 1982 address (cited above) confirms his view that, while fairly begun, the liturgical and catechetical renewal called for by the Council has much further to go.

11. A footnote to the English text of *Nostra Aetate* in the Abbott edition cited above (fn. 2), relates Jules Isaac's report that "after representations made by him in a private audience in 1949, Pope Pius XII made a similar step in this direction in the Good Friday liturgy" (Abbott, *Documents* 665).

12. Cf. Edward A. Synan, *The Popes and the Jews in the Middle Ages* (N.Y.: Macmillan, 1965). A further irony is that of place, given the clarity of the authoritative *Catechism of the Council of Trent for Parish Priests* published by Pope Pius V in 1566, in debunking the collective guilt charge against the Jews for Jesus' death, of which the blood libel charges were an obvious reflex. *The Catechism* had stated that guilt for Jesus' death "seems more enormous in us than in the Jews, since according to the testimony of the Apostle (Paul): 'If they had known it, they would never have crucified the Lord of glory' (1 Cor. 2:8); while we, on the contrary, professing to know Him, yet denying Him by our actions, seem in some sort to lay violent hands on Him." On the blood libel charges, see also Ben-Zion Bokser, *Judaism and the Christian Predicament* (N.Y.: Knopf, 1967) 151, 237–38; and Maurice Samuel, *Blood Accusation: The Strange History of the Beiliss Case* (Knopf, 1966). Yet a further irony can be found in Soviet Russia's recent "updating" of the blood libel charges in a modern context, accusing Soviet Jews of using drugs in their religious rituals.

13. On this effort within the U.S. Church, see Thomas Krosnicki, "From Reproaches to Psalm 22," *Notitiae* (Rome: Vol. 188, March 1982) 160. The Episcopal Church has resolved the question by suppressing the Reproaches entirely. The recent Methodist "Services of Worship for the Seasons of Lent and Easter" (*From Ashes to Fire*, Abindgon, 1979), on the other hand, seeks to make clear that the Reproaches are a confession of sin *by* Christians rather than a false projection of guilt onto the Jews. It modifies the refrain, for example, to read: "O my people, O my Church, what have I done to you . . ." and includes such searching verses as: "I grafted you unto the tree of my chosen Israel, and you turned on them with persecution and mass murder. I made you joint heirs with them of my covenants, but you made them scapegoats for your own guilt."

14. Raymond Brown in "The Passion According to John," in *Worship*, cited in E. Fisher, *Seminary Education*, 38.

15. David Tracy, "Religious Values After the Holocaust," in A. Peck, ed., *Jews and Christians After the Holocaust* (Phila.: Fortress, 1982) 94.

16. Cf. M. Lowe, "Who Were the 'Ioudaioi?" *Novum Testamentum* 18 (1976) 101–103; J. Townsend, "The Gospel of John and the Jews" in A. Davies, ed., *Antisemitism and the Foundations of Christianity* (N.Y.: Paulist, 1979) 72–79; and Gerard Sloyan, "Israel as Warp and Woof in John's Gospel" in *Face to Face: An Interreligious Bulletin* (Vol. 9, Spring 1982).

17. Sloyan, ibid., 19.

18. Cf. E. Fisher "Continuity and Discontinuity in the Scriptural Readings," *Liturgy* (May 1978) 30–37.

19. A recent survey of Christian educators concludes that catechetical reform is incomplete and endangered without concomitant liturgical reform: "If the basic liturgical or doctrinal mindset of most Christian Churches on Sunday morning slants things against a fair image of Jews, then making changes in religious education materials will be at best minor surgery. Until the major components of the Sunday morning problem have been overhauled children and adults alike will not have sufficient basis for changing their presently inadequate images of Jews and Judaism." John Carmody, "Judaism vis-à-vis Christianity: How to Make Changes," *Journal of Ecumenical Studies* (Vol. 21:3, Summer 1984) 520.

20. Cf. *Dei Verbum* 14–16, and the 1974 Vatican Guidelines, Section II, "Liturgy."

21. See Eugene Fisher, *Faith Without Prejudice: Rebuilding Christian Attitudes Toward Jews and Judaism* (Paulist, 1977), 103–107, and Balfour Brickner, *Passover and Easter* (Union of American Hebrew Congregations) for more complete descriptions of these parallels. See also fn. #9, above.

22. I. Greenberg, "Theological Reflections on the Holocaust," in E. Fleischner, ed., *Auschwitz: Beginning of a New Era?* (New York: KTAV, 1977), 48. Pope John Paul II, in a homily at a mass on the Hill of Martyrs in Otranto, Italy on October 3, 1980, movingly linked the foundation of the State of Israel with the tragedy of the Holocaust: "The Jewish people, after tragic experiences connected with the extermination of so many sons and daughters, driven by the desire for security, set up the State of Israel." Cf. E. Fisher, "The Pope and Israel: Rome Looks at Jerusalem," *Commonweal* (Jan. 11, 1985) 16–17.

23. A Yom HaShoah service for joint Christian-Jewish work has been prepared by E. Fisher and L. Klenicki, *From Death to Hope: Liturgical Reflections on the Holocaust* (N.Y.: Anti-Defamation League/Stimulus Foundation, 1983).

The Los Angeles Story

REV. MSGR. ROYALE M. VADAKIN

AND RABBI ALFRED WOLF, PH.D

PREFACE

This anniversary volume provides a wide and comprehensive look into Catholic-Jewish relations since Vatican II. We have been asked to narrow the focus to demonstrate the practical impact of the document *Nostra Aetate* on a single community, Los Angeles.

Pronouncements on the international and national level remain abstract and symbolic until they are implemented on the "grassroots" level. In describing the manner in which the seeds of the Second Vatican Council took root in Los Angeles, we may include experiences similar to those of other communities as well as others which are unique to this city. What is important is that our story gives the reader insight into a vital process which is still developing.

Our story starts in those first days when *Nostra Aetate* awakened great expectations of unprecedented opportunities for dialogue. It is told in six segments. First, we would like to give an overview of Los Angeles. Second, we deal with the choice of one life issue, specifically abortion, as our first subject for dialogue. Third, we describe the entire process of developing a meaningful statement on this sensitive and controversial topic. Fourth, we show how, by succeeding in this venture, we opened the door to a continuing commitment to explore life issues in all their diversity. Fifth, we demonstrate how this success, in turn, served as a powerful impetus to move our two faith communities into wider areas of involvement. Sixth, we present a local experiment: Project Discovery.

I. THE LOS ANGELES SITUATION

Los Angeles is a community known by all and understood by few. The motion picture industry and the stirrings of "new religions" have created a somewhat bizarre image of our city in the minds of many. Without denying all our eccentricities, we shall try to sketch a fuller and more accurate image of our city.

While Los Angeles dates back to the days of Spanish land grants and missions, its great growth came after World War II. Its people represent a record number of ethnic and racial groups, languages and religions. Almost everyone comes from somewhere else and, even locally, moves from section to section. All these factors influence the religious community and often frustrate those who minister here.

The 7.5 million inhabitants of the Los Angeles metropolitan area include the country's largest Roman Catholic Archdiocese—2.3 million communicants—and the second largest Jewish population—550,000 persons.

Both communities are characterized by extensive cultural pluralism and growing immigrant populations. Recent Southeast Asian and Hispanic immigration has swelled the archdiocese, and as a result the sacraments are administered by the Church in 42 languages. At the same time, the Jewish community has experienced a major influx from Iran, the Soviet Union and Israel. The social, educational and health needs of many of these recent arrivals are a major concern to both groups. There has been a rich and extensive history of contacts between the Catholic and Jewish communities. As early as the 1920's friendships developed between Archbishop John J. Cantwell and Rabbi Edgar F. Magnin and they established contacts between their flocks to the extent then possible. The involvement of Jewish leaders in such Roman Catholic social welfare institutions as St. Anne's Maternity Hospital and Holy Family Adoption Service gave early promise of things to come.

In the fifties and sixties, Loyola University—now Loyola-Marymount—became an effective point of contact. Its President, the Rev. Charles Casassa, S.J., introduced a course on Judaism taught by a rabbi and, together with Dr. Neil Sandberg of the American Jewish Committee, developed a rich program of intercultural education. These efforts prepared a number of key persons for leadership in the post-Vatican II era.

While, during this period, Catholic-Jewish relations were largely limited to especially motivated individuals, the proclamation of *Nostra Aetate* opened the door to official institutional contacts. With the accession of Cardinal Manning as Archbishop, the Archdiocesan Commission on Ecumenical and Interreligious Affairs established a working relationship with the Interreligious Activities Committee of the Southern California Board of Rabbis. The great expectations stimulated by Vatican II were not fulfilled by these cordial but still superficial encounters. Difficulties of which we had been unaware now needed to be addressed. As the decade of the sixties ended we left the beginning stage of dialogue and entered into the long search for real communication and understanding.

II. A CALL TO DIALOGUE

The early days of dialogue created a solid core of people determined not to lose what had been experienced and even more determined to expand the exploration. The first tentative steps in the early seventies included the inception of the Interreligious Council of Southern California as a tri-faith body incorporating the Archdiocese, the Board of Rabbis and two area-wide church councils representing the mainline Protestant judicatories. This umbrella organization was later to expand, embracing most of the major world religions. In the same time frame, a priest-rabbi dialogue was initiated by Archbishop Manning.

Planning the tenth anniversary observance of *Nostra Aetate*, an interreligious leadership group from the American Jewish Committee, the Archdiocese and the Board of Rabbis evaluated what had taken place and what would be needed to sustain the exchange. Two clear requirements were structure—an organization able to assume responsibility—and continuity—not "one-night-stands" for the exchange of shallow pleasantries. Responsibility was accepted by the three bodies represented at that *Nostra Aetate* celebration in 1975. Continuity also was achieved, for the ensuing dialogue itself is now approaching its tenth anniversary.

The remaining question—what would be the group's agenda—was also addressed at the anniversary observance. Stimulated by informative sessions with two international authorities, Rev. Charles Angell, S.A. and Rabbi Marc Tanenbaum, the local leadership tackled four agenda items: Israel, Church-State Relations, Anti-Semitism, and Respect for Life.

While each of these four concerns prompted lively discussions, the fourth, Respect for Life, provoked the most intense response. Participants recommended continued discussion of this subject. We hesitated. Concentrating on this controversial and emotion-charged issue might endanger our entire relationship. We came to realize, however, that little would be gained by tackling topics of easy consensus. On the other hand, wrestling with gut issues, confronting our differences and hammering out our difficulties would get us to truly know one another and would help us to grow.

Thus, the three organizations jointly announced the formation of a Los Angeles Catholic-Jewish Respect Life Committee. No specific directives or limits were given to the Committee, other than to venture and create, respecting the basic principles of interreligious dialogue and the dignity of human life.

III. THE RESPECT LIFE COMMITTEE

We intended our committee to be as representative as possible and therefore attempted to balance its membership between Catholics and Jews—the latter to include conservative, orthodox and reform—between clergy and lay people, men and women. We looked for members of relevant professions, such as medicine and law. We wanted people who were recognized in the community for their dedication to life values. Subsequent experience showed that our care in selecting committee members was well worth the effort.

The group's first task was getting to know and to become comfortable with one another. We accomplished this as we discussed our agenda. As earlier we had to choose between major issues, so now we had to select one of the many topics under the umbrella, "Respect Life," such as care for the young, the aged, the single parent, the incurably ill, and the dying. In the climate of 1976, abortion was clearly the life issue of most intense concern. It also was the most controversial. For a brief moment there was fear that we might not survive the selection process.

Eventually we realized that we should not limit ourselves to one topic, that we should pledge to create ourselves as an ongoing committee willing to explore, one by one, the issues heading the various priority lists. There were no winners or losers in this process.

We took the risk of starting with the most controversial subject: abortion. Inasmuch as there was a clear divergence between the two faith traditions, we knew from the start that there was no possibility for our committee to reach a consensus statement. We could agree, however, that our conclusions should reflect both pluralism and harmony.

The technique we adopted was to have, wherever possible, corresponding presentations from the two faiths. At a given meeting there would be a Jewish and a Catholic presentation on one aspect of the issue, such as medical, scientific, legal, or theological. Though no consensus was sought or reached, all participants shared a dawning sense of mutual discovery.

For Roman Catholics there was the discovery of an ancient and continuing Jewish body of legal reflections on pre-and post-natal life and, at the same time, the allowance for differences of opinion in both talmudic and modern Judaism. For the Jewish participants there was the discovery of the very rich, ancient, highly structured and all-inclusive Catholic ethic, along with its vital interest in contemporary legal and scientific studies.

The committee's final product, "Jewish and Roman Catholic Reflections on Abortion and Related Issues," published in September 1977, began with a joint preface and an opening section entitled "Respect Life Reflections" which included selections from the Psalms, the Mishna, the Gospel of John and a 1976 statement by Cardinal John Dearden on "The Challenge of Religious Pluralism."

There followed two major and totally distinct statements: "Jewish View on Abortion" and "Catholic View on Abortion." Neither claimed to be *the* Jewish or *the* Catholic view, but *a* Jewish and *a* Catholic view. Each community felt comfortable in articulating its position with clear perspective and without compromise. The final section, entitled "Joint Expression of Goals," contained the most substantive results of our months of study and discussion.

The following selections give a hint of the posture, tone and direction of the entire statement.

The concluding section from "Catholic View on Abortion": "We believe that any impulse to polemics should be moderated, and strident terminology, which is both unproductive and offensive, should be avoided. Fighting vigorously for principle need not be inconsistent with love for our neighbors."

From "Jewish View on Abortion": "We abhor the infringement of liberties of individuals or institutions and the imposition of civil penalties on those whose ethical and religious codes prohibit their involvement in any fashion in the performance of abortion. At the same time, living in a pluralistic society, we should not stigmatize as "murderers" those individuals or social governmental institutions whose ethics and morality dictate other norms of conduct which are from their point of view in consonance with the right to and respect for life."

From "Joint Expression of Goals": "Jews, Catholics and other religious groups should be encouraged to teach respect for life in their individual communities in accordance with their sacred traditions, to contribute their insights to the general world of ideas, and to develop sensitivity to the points of view of others."

The final "goal" urges the "advocacy of positive alternatives to abortions and promotion of social situations which will encourage the responsible bearing and rearing of children:

(a) Strengthening of families by pre-marital counseling, reinforcement, counseling during crisis situations.
(b) Healing for broken families and assistance to parents who are raising their children alone.
(c) Counseling and assistance during pregnancy especially for the unmarried.
(d) Guidance toward adoption services for mothers unable to care for children.
(e) Instruction in parenting and child raising.
(f) Nurture of stable and caring families so that every expected child will be a welcomed child.

The conclusion: "While Roman Catholics and Jews may not agree to make the prohibition of all abortions American law, nonetheless we should work together to make respect for life, and particularly the joyful celebration of new life, an American ideal."

IV. ONGOING COMMITMENT TO LIFE ISSUES

"The Committee will continue in exploration of the larger Respect Life issue." With these words, in the preface to our abortion statement, we committed ourselves to further deliberations on "broader areas including bio-medical ethics and the society's control over the individual's life at the end as well as the beginning of the cycle."

Both Jews and Catholics are frequently charged with conducting "single issue politics." In the field of "life issues" this charge is most often leveled at Catholics. While abortion was, is and will remain an intense Catholic concern, our two communities have come to understand that Roman Catholics look at abortion in the context of a comprehensive life ethic, and that, moreover, this life ethic is substantially shared by both traditions. In effect, we gained an early insight into what Cardinal Joseph Bernardin later characterized so perceptively as a "Seamless garment Ethic."

With the success of a completed statement behind us, we were faced with a large and varied list of issues from which to choose. After considerable discussion, we agreed to move from pre-birth to near-death by selecting as our topic, "Caring for the Dying Person."

We replaced committee members whose interest was limited to one issue with people possessing expertise in the new area. While earlier we relied on outside sources for much of our research, we now included resource personnel in the Committee membership. The director of a major hospice and the physician in charge of a major burn center were most helpful in our exploration.

This selection process was repeated as we turned to our next topic, this time in the critical area of family ethics, "The Single Parent Family." For the new subject, our "experts" included three single parents, one Jewish, one Hispanic Catholic and one black Catholic. Thus we were able to gain first-hand information on the experience of singleness in three distinct minorities.

While we had developed helpful techniques, we never allowed the Committee process to become routine. Intensive argument led to the selection of the next topic, "The Nuclear Reality." In our lengthy discussion, which focused primarily on the peaceful use of nuclear power, we found that individual differences of opinion were far more pronounced than the differences between the two faith traditions.

Our experience has shown that, in this type of dialogue, medium and message are closely interrelated. Where the two religions are clearly divided on the content of the message, the medium must take the form of two parallel statements. Where there are broad areas of agreement, a single joint statement is preferable. At times, it is essential to emphasize our common scriptural foundations—as in the matter of abortion. At other times, it is sufficient to refer to current concerns and principles—as in discussing "The Nuclear Reality."

In our dialogue process, we learned a few things:

First, that quantitative information alone does not pave the way out of moral dilemmas. Regardless of the massive input we had from highly respected experts—as in the nuclear area—ultimately we had to voice opinions based on our respective ethical commitments.

Second, that we were challenged to speak on behalf of our *religious* communities and to do so in clear, intelligible terms. More than writing skill was required of us, namely clear vision of the moral challenges offered by our religious traditions and precision in applying them to present-day realities.

Third, that the interreligious dialogue demands commitment as well as flexibility, determination as well as patience. It may be necessary to discuss the same subject again and again to gain the necessary insight where agreement can be reached, where compromise is possible and where firm but friendly disagreement must be recorded.

V. THE RIPPLE EFFECT

The tremendous size of Los Angeles notwithstanding, we can demonstrate that our efforts at dialogue have produced a substantial ripple effect. While the Respect Life Committee was motivated, at least in part, by earlier interfaith successes, it inspired other programs and projects in turn.

Earlier activities inspired—or at least made possible—by the spirit of *Nostra Aetate* include:

The Interreligious Council of Southern California, which, since its launching in 1969, has been an ongoing forum for all the major religions, which has sponsored numerous events for the Metropolitan Area, including the sponsorship of religious services to the 1984 Olympics, and which has fostered friendships between individual members of the diverse religions.

The previously mentioned Priest-Rabbi Committee, which prepared and published the following statements: *Lenten Pastoral Reflections* (1974), *Covenant or Covenants?* (1979), and *Notion of the Kingdom* (1982), and which is currently working on a statement entitled *The Liturgical Context of the Passion Narrative*.

Activities initiated subsequent to the Respect Life Committee include:

The Annual Catholic-Jewish Women's Leadership Day, planned and executed by a growing core group of women actively involved in their respective religious communities.

Lectures by Jewish scholars at the annual Religious Education Conferences sponsored by the Dioceses of Los Angeles and Orange and attended by more than 18,000 professional and lay religious educators. Speakers have included Marc Tanenbaum, Samuel Sandmel and Elie Wiesel.

Catholic dialogues with Episcopalians, Lutherans, Moslems and Buddhists as well as Jewish dialogues with Moslems and Protestants, with black and Korean churches.

INTERSEM, an annual two-day conference for students and faculty of Catholic, Jewish and Protestant seminaries in Southern California and the San Francisco Bay area, enabling future ministers, priests and rabbis to meet their counterparts and to understand their neighbors' religions. (This project is co-sponsored by the Interreligious Council of Southern California and the National Conference of Christians and Jews. Camp facilities are made available by the Baruh Fund of Wilshire Boulevard Temple Camps.)

The Seminary Exchange, an intensive sharing of faculty between St. John's Roman Catholic Seminary and the Los Angeles Campus of the Hebrew Union College.

The Annual Model Passover Seder, hosted by the Wilshire Boulevard Temple. With a minimum of pulpit rearrangement and a maximum of imagination, the synagogue's spacious sanctuary becomes the Passover dining room for a "Jewish family" consisting of 800 to 1000 Catholic High School students with faculty members, priests and, the first year, Cardinal Manning. Participants celebrate the Hebrews' exodus from Egypt, reciting traditional prayers, singing traditional songs and tasting traditional foods.

VI. PROJECT DISCOVERY

The growing complexity of our Catholic-Jewish program led us to search for a method of more effective coordination for all our projects. In 1982, a grant from the Wilshire Boulevard Temple Interreligious Fund enabled us to establish Project Discovery. With the authors serving as co-directors, a modest budget covers the cost of a part-time coordinator and limited operating expenses. The coordinator relieves us of many routine duties such as the calling of myriad meetings, does most of our paper work and serves as our collective conscience.

Thanks to Project Discovery, we have been able to publish the most recent papers of the Priest-Rabbi Dialogue and of the Respect Life Committee as well as a report entitled *A Seminary Exchange: The First Decade,* to print a special Passover Haggada for all the participants of the Catholic High School Seder and to produce a professional videotape of the 1983 Seder for national distribution.

In addition to serving as an umbrella for existing exchanges, Project Discovery opened the door for an exciting new venture: the authentic and personalized teaching of Judaism in Catholic high schools. While the annual Model Seder provides a one-time encounter with Judaism for approximately 1,000 students a year, we felt that a more intensive experience was needed. In cooperation with the Hebrew Union College we developed an intern program beginning with two Catholic high schools.

The intern is a rabbinic student or a graduate student in Jewish education selected by the College faculty for both competence and interreligious sensitivity, and is guided by the director of the School of Education as well as by a member of the rabbinic faculty. The first two Catholic schools were chosen for the presence of master teachers able to give expert direction and to make the newcomer comfortable in an unfamiliar environment.

The intern is on campus for an entire morning during each week of the school year, is readily available to answer questions about Jews and Judaism, and becomes a familiar figure to faculty and students. More important, the school now has a ready resource for a variety of situations: instructing a religion class that deals intensively with Judaism in the intertestamental period or briefly explaining the roots of Easter in the Jewish liturgical year; responding to a social studies teacher's request for information on Nazi concentration camps or a literature instructor's need for information on Jews in the American novel. Students in this type of experience not only get to know facts about Judaism but encounter a person modeling Judaism as a living faith.

The experiment is also beginning to show incidental results. Extensive notes on the "minilessons" on Judaism taught in varied classes of the Catholic high school curriculum may benefit future teachers in this and similar programs. The interns themselves are getting an education about the Catholic Church, its institutions, its leaders and its people which is bound to enrich their personal and professional lives.

Project Discovery will continue this intern program. We have moved from two Catholic high schools to four at the present time and will explore ways to further expand it, as well as the other aspects of our interreligious dialogue. It is our hope that, by these efforts, Catholic-Jewish relations will take strong and stable roots in every segment of our diverse communities.

SUMMARY

We are under no illusion that our particular angle of "The Los Angeles Story" will swell the tide of easterners anxious to make their homes on our blessed western shore or change the mind of even one reader who believes that "Los Angeles is a nice place to visit, but I would not want to live there." We have not wanted to paint a picture that appears more rosy than reality. We know that it takes far more than cosmetic treatments and public relations programs to achieve our goal which is nothing less than changing perceptions and attitudes.

This goal can not be reached by merely correcting mutual misinformation and replacing it with accurate facts. It requires thinking and feeling with "the other." The wisdom of the Plains Indians advises walking in "the other fellow's moccasins." The *Ethics of the Fathers* urges not to judge the other person "until you have stood in his place." The "I-Thou" relationship requires meeting. Meeting, therefore, is what the varied aspects of our "Los Angeles Story" have in common: representatives of the major world religions meeting monthly in each other's places of worship as an Interreligious Council; members of the Priest-Rabbi Dialogue and of the Respect Life Committee meeting year after year; Catholic, Jewish and Protestant seminarians, Catholic and Jewish women, meeting for solid blocks of time. What is destroyed is more than misinformation—it is stereotypes. What is conveyed is more than facts—it is understanding.

Attitudes are qualities which may be difficult to measure, but they are real and they shape the realities of life. For two thousand years, Christian attitudes toward Jews have been shaped too frequently by what Jules Isaac called "the teaching of contempt." Attitudes, on the other side, were formed by what Father Edward Flannery described as "the anguish of the Jews." *Nostra Aetate* gave the signal to the Catholic Church, indeed to the Christian world: "The time for a change is at hand," and to the Jews: "There is a chance for change."

The wrongs of two millennia cannot be righted in two decades. But we have made a beginning.

PART III

New Trends in
Catholic Religious Thought

REV. JOHN T. PAWLIKOWSKI, O.S.M., PH.D.

In the two decades since the Second Vatican Council issued its ground-breaking declaration on the Church and the Jewish People some significant developments have taken place in Catholicism's theological approach to the Jewish People. The Council itself undercut many of the prevailing theological outlooks. *Nostra Aetate* stressed Christianity's profound debt to Judaism. Picking up the imagery of St. Paul in Romans 9–11 it saw the church as grafted onto the tree of salvation whose trunk was Judaism. By implication such imagery implies a continuing life for Judaism from a Christian theological perspective, for if the trunk has died the branches can hardly stay healthy.

Likewise in putting to rest the historic deicide charge the Council destroyed any credibility for the so-called "perpetual wandering" theology which basically argued that Jews were an accursed race perpetually doomed to roam the face of the earth in a degraded state for murdering the Messiah. This theology was responsible for much of the persecution of the Jews during the course of history and for Catholic opposition, including some opposition at the level of the Vatican, to the early calls for the restoration of a Jewish state in Palestine.

The statement on the Jewish People is also most interesting in another respect. Though the text stresses the close connection between the church and the Jewish People, its placement in the document on the church's relationship to non-Christian religions seems to support the notion of Judaism and Christianity as two clearly distinct religious traditions. There was much controversy over this question at the Council. Most of the proponents of a statement on Catholic-Jewish relations would have preferred its inclusion in the document on the church, thereby making the point of the intimate connection. In retrospect it may have been a good decision to include it with non-Christian religions while stressing the close bonds in the text itself. For this conveys a message to Catholics of equal significance to that of Christian-Jewish mutuality: Judaism is not simply biblical Judaism; the synagogue has developed a rich legacy of faith insight and faith expression based on post-biblical experiences that often do not parallel that of Christianity. Thus, post-biblical Judaism (rabbinic, mystical, medieval and modern) may have even more that is distinctive to offer Christianity through the contemporary dialogue than is the case for biblical Judaism. Recovery of the spirit and teachings of biblical Judaism is vital for a healthy Christianity. Without such a recovery we are presenting a truncated version of Jesus' message. But Catholics must also come to recognize Judaism as an ongoing, vigorous tradition that stands independently of Christianity.

The discussion on this question of the best model for describing the relationship between church and synagogue has not ended. Some Catholics still prefer a closer link with the church. But in my estimation the Council did us a favor in placing its reflections on the Jewish People where it did.

The Second Vatican Council did not offer us an elaborated theological perspective on Judaism from the Catholic point of view. But a statement emerging from a 1969 plenary session of the episcopal members of the Secretariat for Promoting Christian Unity gives us an early indication of the theological directions in which the Council wished the church to move in light of *Nostra Aetate*.[1] This document stressed that the understanding of Judaism is central to any authentic Catholic ecclesiology: "The problem of the relations between Jews and Christians concerns the *church as such,* since it is in 'searching into its own mystery' that it comes upon the mystery of Israel." It also affirms the enduring value of the Hebrew Scriptures for Christian faith expression, maintaining that this is in fact the direction set by the New Testament. As a result, Catholics must begin to draw upon the resources of the Jewish tradition for interpreting these books. This is a critical step. For it had been customary, as a consequence of the theology of fulfillment, for the church to bring a distinctive exegesis of its own to the interpretation of the Hebrew Scriptures, one which primarily looked for foreshadowings of the Christ Event and the teachings associated with it in these pre-Christian texts. Because Jewish interpreters did not share in the Christian faith perspective their insights into these books of the first testament were considered of little relevance for Christian theology. Thus, at least implicitly, this call to take seriously Jewish interpretations of the Hebrew Scriptures represents a measure of affirmation regarding the ongoing validity of the Jewish covenantal tradition.

Another significant point made in this 1969 document concerns the Jewishness of Jesus. This reverses a predominant exegetical trend which tended to downplay Jesus' deep involvement with the Jewish community of his time and emphasized the Hellenistic background of New Testament teachings. This interpretative school also frequently turned Jesus into a "universal" person, ignoring his Jewish roots. The primary criterion of Christian faith became the immediate personal decision of the believer to the person of Jesus and his teachings. The dominance of this exegetical school meant that students of the New Testament received little or no introduction to the Jewish materials from Jesus' time which we are increasingly recognizing as essential for any authentic exposition of his message. This trend is now being slowly reversed as a result of modern scholarship and *Nostra Aetate*.

Finally, the bishops meeting in 1969 brought to our attention another preconciliar theological model which they felt Vatican II had rendered obsolete. Though this model had a greater impact historically within Protestantism, it was to be found in Catholic Christianity as well. Succinctly stated, this theological approach contrasted Judaism and Christianity as religions of law and gospel, law and grace, or law and freedom. The prevailing ethos of this description of the Jewish-Christian relationship was the absolute superiority of Christianity which provides the believer with an immediate union with God through grace without the mediation of the law and which liberates humanity from the legalism of the Torah approach to religion. Taking their cue from *Nostra Aetate,* the bishops argue that these contrasts no longer represent an appropriate way to describe the link between the two faith communities: "The Old Testament and Jewish tradition should not be opposed to the New Testament in such a way as to make it appear as a religion of justice alone, a religion of fear and legalism, implying that only Christianity possesses the law of love and freedom."

We need to be reminded of this admonition today since this contrast has surfaced once more in some versions of Catholic liberationist and feminist theologies. While I support the legitimacy of the need to construct a liberationist interpretation of the gospel for our time, such an interpretation need not fall back into the old law-gospel model repudiated by the spirit of *Nostra Aetate*. A theology of Christian freedom must not be constructed on the back of Judaism. On the contrary, a proper understanding of the Exodus tradition and the developments within the Second Temple will show us that Judaism can be a resource for such a positive theology of liberation and not an obstacle preventing it as some liberation theologians such as Jon Sobrino and Leonardo Boff would seem to imply.[2]

It is clear, therefore, that *Nostra Aetate* and its initial interpretation by the 1969 Vatican document had put Catholicism on a new theological track relative to the meaning of Judaism. Overall, however, we still appear to be immersed in the "mystery" approach which first appeared in the years just prior to the Council and was endorsed by prominent European Catholic theologians such as Charles Journet,[3] Jean Daniélou,[4] Hans Urs von Balthasar,[5] and Augustin Cardinal Bea[6] who played such a pivotal role in the passage of *Nostra Aetate* in the Council. While each of these theologians has a distinctive twist in his appropriation of this Pauline idea from the Letter to the Romans, they all remain uncompromising on the question of the centrality of Christ and the fulfillment that his coming brought to salvation history. Although they all found ways to leave some theological space for Judaism after the Christ Event, they made no sustained effort to reconcile the apparent tension resulting from these twin assertions. Rather, they simply fell back on the Pauline contention that their compatibility remains a "mystery" in the divinely instituted plan of human salvation.

As we move on into the seventies, Catholic theologians begin to abandon this Pauline "mystery" approach and to look for bolder ways to restate the church-synagogue bond theologically. In general, three models have surfaced: (1) there is a single covenant embracing both Jews and Christians; Christ was the point of entry for the Gentile world into the ongoing covenant established at Sinai; (2) Christianity and Judaism are distinctive religions with many complementary features and a shared biblical patrimony; (3) both Sinai and the Christ Event represent authentic messianic experiences of which there can be an undetermined number.

An example of the single covenant perspective can be found in the writings of Monika Hellwig, though it is not fully developed up to this point. She views Judaism and Christianity as both pointing toward the same fundamental eschatological reality which still lies ahead. The two faith communities share a common messianic mission in terms of this reality, though each may work somewhat differently in carrying it out. For Hellwig there is "a most important sense in which Jesus is not yet Messiah. The eschatological tension has not been resolved. . . . Logically the Messianic Event should be seen as lengthy, complex, unfinished and mysterious."[7]

The one covenant forged at Sinai continues in force. What happens in the Christ Event is not the fulfillment of messianic prophecies, but the possibility of all Gentiles encountering the God of Abraham, Isaac and Sarah. Jesus has allowed the Gentiles to enter the election first bestowed on Israel and experience the intimacy with God that this election brought to the Jewish People. Hence Christians must look to God's continuing revelation in contemporary Jewish experience to fully understand God's self-revelation today. By implication, though this is not explicit in Hellwig's thinking, the experience of the church would seem to become some barometer for Jewish faith expression as well. Hellwig has not really refined her original statement on the relationship, and hence there remain many ambiguities in her approach. She does not elaborate on the question whether there are any unique features to the Christian appropriation of the original covenant through the Christ Event and, if in fact there are, whether they need to be a central component of every adequate understanding of human salvation. From what she has given us this far she would seem to be theologically allied with those Christian thinkers, most prominently the Episcopalian scholar Paul Van Buren,[8] who interpret Christianity as fundamentally Judaism for the Gentiles.

Monika Hellwig appears to be the only Catholic theologian thus far to suggest a rethinking of the Christian-Jewish relationship within the context of a single, expanding covenant. Most Catholics who have addressed the question in some measure prefer to work with the idea of twin covenants. Three prominent names in this regard are Gregory Baum, Clemens Thoma and Franz Mussner.

Like Hellwig, Baum has not formulated a comprehensive statement on the meaning of the Christ Event in light of Judaism.[9] But he lays down several cardinal principles for an adequate Christian theological approach to Judaism following up upon *Nostra Aetate*. Two are especially crucial in his perspective: (1) Judaism is not destined to disappear after the coming of Christ, but continues to play a pivotal role in the completion of the divine salvific plan. God's saving presence remains alive within the Jewish People after the Resurrection. (2) Central to any reformulated Christology that aims at affirming the ongoing theological significance of Judaism must be the abandonment of any claim that Jesus is the one mediator without whom salvation is impossible to attain. Baum rejects any attempt to circumvent this difficulty by referring to Jews and other non-Christians as "anonymous Christians" in the manner of Karl Rahner.

Baum apparently would retain a central significance for the Christ Event that involves more than integrating the Gentiles into the original covenant. His position, however, is not entirely clear on this point. In his introduction to Rosemary Ruether's *Faith and Fratricide* he speaks of an absolute, all-embracing dimension to the revelation brought through Jesus. Yet Baum seems to endorse Ruether's main line of argumentation which rules out any necessarily universal significance. In fairness it must be said that Baum's understanding of this universal significance is considerably different from classical interpretations. What occurred in the Christ Event was the realization that God's full victory is assured, even though not totally realized at present. Hence all messianic statements relative to the Christ Event must be spoken of in terms of the future. None of these messianic claims automatically invalidate the continuing significance of Judaism or any other religion. But even with this new approach to universal significance the Christ Event still comes off as more decisive and central for Baum than for Ruether. Unfortunately Baum has not told us how he himself reconciles his support for Ruether with this continued insistence on universal significance even in his reformulated sense of the term.

Jesus will become the Christ in the full sense, according to Baum, only at the onset of the eschatological era. In the interim Christians bear witness to a divine reality that can be discovered by all peoples though they may in fact articulate this discovery through different sets of theological symbols and languages. Thus, for him, theological reality is far more crucial than the particular set of words and images Christians have associated with the Christ Event. The following statement by Baum summarizes well the main thrust of his approach:

> What is this Christian witness with universal significance? . . . I propose that the Church's witness with universal meaning and power is the message of God's approaching kingdom. Jesus Christ is the unique instrument and servant of this kingdom, and through his humiliation and glory we have been assured of God's ultimate victory over evil, already pressing in upon us now. . . . The Church's eschatological witness constitutes its universal vocation.[10]

Baum's approach certainly creates theological space for Judaism. But it offers no special role for Judaism over against Christianity, or for any other religion for that matter. Baum seems to claim that all religions are capable presently of attaining more or less the same understanding of the God-human community relationship though they may express this understanding differently. None of them, however, appear to have the unique insight into the future resulting from Christianity's revelatory experience of the Cross and the Resurrection. As Michael McGarry perceptively comments, the position advocated by Baum might be pushing Christians to do nothing more than postpone the traditional notion of Judaism's invalidation by the Christ Event one step back to the end of time.[11] If this is the case, then Baum's position would not really qualify as a positive reappraisal of the theology of the Christian-Jewish relationship.

A somewhat more biblically-based interpretation of the Christian-Jewish relationship which stresses unique features in the Christ Event is to be found in the writings of Clemens Thoma.[12] Thoma places great emphasis on the profound connections between Jesus' teachings and the Jewish tradition both prior to and contemporaneous with him. The Hebrew Scriptures occupy a central position in any expression of Christian faith for Thoma and, in concert with the 1969 Vatican statement, he cautions against interpreting them solely through the eyes of the New Testament. He also is strong regarding the significance of post-biblical Judaism and of events such as the Holocaust for Christian statement about the Christ Event today.

Thoma clearly rejects any attempt to describe the basic theological tension between the Church and Israel as rooted in the acceptance/rejection of Jesus' Messiahship:

> It is not correct to say that the decisive or even the sole difference between Judaism and Christianity consists in the Christian affirmation of Jesus as the messiah and its denial by Jews. There are certain asymmetries and considerations on both sides that render unacceptable such absolute statements on the messianic question. For a better evaluation we must consider and compare the relative importance and place accorded the question in Judaism and Christianity. . . . In the last resort, neither in Judaism nor in Christianity is it a question

of the messiah but of the Kingdom of God, of "God who is all in all" (1 Cor 15:28).[13]

There is no consistent, univocal notion of the Messiah in Jewish thought at the time of Jesus. Many diverse understandings were floating about in the period and some Jews even considered the notion of messiah dispensable. As a result, there is really no one Jewish expectation to which Jesus can be compared and no grounds for alleging Jewish rejection of Jesus' fulfillment of this expectation.

Thoma believes that the uniqueness of Jesus is to be found in the absolute fashion in which he linked the Kingdom of God to his own activities and person. The apocalyptic Jewish tradition of which Jesus drank deeply shared his perception of the intimate presence of God. It was imbued, as he was, "with the penetrating, assertive power of God in the world."[14] Thoma puts it this way:

> In his relationship to the God and Father, Jesus gathered together Old Testament Jewish traditions of piety in an original way and endowed them with new beauty. Yet, it would be a radical mistake to represent Jesus, on principle and in any way at all, as being in opposition to the God of Torah. However, he did experience this God in a uniquely close and intimate way.[15]

One observation is in order relative to Thoma's model which needs further development and fine-tuning. While he stresses both the shared religious perceptions of Judaism and Christianity and the unique features found in Christian theology, he never discusses anything about Jewish uniqueness. Without some sense that Judaism continues to preserve elements of authentic faith expression that are underplayed or missing in Christianity, the combination of shared perspectives/unique features that he presents will still result in an imbalance in the relationship that will weigh heavily in the church's favor. This is an area Thoma needs to pursue much more than he has to date.

A third important Catholic voice in the effort to theologically rethink the Christian-Jewish relationship is the German scholar Franz Mussner. His approach is similar to Thoma's in many respects. He too emphasizes Jesus' profound and positive connections with the Jewish tradition and how important it is for contemporary members of the church to appreciate and understand this. And he likewise rejects any interpretation of the Christ Event over against Judaism in terms of Jesus' fulfillment of biblical messianic prophecies. Rather the uniqueness of the Christ Event must be sought in the complete identity of the work of Jesus, as well as his word and actions, with the work of God. The Christian Scriptures have spoken about God, as a result of the revelatory vision in Christ, with an anthropomorphic boldness not seen to the same degree in the Hebrew Scriptures. In answer to the question of what the disciples finally experienced through their association with Jesus of Nazareth, Mussner answers as follows: "A unity of action extending to the point of congruence of Jesus with God, an unheard-of existential imitation of God by Jesus."[16] Mussner reiterates, however, that the imitation of God is quite consistent with Jewish thinking. The uniqueness is to be found in the *depth* of that imitation on the part of Jesus. So the most particular feature of Christianity when contrasted with Judaism is located by Mussner in the notion of Incarnation rather than prophetic fulfillment. And even this particular feature is an outgrowth of a sensibility deeply Jewish at its core.

Having laid out the basic principles of his approach to a theological expression of the Jewish-Christian relationship, he then amplifies his model with a discussion of "prophet Christology" and "Son Christology." The "prophet Christology" is the earlier of the two. It views Jesus as in the line of the prophets who made manifest the "pathos" of God and joined their words and actions to the divine plan for human salvation. Christianity never completely abandoned this "prophet Christology," not even in the gospel of John where the "Son Christology" most clearly predominates. The two are not fundamentally antithetical. But the "Son Christology" does "break through" the "prophet Christology" in a way that makes the differentiation between Christian and Jewish belief more pronounced: "Beyond the experience of Jesus as prophet there was added the experience of Jesus as *meizon* ('greater than') and *pleion* ('more than'). . . ."[17]

But Mussner wishes to avoid the trap of leaving the impression that the "Son Christology" is totally devoid of Jewish origins. This is simply not the case, and the claims in the past for an essentially non-Jewish basis for this "high" Christology are unfounded. This "Son Christology" owes much of its language and imagery to Judaism, especially the Wisdom tradition. Seen in this light such a Christology "is not the paganization and the acute Hellenization of strict monotheism as Judaism and Islam represent it. Rather, it lies much more along the line of the teaching of the self-expression and self-emptying of God into the world."[18] Mussner has no illusions that bringing to the surface this connection between "Son Christology" and the Jewish tradition will suddenly wipe out objections to it by both the synagogue and the mosque. But such an understanding might provide us with a more fruitful context for discussing it within the setting of the dialogue.

In a discussion of the notion of "redemption" toward the end of the volume Mussner hints at a continuing role for the Jewish People after the Christ Event in the process of human salvation. Here he stresses once more that the promises of the prophets of Israel have at best been partially fulfilled in Jesus of Nazareth. Hence there is no way the Christian church can really call him the Promised One. There remains "an 'excess,' a large remnant which must yet be brought to fulfillment and to which the Jew constantly points, perhaps even with irony and sarcasm. . . ."[19]

From the above comments it would seem that Mussner sees in the Jewish "no" to Jesus a continual reminder to Christians of the work that still remains. Jews in his model are the prime examples of those who still need to be incorporated into the unification of humanity that is integral to the salvific process. And Christ cannot truly be called the Promised One until this occurs. I must admit to some grave reservations about this model, especially when Mussner speaks of Jesus having abolished the Torah without any qualification and having established a totally new center of human unity in his person. Such a model is still ripe for activist attempts at converting Jews, something from which the church seems to be moving away. More will be said about this point later on in this essay. This model leaves Jews with a very modest positive model—protecting any false messianic interpretations that fail to do justice to the Jewish context of Jesus' teaching. But like Thoma, Mussner leaves little room for a creative contribution by Judaism to the Christian vision of salvation. Put another way, it does not appear that Mussner is ready to admit any deficiency in the Christian notion of human salvation that Judaism can overcome.

There are a number of other Catholic scholars who have looked at specific aspects of the Jewish-Christian relationship from a theological point of view, but have not attempted a full-scale examination of the issue in the manner of Thoma or Mussner. The names include Eugene Fisher, John Oesterreicher, Lawrence Frizzell and Michel Remaud. All in one way or another stress the Jewish context of Christianity and the continuing validity of the Jewish covenant after the Christ Event. All of them appear to hold the position that there is no fundamental antagonism between this affirmation by Christians and the expression of their Incarnational beliefs. None of them seem to think any major reformulation of Christological belief is necessary. The negative theology of Judaism in Christian circles in the past is largely due to the misunderstanding of Jesus' actual relationship to Judaism. Once this is overcome a constructive theology of Judaism can be built by Christians from the resources provided by the New Testament. In other words, anti-Judaism is in no way integral to a Christian theology that is authentically rooted in the New Testament. I list the scholars under the double covenant column because, while their positions remain underdeveloped, they seem to hold out for some distinctive features in Christianity. In this sense they are somewhat beyond the single covenant model. Some of them take their cue from the Pauline mystery theology but they go beyond the earlier versions of this approach that one finds, for example, in the writings of Cardinal Bea.

The French Catholic scholar Michel Remaud comes closest of the above group to presenting the outlines for a possible Christian theological model with respect to Judaism. Remaud emphasizes that the churches are only at the outset of reassessing their relationship to Judaism theologically. He warns that in undertaking this process the church must studiously avoid any theology of "substitution," or any form of self-expression that would appropriate for the church the identity of the Jewish People. This point is also made quite strongly by Gerard Sloyan in his writings.[20] Both the Shoah and the Jewish return to the land, Remaud insists, must play a role in such new theological reflection within Christianity.

Remaud goes back to the "mystery of Israel" approach for his starting point. But he then proceeds to interpret "mystery" in a different light than the previous supporters of this position. For him "mystery" essentially means "spiritual reality." Both Israel and the Church participate in this same spiritual reality which has several dimensions. Israel's distinctive role is to highlight the messianic hope in this spiritual reality; the church, on the other hand, bears witness to the already existing hope that is central to this one, though complex, spiritual reality.[21]

This contribution by Remaud is intriguing, though in need of much greater elaboration. It represents a new way of building from Romans 9–11. The proposal, especially its interpretation of "mystery," may not stand the test of careful scholarly scrutiny. But it is to be welcomed as an important contribution for further reflection. It has the decided advantage of providing a continuing, *distinctive* mission for Israel after the Easter event.

My work on Christology and Judaism, developed most fully up till now in my volume *Christ in Light of the Christian-Jewish Dialogue,*[22] generally falls into this second category of Christian theological positions in the dialogue. Several convictions are key to my approach. They are: (1) that the Christ Event did not invalidate the Jewish faith perspective; (2) that Christianity is not superior to Judaism, nor is it the fulfillment of Judaism as previously maintained; (3) that the Sinai covenant is in principle as crucial to Christian faith expression as the covenant in Christ; (4) that Christianity needs to reincorporate dimensions from its original Jewish context. Behind these convictions stands the realization that a Christology has to be developed which recognizes central and unique features in the revelation of the Christ Event, mostly associated with the Incarnation, without thereby implying that these represent the totality of revelation. Such a Christology needs to make room both for the ongoing validity of the Jewish covenant and for the recognition of its unique and central insights that presently are not incorporated, or are at least understated, by the Christian church. This approach, let me add, needs to be extended relative to other world religions as well. My own approach thus has much in common with the orientation given the question by Thoma, Mussner and, to some extent, Remaud.

The third position relative to a theology of the Christian-Jewish relationship—Sinai and the Christ Event as two among an undetermined number of messianic experiences within humanity—has been articulated most completely in the writings of Rosemary Ruether. She is firmly convinced that a positive theology of Judaism cannot arise in the church without a thorough reworking of the traditional Christological statement. This is due in large part to the anti-Jewish Christologies fashioned by the Church Fathers in the earliest period of the church's existence. Until these patristic Christologies are rooted out of the church's proclamation, little headway will be made in her estimation.

Ruether joins the other Christian theologians associated with the dialogue with Judaism in rejecting any claims about the Messianic Age having been fulfilled with Christ's coming. The realities of the human condition will not permit such an assertion. If the church persists in affirming that the term "Christ" signifies the Messiah of Israel's hope, then it must likewise appreciate that

> . . . from the standpoint of that faith of Israel itself, there is no possibility of talking about the Messiah having come (much less of having come two thousand years ago, with all the evil history that has reigned from that time until this) when the reign of God has not come.[23]

Ruether maintains that Judaism can envision no separation between the coming of the Messiah and the appearance of the Messianic age. The two are simultaneous—in actuality, one and the same event. The problem is that Christianity picked up this traditional Jewish belief in the Messianic age of the future and "imported" it into history. Christianity declared that evil had in fact been overcome once and for all through the Christ Event. The end result of this was a false solution to the ultimate crisis facing human existence, the crisis that divides the historical from the eschatological. Both Christian antisemitism and the structures of political totalitarianism and imperialism found in the nations of the West ultimately spring from this unwarranted assumption by the church of eschatological fulfillment.

As Ruether sees it, the traditional idea of the Christ Event as the final Messianic revelation and hence as the replacement for the Jewish Messianic vision needs to be totally reformulated. She unqualifiedly affirms that "what Christianity has in Jesus is not the Messiah, but a Jew who hoped for the kingdom of God and who died in that hope."[24] In her published works, principally *Faith and Fratricide*,[25] she has not provided any comprehensive reformulation. But she has provided some general directions in which such a reformulation must move. Ruether has also written a more thorough reformulation, still unpublished, whose basic thrust has been summarized in Michael McGarry's *Christology After Auschwitz*.[26]

No Messianic notion can be authentically proclaimed by Christianity, in Ruether's view, which does not primarily look to an ultimate, future event that will abolish all suffering and injustice on this earth. Jesus' ministry provided such a future vision. Hence it can be said to have a paradigmatic and anticipatory value relative to the eschatological age. The man Jesus stands as a model of the hope that this eschatological ideal is in fact possible of realization in the future. Christ constitutes the theological symbol for the fulfillment of the hope. Jesus Christ represents the unification of the human community with its ultimate destiny which is yet to come and in whose light men and women can continue to hope and to struggle for the realization of that unity. For Ruether the Christ Event also reveals the ultimate overthrow of evil and the establishment of God's reign even though evil still holds sway on many fronts.

But the Christ Event constitutes an authentic eschatological paradigm only for the people who have consciously accepted it as such. Others who have turned to alternate paradigms which have emerged compellingly from central experiences in their own respective histories should not be looked upon by Christians as unredeemed. The Exodus Event, for example, does the same for Jewish identity that the Christ Event does for Christianity. It is the foundation of hope and a statement about the ultimate conquerability of evil. The Christ Event in no way invalidates the value of the Exodus experience as a paradigm, nor vice versa. Each speaks to a different group of people.

Ruether's writings have brought the Christological question in the dialogue to a head in a singular way. She makes a distinctive contribution with her bold challenge to classical Christian claims about Jesus' fulfillment of Judaism. She has helped significantly in bringing out the shadow side of what she calls the ''historicizing of the eschatological'' process. And her insistence that Christian faith needs to be reanchored in the flow of human history can be enthusiastically supported. But, on balance, she has relativized the Christ Event far too much. And she has failed to indicate whether the revelations in the Exodus and in the Christ Events differ in any manner. We do not have to maintain the traditional fulfillment/superiority model for the Christ Event relative to Judaism to continue to argue for some measure of its uniqueness and centrality. In fact, if we cease making such claims totally, there seems little reason for maintaining Christianity as a distinct religion.[27]

A recent Catholic contribution to the rethinking of Christianity's relationship to Judaism and other world religions that might also be included in this more radical category with Rosemary Ruether is Paul Knitter's *No Other Name?*[28] In one section of the volume Knitter summarizes various options for rethinking Christology that have arisen from the Christian-Jewish dialogue in the last several decades. He seems particularly responsive to Ruether's attempt to relativize the authentic Messianic hope associated with the Christ Event. He proposes a theocentric Christological model which revolves around a notion of "relational uniqueness" for Jesus. This model affirms that

> Jesus *is* unique, but with a uniqueness defined by its ability to relate
> to—that is, to include and be included by—other unique religious
> figures. Such an understanding of Jesus views him not as exclusive
> or even as normative but as *theocentric,* as a universally relevant
> manifestation (sacrament, incarnation) of divine revelation and sal-
> vation.[29]

Knitter insists, however, that such uniqueness claims for Jesus cannot be presumed, but must be tested through concrete dialogue with other world religions.

Knitter thus stands somewhere on a bridge between Ruether and the theologians included in group two. He seems not to relativize the Christ Event quite as much as Ruether, but like her, he does not automatically make this event central or singularly important in the history of religions. As a Christian theologian he seems prepared to place in principle the fundamental orienting experiences of Judaism and other world religions on a par with the Christ Event. Since his basic goal is to provide principles for a theology of religious diversity he does not really go into the question of what unique features Judaism or any other world religion might bring to Christianity's self-awareness. He is content for the moment to argue the more basic premise.

Knitter's approach has some definite possibilities for application to the construction of a theology of the Christian-Jewish relationship. It would need to deal more fully with the special link that exists here and which is not present in the church's relationship with the other religions except perhaps Islam. He would also have to spell out more fully the meaning of Jesus' uniqueness which he seems to locate in the Incarnation.

At this point it would be useful to add a word or two about developments in Catholic systematic theology generally relative to the continuing role for Judaism in the process of human salvation. The majority of Catholic theologians have never raised the issue in a direct fashion. Eva Fleischner points this out very clearly in her analysis of leading German theologians such as Karl Rahner and Walter Kasper.[30] Others, such as Hans Küng,[31] have written very sensitive chapters on the contemporary Jewish-Christian relationship, but have done little to raise this question within the main body of their theological thought.

Among the leading writers on Christology in present-day Catholicism the best possibilities for a positive inclusion of Judaism seem to lie with Edward Schillebeeckx[32] and Gustavo Gutierrez.[33] Though they do not treat many of the specific issues of the dialogue, the Christological themes they highlight are the least antithetical to a continued salvific function for Judaism. The primacy Schillebeeckx gives the "Abba" notion in his understanding of the Christ Event and the positive link Gutierrez establishes between the liberation central to the Sinai covenant and the freedom found in Jesus are both potential building blocks for a constructive Christian theology of Judaism that could co-exist with an ongoing stress on the unique features of the Christ Event.

To bring this discussion of developments since *Nostra Aetate* regarding theological foundations for the Christian-Jewish relationship to a close, it would be important to focus briefly on three outlooks which I consider essential if we are to witness further progress in this area. The first has to do with the handling of New Testament data on the meaning of the Christ Event. With Knitter we need to recognize a certain evolution of Christological awareness in the New Testament, away from what I call "messianic fulfillment" Christology and what he terms "prophet Christology," found principally in the synoptics, to "consciousness Christology" or "Son Christology" which dominates the gospel of John and the later Pauline writings. The methodological principle that is critical here is the willingness to say that not everything in the New Testament is of equal value. This is an interpretive principle advocated by Raymond Brown for solving some of the antisemitism he finds in the New Testament. This principle, applied to the problem at hand, would allow us to take the later "Son" or "consciousness" Christology as our starting point for a constructive theology of Judaism over the earlier version whose *fulfillment* emphasis seems to erode a continuing salvific function for Judaism.

The second outlook is the assertion that revelation is developmental rather than static and that it continues to offer new insights as the church advances the building of the kingdom through its participation in the flow of history. This outlook will likewise permit the selection of "Son Christology" as our basis for a theology of the Christian-Jewish relationship, not only because it seems to be the product of mature apostolic reflection rather than initial faith enthusiasm but because subsequent revelation through history has shown us the unsuitability of any fulfillment claims in light of the continued presence of evil and suffering and the tenacious vitality of the people Israel despite events such as the Nazi Holocaust.

Third, we must be prepared to move beyond an attitude of toleration with respect not only to Judaism but to all world religions as well to a positive affirmation of religious pluralism. Such a constructive theological approach to religious diversity may not necessarily entail the wholesale abandonment of eschatological truth claims for which the Israeli scholar David Hartman has called.[34] We may still view our respective truth claims as central for the redemption for all humanity. But we can no longer regard them as exclusively so. A certain recognition of incompleteness must enter our self-awareness, an incompleteness that can be overcome only by interaction with other religious traditions. Other religious traditions exist for our spiritual enrichment as well as their own, for our salvation as well as their own. This is a key principle for building a valid theology of religious pluralism in which a theology of the Christian-Jewish relationship must be set.

A theology of religious pluralism might allow us to say that we have more than others, but never could it permit us to say that we have a hold on all significant religious insight. This does not mean that each religious tradition is incapable of providing salvation for its adherents. What we need to recognize ⟵ is that all of us are saved in our incompleteness. All this needs further discussion, however, since the theology of religious pluralism is very much in its infancy in both Catholicism and Judaism.

It should also be recognized that the extent to which we create theological space for Judaism against which we originally defined Christian identity, to that same extent do we moderate, albeit implicitly, any absolutist claims about Christian faith. Because Christianity has so often cast its relationship to Judaism in "over-against" terms, far more than has been the case with the other religions, any changes in the theological conception of the Christian-Jewish relationship will automatically redound favorably on the Church's theological ability to relate to these religions as well. Gerald Anderson has correctly perceived that any substantial changes in the Christian theological understanding of Judaism will have a "domino" effect with respect to the other world religions.[35]

A final point needs to be added here regarding the reformulation of the theology of the Christian-Jewish relationship. It concerns the *liturgical* expression of this theology. The incorporation of any revamped theology in this regard into the consciousness of the Catholic faithful will only come about if we are prepared to significantly alter parts of our liturgy. So much of the current liturgy, especially during the key seasons of Advent, Lent and Eastertime, revolves around the notion of Jesus as fulfillment of the biblical promises about the Messiah and the Messianic age. Yet we have seen that all the Catholic theologians who have reflected on the Jewish-Christian relationship since Vatican II reject any simple prophecy-fulfillment Christology. Unless we address this difficult and pivotal problem, our reformulated Christology will remain in the realm of pure theory with little effect on the average Christian's attitudes toward the Jewish People.

This chapter was focused almost exclusively on the theology of the Jewish-Christian relationship, especially its impact on Christological expression, because this has been the historic source of tension between Christianity and Judaism over the ages and the cause of so much persecution of the people of

Israel. But there are other theological issues that have been pursued in the last twenty years relative to the Christian-Jewish encounter and which require further elaboration.

The first is the relevance of the experience of the Nazi Holocaust for thinking about God in both our traditions. This process is far more advanced in Judaism[36] than in Christianity. It is imperative that Christians enter this discussion to a far deeper extent than has been the case up till now. David Tracy makes this point very well:

> The ultimate theological issue, the understanding of God, has yet to receive much reflection from Catholic theologians. And yet, as Schleiermacher correctly insisted, the doctrine of God can never be "another" doctrine for theology, but must pervade all doctrines. Here Jewish theology, in its reflections on the reality of God since the *Tremendum* of the Holocaust, has led the way for all serious theological reflection.[37]

There is considerable controversy at present as to whether the Holocaust has significantly modified (or even rendered null and void) the covenant at Sinai. David Hartman, Michael Wyschogrod, and Eugene Borowitz say no; Richard Rubenstein, Irving Greenberg, Emil Fackenheim and Arthur Cohen claim it does. There is little doubt that the resolution of the God-question after the Shoah will have a profound influence on any Catholic attempts to restate theologically the relationship between the Christian and Jewish covenants. This is also true for Christology in general.[38] It is encouraging that a number of prominent Catholic scholars, in addition to David Tracy, are beginning of late to take greater interest in the theological implications of the Holocaust. They include Gregory Baum, Marcel Dubois, and especially Johannes Metz. Metz now argues that any statement of Christian theodicy, any attempt to express religious meaning, must be considered "blasphemy" if it does not meet the test of this central event in human history.[39]

There are also other theological issues which need discussion in light of the Holocaust. Many of them relate to the sphere of ethics.[40] One especially important one from the Christian standpoint is ecclesiology, particularly the church-world relationship. The Austrian Catholic philosopher Frederich Heer has urged the church to reclaim Judaism's more positive attitude toward the world in light of the Shoah as a way of saving the world from nuclear disaster. Catholic ecclesiology has been far too anti-worldly in the past.[41] And Professor Gordon Zahn, a long-time leader in the Catholic peace movement, has argued that the Holocaust experience should lead us to a Catholic ecclesiology that refrains from involvement with the state and understands itself primarily as prophetic presence to the nations.[42] One may not fully agree with either of these viewpoints, but there is no escaping the need to rethink the church-world relatjonship as a consequence of the Holocaust.

Another area calling for further theological reflection concerns the legitimacy of mission to the Jewish People. This has been to say the least a very controversial issue in the dialogue, though the controversy has been somewhat more intense in Protestantism than Catholicism since the former has had a much greater commitment historically to the proselytization of Jews.[43] Some Catholics have addressed this question since *Nostra Aetate*. Gregory Baum holds that the only "moral" mission to the Jews after Auschwitz is that of genuine service.[44] Perhaps the most comprehensive Catholic statement with regard to mission and the Jews has come from Professor Tommaso Federici of the San Anselmo Pontifical Theological Faculty in Rome. Speaking to a meeting of the Vatican-Jewish international dialogue in Venice in 1977, Federici introduced a basic distinction between proselytism and *witness*. Witness remains an obligation of the church, but it ought to take place in the setting of dialogue. Undue proselytizing is now out of the question for Federici in light of *Nostra Aetate*. Included under this ban are all forms of preaching or witness which in any manner constrain individual Jews, or the Jewish community as a whole, whether that constraint be of the physical, moral, psychological or cultural variety. Any presentation of Christian belief in Christ must take place in an atmosphere of reverent dialogue. Such dialogue, if it is to be genuine,

> demands authentic self-discipline. Every temptation to exclusivism must be eliminated as also any imperialism or self-sufficiency. On the other hand there must be fidelity and dedicated personal searching, avoiding any form of relativism and syncretism that would try artificially to combine irreconcilable elements. Once the spiritual identity of the one and the other is guaranteed, there must be mutual esteem and respect (theological as well), and the conviction that every growth and bettering in the spiritual field comes about with the other's contribution.[45]

If a criticism can be made of Federici it is that he does not go far enough in his rejection of the "total fulfillment" Christology that has been at the heart of Christianity's superiority complex relative to Judaism and the basis of its traditional approach to missionizing Jews. Until such repudiation occurs, until the kind of Christological reformulation discussed earlier on in this chapter gains widespread support, any rejection of a proselytizing attitude toward the Jewish People will look to many like a failure in carrying out the supposed gospel mandate to preach the good news to all nations. Until Christians recognize their own salvific nakedness and stand ready to learn from Judaism because it is clear that Judaism has preserved aspects of the full biblical revelation better than Christianity, the old theology of mission will not be overcome once and for all.[46]

The theological phase of the Christian-Jewish dialogue will also need to give attention to the Jewish land tradition. Here Catholic theologians will need to pick up on the reflections of several Protestant scholars, especially Walter Brueggemann and W.D. Davies. The former has argued that recovery of this land tradition is vital to the necessary rehistoricizing of Christian faith understanding; the latter has clearly shown that when Jews introduce the question of Israel in the dialogue they are not simply trying to politicize the discussion but calling on a classical theological theme in the Jewish tradition.[47]

Finally, we must take a look at the meaning of tradition. This will prove an especially enriching theological discussion for Jews and Catholics, both of whom recognize something besides the Scriptures as a source of revelatory meaning. Is there a way we can develop through common reflection a joint hermeneutic of "retrieval," as David Tracy has called it? To what extent does the Holocaust affect our discussion of such retrieval? Tracy says considerably.[48]

It is my firm conviction that the appropriation of tradition's content and the use of tradition as a principle of ongoing interpretation and modification of that content are critical to the development of a reformulated theology of the Christian-Jewish relationship as well as a more generalized theology of religious pluralism. The Christian-Jewish discussion of this issue will prove especially beneficial because the notion of *oral Torah,* perfected in Pharisaic-rabbinic Judaism, was behind the development of the concept of tradition as a source of revelation within early Christianity.

Two Catholic theologians have made important contributions to such a discussion of tradition within the Christian-Jewish dialogue. Peter Chirico speaks of tradition as something more than the "mere exegesis of Scripture." Rather it involves the expression by the Christian community "of the progressive unfolding of revelation that is taking place within it and the world at large in the course of history."[49] And Robert Schreiter in discussing implications of Edward Schillebeeckx's Christology for Christian-Jewish relations attempts to relate the classic notion of tradition to the insights of modern language analysis. Schreiter underscores Schillebeeckx's proposal that statements about Christian fulfillment need to be understood as anticipatory and proleptic instead of participatory with respect to God's eschatological reign. This notion of tradition manifests the need to reread the classic Christian texts in the light of new experiences by the church. Schreiter sees many of the eschatological and messianic texts of the New Testament as efforts to mediate the felt presence but equally realized absence of Jesus in the midst of his disciples. Recognizing that every religious affirmation will involve some non-meaning, and conscious of the anticipatory nature of many of the earliest Christian Christological affirmations, it is possible for us today with such a concept of tradition to develop new insights as a result of new experiences of meaning. The living encounter with Jews as a faith community can provide the church as a whole with new meaning regarding the Christian-Jewish relationship considered theologically.[50]

As an overall assessment, theological developments since *Nostra Aetate* show considerable progress. There is still need to move these reflections to the mainstream of Catholic and Jewish theology which is only beginning to happen of late. But there is little doubt that the Second Vatican Council opened up a profound re-evaluation of the church's relationship to Judaism that will have lasting impact.

NOTES

1. For the text of this document, cf. Helga Croner (ed.), *Stepping Stones to Further Jewish-Christian Relations.* London/New York: Stimulus Books, 1977.

2. For an extended discussion of Judaism in contemporary Latin American liberation theology, cf. my volume *Christ in Light of the Christian-Jewish Dialogue.* New York/Ramsey: Paulist Press, 1982, 59–73. On the Jewish-Christian relationship and Feminist theology, cf. Deborah McCauley and Annette Daum, "Jewish-Christian Feminist Dialogue: A Wholistic Vision," *Union Seminary Quarterly Review,* 38:2 (1983), 147–190.

3. "The Mysterious Destines of Israel," in *The Bridge,* Vol. II, John Oesterreicher (ed.), New York: Pantheon Books, 1956, 35–90.

4. *Dialogue with Israel.* Baltimore: Helicon Press, 1966; *The Theology of Jewish Christianity.* Chicago: Henry Regnery, 1964. Also cf. Jean Danielou and Andre Chouraqui, *The Jews: Views and Counterviews.* New York: Newman Press, 1967.

5. *Church and World.* New York: Herder and Herder, 1967.

6. *The Church and the Jewish People.* London: Geoffrey Chapman, 1966.

7. "Christian Theology and the Covenant of Israel," *Journal of Ecumenical Studies* 7 (Winter 1970), 49.

8. Cf. *Discerning the Way.* New York: Seabury, 1980, and *A Christian Theology of the People Israel.* New York: Seabury, 1983.

9. Baum's principal writings on the question include: "The Jews, Faith and Ideology," *The Ecumenist* 10 (1971/72), 71–76; "The Doctrinal Basis for Jewish-Christian Dialogue," *The Month* 224 (1967), 232–245; "Introduction" to Rosemary Ruether's *Faith and Fratricide.* New York: Seabury Press, 1974; and "Rethinking the Church's Mission after Auschwitz," in Eva

188   *Rev. John T. Pawlikowski, O.S.M., Ph.D.*

Fleischner (ed.), *Auschwitz: Beginning of a New Era?* New York: Ktav, 1977, 113–128.

10. "Rethinking the Church's Mission," 127.

11. *Christology After Auschwitz.* New York: Paulist, 1977, 83.

12. Cf. *A Christian Theology of Judaism,* trans. by Helga Croner. New York/Ramsey: Paulist Press, 1980.

13. *Ibid.,* 134–135.

14. *Ibid.,* 114.

15. *Ibid.,* 115.

16. *Tractate on the Jews: The Significance of Judaism for Christian Faith,* trans. with an introduction by Leonard Swidler. Philadelphia: Fortress Press, 1984, 226.

17. *Ibid.,* 227.

18. *Ibid.*

19. *Ibid.,* 241.

20. "Who Are the People of God?" in *Standing Before God,* edited by Asher Finkel and Lawrence Frizzell. New York: Ktav, 1981, 103–116, and *Is Christ the End of the Law?* Philadelphia: Westminster, 1978.

21. *Chrétiens Devant: Israël Serviteur de Dieu.* Paris: Les Editions Du Cerf, 1983, 147–148.

22. New York/Ramsey: Paulist Press, 1982, 76–135.

23. "An Invitation to Jewish-Christian Dialogue: In What Sense Can We Say That Jesus Was 'The Christ'?" *The Ecumenist* 10 (January/February 1972), 17.

24. "Christian-Jewish Dialogue: New Interpretations," *ADL Bulletin* 30 (May 1973), 4.

25. New York: Seabury, 1974. Also cf. *Disputed Questions: On Being a Christian.* Nashville: Abingdon, 1982.

26. New York: Paulist Press, 1977, 87–91.

27. For other critiques of Ruether, including my own, cf. Alan T. Davies, *Antisemitism and the Foundations of Christianity.* New York/Ramsey/Toronto: Paulist Press, 1979. Also cf. Franz Mussner, *Tractate,* 227–233, and John Oesterreicher, *Anatomy of Contempt.* South Orange, NJ: Institute of Judaeo-Christian Studies, 1975.

28. Maryknoll, NY: Orbis, 1985.

29. *Ibid.,* 171–172.

30. *Judaism in German Christian Theology Since 1945: Christianity and Israel Considered in Terms of Mission.* Metuchen, NJ: Scarecrow Press, 1975.

31. *On Being a Christian.* Garden City, NY: Doubleday, 1976.

32. On this potential in Schillebeeckx, cf. Robert Schreiter, "Christology in the Jewish-Christian Encounter: An Essay-Review of Edward Schillebeeckx's *Jesuz het Verhaal van een Levende,*" *Journal of the American*

Academy of Religion 44 (December 1976), 702–723, and my volume *Christ,* 50–58.

33. On this potential in Gutierrez, cf. my volume *Christ,* 59–65.

34. "Jews and Christians in the World of Tomorrow," *Immanuel* 6 (Spring 1976), 79. Also cf. "Creating Space for the Integrity of the Other," SIDIC (English Edition), 15:2 (1982), 5–10. For a less radical Jewish viewpoint, cf. Shemaryahu Talmon, "Towards World Community: Resources for Living Together—A Jewish View," *The Ecumenical Review* 26 (October 1974), 610–629.

35. "Response to Pietro Rossano," in *Christ's Lordship and Religious Pluralism,* Gerald H. Anderson and Thomas F. Stransky (eds.), Maryknoll, NY: Orbis, 1981, 118–119.

36. Cf. David Hartman, "New Jewish Religious Voices II: Auschwitz or Sinai?" *The Ecumenist,* 21:1 (November/December 1982), 1–9; Eugene Borowitz, *Choices in Modern Jewish Thought: A Partisan Guide.* New York: Behrman House, 1983; Richard Rubenstein, *After Auschwitz.* Indianapolis; Bobbs-Merrill, 1966; Emil Fackenheim, *The Jewish Return into History.* New York: Schocken Books, 1978; Irving Greenberg, "The Voluntary Covenant," *Perspectives* #3. New York: National Jewish Resource Center, 1982; Arthur Cohen. *The Tremendum: Theological Interpretation of The Holocaust.* New York: Crossroad, 1981.

37. "Religious Values after the Holocaust: A Catholic View," in Abraham J. Peck (ed.), *Jews and Christians After the Holocaust.* Philadelphia: Fortress, 1982, 101.

38. Cf. my essay "L'Holocauste et la Christologie Contemporaine," in *Le Judaisme après Auschwitz: Une Question Radicale,* E. Schüssler-Fiorenza (ed.), *Concilium* #195. Paris: Beauchesne, 1984, 71–81. This same essay is available in the other language editions of *Concilium.*

39. *The Emergent Church.* New York: Crossroad, 1981, 19–20. Also cf. Gregory Baum, "Catholic Dogma After Auschwitz," in Alan Davies (ed.), *Antisemitism,* 137–150; and Marcel Dubois, Christian Reflection on the Holocaust, SIDIC 7:2 (1974), 10–16. My own writings on the topic include *The Challenge of the Holocaust for Christian Theology* (Revised Edition). New York: Anti-Defamation League, 1982, and a chapter "Christian Ethics and the Holocaust—A Dialogue with Post-Auschwitz Judaism," in the forthcoming volume *The Future of Holocaust Studies: A Search for Directions,* F. Burton Nelson (ed.).

40. Cf. my essays, "The Holocaust: Its Implications for the Church and Society Problematic," in *Christianity and Judaism: The Deepening Dialogue,* Richard W. Rousseau, S.J. (ed.). Montrose, PA: Ridge Row Press, 1983, 95–106; "Christian Perspective and Moral Implications," in *The Holocaust: Ideology, Bureaucracy, and Genocide,* Henry Friedlander and Sybil Milton (eds).

Millwood, NY: Kraus International Publications, 1980, 295–308. On the implications of the Holocaust for contemporary worship, cf. my essay, "Worship After the Holocaust: An Ethician's Reflections," *Worship,* 58:4 (July 1984), 315–329.

41. *God's First Love.* New York: Weybright and Talley, 1970.

42. "Catholic Resistance? A Yes and a No," in *The German Church Struggle and the Holocaust,*" Franklin Littell and Hubert G. Locke (eds.). Detroit: Wayne State University Press, 1974, 203–240.

43. For an introduction to this controversy cf. Balfour Brickner, "Christian Missionaries and a Jewish Response," *Worldview,* 21 (May 1978), 37–41 and "Christians Challenge the Rabbi's Response," *Worldview* 21 (July/ August 1978), 42–46.

44. "Rethinking the Church's Mission" (see Note #9).

45. *Origins,* 8 (October 19, 1978) and *Encounter Today* 13 (Winter/ Spring 1978), 18–36.

46. For a further elaboration of my view on this subject, cf. *Christ in Light,* 148–154.

47. Brueggemann's principal work is *The Land.* Philadelphia: Fortress Press, 1977. For Davies' views, cf. *The Gospel and the Land.* Berkeley, CA: University of California Press, 1974, and *The Territorial Imperative of Judaism.* Berkeley, CA: University of California Press, 1982.

48. Cf. "The Interpretation of Theological Texts After the Holocaust," unpublished lecture, International Conference on the Holocaust, Indiana University, Fall 1982.

49. "Christian and Jew Today From a Christian Theological Perspective." *Journal of Ecumenical Studies* 7 (Fall 1970), 748–749.

50. Cf. Note #32.

The Relationship of Judaism and Christianity: Toward a New Organic Model

IRVING GREENBERG

INTRODUCTION

This paper does not focus on the Holocaust but in part it is a response to the Holocaust. I believe that nobody should use the Holocaust to simply uphold the validity of his/her own views or categories. Rather, people must challenge themselves in light of the Holocaust to correct any weaknesses revealed in themselves.

Pope John XXIII's regret at Christianity's teaching of contempt for Judaism led to the statement on Judaism in Vatican II's Declaration on the Relationship of the Church to Non-Christian Religions. The repudiation of the deicide charge and the call not to teach Scripture so as to malign the Jews was a sign that the Church was alive, for inability to repent is a sign of spiritual death. Later declarations have gone beyond *Nostra Aetate* in affirming the dignity of Judaism and distancing from past Christian anti-Judaic polemics. These are proof positive that inspiration has not abandoned the Church.

The most powerful proof of the vitality and the ongoing relevance of Christianity is the work of people like Alice and Roy Eckardt whose fundamental critique of Christianity is surely one of the most sustained and devastating moral analyses in its history. But their work, and that of others like them (Paul van Buren, Rosemary Ruether, Eva Fleischner) is both healing and affirming of Christianity.

In the light of the Holocaust, the willingness to confront, to criticize, and to correct is the ultimate test of the validity and the vitality of faith. One might say that that religion which is most able to correct itself is the one that will prove itself to be most true. Those that claim that they have the whole truth and nothing but the truth and there is nothing to correct thereby prove how false and how ineffective their religious viewpoint is.[1]

In that spirit, this paper is an attempt to ask Jews and Jewish thinkers to focus not only on Christian failure and the Christian tradition of teaching of contempt. "The Holocaust cannot be used for triumphalism. Its moral challenge must also be applied to Jews."² This paper asks whether it is possible for Judaism to have a more affirmative model of Christianity, one that appreciates Christian spiritual life in all its manifest power. If for no other reason, let this be done because if we take the other's spiritual life less seriously, we run the great risk of taking the biological life less seriously, too. It was the Christian theological negativism and stereotyping of Judaism that created that profound moral trap into which all too many Christians fell during the Holocaust. At the least, it encouraged relative indifference to the fate of the other. In the light of the Holocaust, Jews have to ask themselves: Is there anything in Jewish tradition or the Jewish model of other religions such as Christianity that could lead to some indifference to the fate of others? If there are such phenomena, they must be addressed.

After the Holocaust, a model of the relationship of Judaism and Christianity ideally should enable one to affirm the fullness of the faith claims of the other, not just offer tolerance. It is important to avoid a kind of affirmation of the other that is patronizing. Take Martin Buber, our master and teacher. In Buber's book, *Two Types of Faith,* and other writings on Christianity, one is fascinated by the incredible openness (which profoundly affected me). Martin Buber speaks of "my brother Jesus." (The daring and the power of that statement! I could never use that term.) Yet in Buber's approach, Jesus' true religion is the subterranean religion which runs through Judaism also. The Christianity which Martin Buber loves turns out to be suspiciously like the Judaism that Martin Buber loves. That religion, theologically misled by Paul, turns into the Christianity we all know. Now Buber in his own way was a remarkable pioneer, but is that ultimately the message—that Christianity is a wonderful religion when it fits (our) Jewish ideas? Should not Jewish theology seek to be open to Christian self-understanding, including the remarkable, unbelievable claim of resurrection, incarnation, etc.? Can one, as a Jew, take these claims seriously without giving up one's Jewishness? Up to now, the agreed response is that if you take such claims seriously, there is nothing further to be as a Jew. This is why Jews who are serious Jews have rejected these claims in the past.

This paper seeks to articulate a model that would allow for the Christian possibility without yielding the firm conviction that Judaism is a covenant faith, true and valid in history. I believe that Judaism has never been superseded, and that its work is yet unfinished. We need a model that would allow both sides to respect the full nature of the other in all its faith claims. (One must recognize that there is a whole range of Christian self-understanding and a whole range of Jewish self-understanding, from the most secular to the most fundamentalist. Ideally, a model should allow room for that range of model, and still not exclude the fullness of the faith claims of the other.) Last, but not least, the model is willing to affirm the profound inner relationship between the two, and to recognize and admit how much closer they are to each other than either has been able to say, without denying the other. Up to now, the affirmation that the two religions are internally close was made by Christians who claimed that Christianity grows organically out of Judaism in the *course* of superseding Judaism. To the extent that there have been Christians who have affirmed Judaism as valid, they have had (to a certain extent) to overemphasize Jewish differentiation in order to make space for Jewish existence. To the extent that there were Jews willing to see Christianity as a valid religion, they also tended to stress the differences, in order to protect Judaism. This model will seek to reduce the gaps without denying the authenticity of the other.

I. THE SCRIPTURAL MODEL

Judaism is a religion of redemption. The fundamental teaching of Judaism is that because this world is rooted in an infinite source of life and goodness, which we call God, life within it is growing, increasing, perfecting. Life is developing to become more and more like God. The ultimate achievement so far is the human being. The human being is in the image of God, so much like God that one can literally use the imagery of a human like God. In the case of the human, life is of infinite value, equal and unique. Judaism claims that this process will continue until life's fullest possibilities will be realized, until life finally overcomes death.

If that is not incredible enough, Judaism makes a further claim. The world that we live in, in the realm of the history of humans, is where this perfection will come. There is another realm—rabbinic Judaism affirms a world to come. But this perfection of life will be achieved in the realm which the five senses can see and measure, in the realm of history. Sickness will be overcome; poverty and oppression will be overcome; death will be overcome. The political, economic, and social structures will be restructured, to support and nurture the perfection of life. Now thousands of people will die this year of various diseases which could be treated at this very moment. In many cases, people will die not because of evil, not even because of prejudice, but simply because the community could not afford the treatment. Therefore, when Judaism speaks of a world that will respect the infinite value of humans, it is speaking of a world that is fabulously wealthy. It would take enormous productivity, industry, and wealth to support such dignity. Indeed, the opening chapter of Genesis, which is the program of the Torah (the ultimate dream is the original dream), describes a world in which every human being is of infinite value in the image of God. That world is a Garden of Eden, totally at the service of two people.

Finally, Judaism said that if God is good and God is a source of infinite life and infinite goodness, no one should have died in the first place. To perfect the world, it would not be enough to overcome death prospectively. Judaism goes on to say there will be resurrection. All those who have died will come to life. Then all will know that everything about God is true.

Faith is not a fairytale. If all this does not happen, then the whole Torah is an illusion, a fable. This affirmation is part of the courage and daring of Judaism. It set the test of its truth not in another world which cannot be measured, not in a world from which there are no travelers who have returned with first-hand reports. Judaism insisted that redemption is going to happen in this world, where you can see it, measure it—and if it does not happen, then the religion is revealed to be an illusion.

This vision of Judaism was set in motion by a great event in Jewish history—the Exodus. Out of this great redemption of the Hebrew slaves grew the model that not just the Hebrew slaves but all of humanity will be free. Not just the power of the oppressor Pharaoh will be broken; all oppressor power will be broken. Not just the Jews will reach the Promised Land and freedom and equality; all people someday will get there. Therefore, the faith which starts with Exodus, which is codified in the revelation of Sinai, is in fact pointing toward a future goal—a future goal which obviously is greater than the initial point. In the future, that which happened to this small group—while the rest of the world remained in suffering, sickness, and slavery—will happen to the whole world.

By its own definition, Judaism is a religion which must be open to further events in history. Judaism is a way: a way from the present reality toward that final perfection, a way in history. In its view, the final act will be greater than the first one. To put it another way: Judaism has built into its model, into its own self-understanding, that it must generate future messianic moments. If it does not generate a future messianic moment, it is a failure and a falsehood. Thus, Judaism is a religion that, starting with a great initial event, must look forward to future events, at least one of which may be greater than the initial event, as further revelation of its way. In the words of Jeremiah, "Behold the day will come, says the Lord, it shall no more be said: 'As God lives who brought up the children of Israel out of Egypt,' but, 'As God lives who brought up the children of Israel from the land of the north, and from all the countries where He had driven them, and I will bring them back into the land that I gave to their fathers.' " In Jewish tradition, the Sabbath is celebrated in memory of the Exodus. The great holidays are in reenactment of the Exodus. Jeremiah predicts that there will be a future moment of redemption which will be so extraordinary that people will stop talking about the good old days of the Exodus, and will speak of the God who carried out this "new Exodus."

The central revealed metaphor that guides this process from the beginning—from the initiation of Exodus and redemption to that final moment of total triumph of life and resurrection—is covenant. Covenant means that this achievement of the total perfection of the world will take place as the result of efforts undertaken as the outcome of a pledge of obligation between two partners. One might say that only God could make such an incredible set of promises. The total promise seems beyond human capacity. But Judaism did not say that. It insisted that there are two partners; the covenant is between God and Israel. Implied in the Scriptures is that the Divine respects the free will of humans. Therefore this final perfection cannot simply be given by God or brought by force to humanity. The Divine self-limits to enable humans to attain perfection with dignity. God first threatens to kill Adam and Eve if they sin, but does not. After God brings the Flood, God covenants never to do this again. God's turning to Abraham in further covenant is part of the process of the Divine accepting human freedom.

A Rabbi of mine once asked, "What is the Jewish dream? It is that all human beings live like Adam and Eve in the Garden of Eden. That is what will happen at the end of days. Well, if the world started with the Garden of Eden and Adam and Eve and is going to end at the same place, why have the whole process? Why did we not stay there in the first place?" The answer is not merely that Adam and Eve sinned. The main difference is that the first Garden of Eden experience was handed to humans on a silver platter. To be given everything is not to be free; it is to be a child, to be infantile. The second Garden of Eden will be earned, arrived at out of maturity and co-responsibility. The first Paradise was vulnerable to error and to sin, to misunderstanding, failure and betrayal. The second will be achieved after all those phenomena and therefore will be beyond them.

What then makes possible this process of getting to the final redemption? The answer, again, is covenant. The covenant is Israel's commitment not to stop short of perfection. It is the pledge to testify, to teach the world, to witness to other human beings. If God is not going to force humanity to be free, what will set this process of freedom in motion? The answer is: a human model— through witness, testimony, teaching. Tell people they are not to settle for the world they are living in; tell people not to settle for sickness and poverty; they are entitled to infinite value and dignity. This teaching will generate in them the will to achieve that state. Judaism and Jewry come into existence out of God's respect for human freedom. Let there be at least one group (it turns out there may be more than one) that can witness and teach others not to settle for less than perfection, to offer this promise and this hope. Further, the group in its own life can create a model of how to get there. Israel is a community that can show in its own limited way how one can begin to work toward the final perfection. It is a community that pledges not to say "might makes right," not to take advantage of the world as it is, but rather disciplines itself to respect the widow and the orphan, to free the slaves, and so step by step to walk toward that final perfection. This is done in the hope that as Israel does it, others will see the model and apply it in their own lives as well. This is what the covenantal community is all about.

Implicit in the dynamics of a covenant idea is another idea as well. If I intend to perfect the world, what do I do now? Am I prepared to try to realize total perfection right now? In total perfection, there will be peace. In total perfection, there will be no war. But suppose this people—suppose the state of Israel—were to decide tonight to live in a most perfect world and, in order to get there, would voluntarily renounce all its arms and all its armies. It would be totally destroyed.

How, then, does one get there? The answer is: step by step. Use an army to reduce the possibility of war. If one has to fight, kill as few people as possible. That is how one gets to the final perfection. If one attempts to perfect the world in one step, the only way to do that is to kill off all the humans, because they get in the way. (It would be a wonderful world if there were not all those people around who keep messing it up.) If you intend to have a perfect world in this generation there is only one way to do it: kill them all! Mao Zedong and Joseph Stalin showed how to do it. First, kill off the rich Kulaks; then, kill off the next group and the next group. Of course you end up not with perfection, but with more repression.

The alternative is the Biblical way of doing it step by step, which involves a constant process of compromises. The Bible proclaims freedom but it starts by codifying a law that there will be no more *Hebrew* slaves. (Even then, for six years, you can keep them as bonded servants.) It does not sound very noble. But that is how slavery was abolished among Jews—one step at a time.

Covenant makes this process morally possible. What saves compromise from being a sellout? It is a pledge not to rest—if you do not make it, you will try to get your daughter or your son after you to carry it on—until that final perfection. What makes both living in history and redemption in history possible is the covenantal commitment not to stop, not to surrender the goal. It is the promise to compromise temporarily for the sake of progress, but to continually renew the process until the final perfection. Implied in this model, then, is that the vision of redemption is open to development in history. A commitment to achieve perfection step by step means that the model of perfection itself unfolds in history. The covenant itself is constantly seen in a new light during the struggle. If there is an open-ended commitment to perfection, then what is possible under the rubric "perfection" in this generation may be less than is possible in the next. So the covenant is continually open to new reflection and new insight. To put it in Biblical language, "Not with you alone do I establish this covenant and this oath, but with the one who is here today and the one who is not here with us today." This is also why Judaism is open to someone joining the Jewish community. This covenant formula means that Judaism is open to converts in future generations. Finally, at least in retrospect, its openness can be interpreted to mean that it is open to *other people* as well.

To summarize: Judaism is a religion of redemption and perfection, rooted in history, operating through a covenant, illuminated by history, open to further events of revelation which will clarify its message, with an implied pedagogical model of the relationship of God and humans in which God will help the humans unfold, but will not force them to be free. God will operate out of respect for the human capacity to grow. One might say that human response to further events in history can contribute to the unfolding of the covenant, although whether this implication was fully understood by humans—and, possibly, even by God—is not clear in the Biblical accounts.

II. JUDAISM AND CHRISTIANITY

In light of all this, to be a faithful Jew is to look forward to further events of revelation and redemption beyond the Exodus—events that will illuminate the covenantal way and guide it forward. When should one most look forward to those kinds of events? In time of great despair and setbacks. That is the time to anticipate the Messiah. To those committed to the triumph of life, goodness, and justice, the moment of great injustice is the time to look forward even more to messianic redemption. When evil reigns supreme, the true balance and direction of history has been disturbed. The only event that can correct such imbalance is a major redemptive move on the other side.

The logic of covenantal redemption explains why Judaism, in fact, generated Christianity. One might argue that Christianity is a necessary sign of Judaism's vitality, i.e., it is a sign that the dynamics of the covenant are operating. If Judaism did not stimulate messianic expectations, did not generate a Messiah, it would be a sign that it was dead. As long as Jewry is generating Messiahs, it is faithful to its own calling. If Judaism does not give rise to would-be Messiahs—at least until the final Messiah does come and straighten out the whole world—then there is something wrong.

(In the writing about the Holocaust, I once wrote that I was ashamed of the fact that, in this generation, there was not at least a false Messiah. A false Messiah would show that the Jews were truly living up to their vocation, which is to hope and expect the Messiah, particularly in such tragic times. If one hopes for the Messiah and a false one shows up—well, it is regrettable but at least one has tried. Not to generate even a false Messiah is a sign that people are complacent; they have either lost hope or do not care.)

The later event which illuminates the earlier event and guides us to its fulfillment is the Messianic moment. Like good, faithful Jews, the early Jew-

ish followers of Jesus were looking for the Messiah, particularly in a difficult
century. Lo! and behold! in Jesus' life they recognized his arrival. To recognize that the Messiah has arrived, and to respond, is a very faithful response
on the part of a Jew. Therefore, a Jew does not initially forfeit the state of
faithfulness by recognizing someone as Messiah—even if he or she has erred.

Caution: Whenever one responds to a new event, believing that this event
illuminates the original event, there is a risk. On the one hand, the response
shows faithfulness. On the other hand, there are great dangers. One risk is to
give your trust and faith to a false Messiah—the new arrival may turn out not
to be the true Messiah. There is a further risk—the new developments may
lead to a transformation of the original ideas. Then, out of trying to be faithful
to the new experience, one may find oneself in some way leaving behind or
betraying the original commitments. Which then are true: the old ideas or the
new ones? Or both? The answer, of course, is that there is no guarantee in
advance. Wait until it is all clarified and it will be too late. One must respond
right now. Faith response is a wager of one's own life, out of faithfulness.

The early Christians were equally faithful—and equally acting out of loy-
alty to their Jewish understanding—when they responded to a further event,
one they had not fully anticipated: namely, the Messiah's death.

Consider the Jewish *Sitz im Leben* of those faithful Jewish Christians responding to the Messiah. Here was this man whom they experienced as the
Messiah. He was shockingly killed. It was a terrible degrading death. Equally
shocking: the Messiah was supposed to bring the final perfection: peace, dignity, prosperity, independence. Instead of doing all this, this Messiah died mi-
serably—according to some reports, even in despair and self-denial.

Now, as a believing Jew—the group still wasn't Christian—how does one
respond to this death? Does one say, "He was a false Messiah"? Does one
betray the original insight that this person is the Messiah? Or does one think:
"Maybe this death is another event that illuminates the meaning of the previous event?" Maybe the crucifixion is not a refutation of Jesus' being the
Messiah, but rather a clarification of the nature of redemption. Up to now, one
thought that the Messiah will straighten out the political and economic world—
because that was the mental image of what it means to perfect the world. But
if I know this was the Messiah but he did not bring worldly liberation, there
is an alternative to yielding faith. The alternative is to say that the death is
teaching a lesson. The lesson is: true redemption is not in this world. The Kingdom of God is within you. Faith leads to a world of spiritual perfection; even
though I am a slave, I am free in Christ.

The Christians responded faithfully but later history suggests they made
a hermeneutical error. To put it another way: in retrospect, it was a mistake to
say that the explanation of the crucifixion is that the redemption is beyond history. That judgment generated a fundamental continuing problem of Christi-

anity. In its faithfulness to its vision of Christ come—pitted against the shocking reality of a world of suffering and evil and poverty—Christianity is continually tempted to answer, "This vale of tears is not the real world. The world of suffering and oppression does not matter. It is trivial or secondary. The world that really counts is the spiritual world. That is where you can be born again—and free right now." But this finding betrays the fundamental claim of Judaism that life itself and not only afterlife will be perfected.

As they struggled with the meaning of their faithfulness to Jesus, Christians went on to make a second error, when the Destruction of the Temple came a generation later. But this error was again the outgrowth of a response of faith to a great historical event. (It should be noted that to respond with religious interpretation to great historical events is a classic Jewish faith paradigm.) In light of the Destruction, Jewish and Gentile Christians concluded that their initial conception that Jesus was the fulfillment of the Jewish promises within the bounds of Jewish life and hope was an error. If the Jews do not accept Jesus, even after their Temple is destroyed, is this not a proof that God has in fact rejected them? And using the same hermeneutical model, would not Gentile Christians conclude that the acceptance of Christianity in the world proves that Jesus came not to continue the old and the original covenant, but rather to bring a new covenant to humanity? And since the Jews failed to understand, have they not forfeited the promise? In short, the classic Christian interpretation that Christianity has superseded Judaism is an understandable hermeneutic, rooted in Jewish models of interpretation and capable of being derived in consistency with past Jewish modes of thinking.

With hindsight, one can say that this reasoning was deeply flawed in that it ignored God's fundamental faithfulness to the existing covenant. Even if newcomers were being chosen, and a new dimension of revelation was unfolding in Jesus' life and death, it did not necessarily follow that God was repudiating the Jews. The Divine love can hold "contradictory" covenantal positions and a variety of peoples in its embrace simultaneously. Understandably and very humanly, the people involved prefer to think that they have a new monopoly—but that is a very egocentric assumption.

The sad paradox is, that although "Judaic" thinking was involved in arriving at a supersessionist interpretation, the conclusion itself was devastating for future Jewish-Christian relations. In effect, the response to the Destruction created a model of relationship in which the mere existence of the Jews is a problem for Christianity. The obvious temptation—continually given in to—was to solve the problem by getting rid of the Jews.

There were and are three classic Christian ways of removing the Jewish problem. One was to insist that the Jews were not really alive—Judaism was a fossilized religion; Jews are children of the Devil: they are dead, but the Devil is pumping them up, etc. This is the way of caricature and dismissal; of stereotypes of legalism and spät Judentum, etc. In taking this tack, Christians did not deal with the possibility that God was keeping the Jews alive because God wanted their testimony to go on until the world itself was redeemed. The second way was to convert Jews to become Christians: so there would be no problem. However, by and large, the Jews declined to yield their witness.

The third way, if the other two did not work, was to kill the Jews—then there was no contradiction between Jewish existence and Christianity anymore.

The supersessionist interpretation continually tempted Christianity into being neither the gospel of love it wanted to be, nor the outgrowth of Judaism seeking to outreach and realize Israel's messianic dream that it could have been. Christianity was continually led to become an otherworldly, triumphalist religion that put its own mother down; it spit into the well from which it drank.

The Rabbis and the Jews had a similar problem from the other side. After all, they sensed the profound continuity from Judaism into Christianity. The hermeneutical language of Hebrew Scriptures makes many of the same claims. What made it worse, or more difficult, was that Christianity triumphed. Christianity became a world religion, far greater in its numbers than Judaism. How can one account for that, if one believes that Judaism is true and the Messiah has not come yet? In Jewish terms, could there be more clear proof of Christian claims than the fact that it triumphed in history?

The Jews, too, handled the problem by a series of responses. First: the Christian victory was not really a victory. Look how evil the world is even after Jesus' career. This is the bedrock of Jewish response to Christianity but it did not deal with the possibility that the nature of redemption was being redefined—or widened—or partially realized.

Second, Christianity is neither a gospel of love nor God's message—because look how cruel Christians are to Jews. Far from bringing redemption, Christianity has brought a whole new sum of evil and cruelty into the world. That is the best proof Christianity is not a true religion.

Third, Christians claim to supersede Jewry. Christians themselves say that if Christianity is the true faith, then Judaism does not exist or has no right to exist. But Jewry knows that it is alive and vital. Obviously, Christianity must be false. If your truth means that I am not valid, but I know my own validity—then you must be false.

The fourth Jewish response was that Christianity triumphed among the Gentiles. No Jew would fall for that fairytale of a virgin mother. If you were pregnant from someone else, what would you tell your husband? This is fundamentally how medieval Jews handled Christianity. Joseph was a fool enough to believe. With one Jew, you never can tell. But the Jews as a whole would not buy it. That a whole world would buy it proves that Gentile heads can be filled with anything. This understanding bred contempt for Gentiles rather than appreciation for their joining in the work of achieving total redemption, i.e., both worldly and spiritual. Of course, the contempt was earned and reinforced by Christian mistreatment of Jews.

Just as Christians were tempted to step out of history—because the Messiah had come already and the ongoing suffering was a problem, so the answer was history does not matter—so Jews were also tempted to step out of history—because in that arena, Christianity had won. To which the Jewish answer was that what happens in history now is unimportant. Christianity has triumphed—temporarily. When the final redemption comes, all these huge statues and towers will come crashing down, and humanity will know the truth. Jewry, this small, pitiful people which had no political clout, was really the heart of the world. All the rest was just a big, flashy show, up front—temporarily. Therefore, Judaism also stepped out of history to wait for its final redemption.

Rabbinic Judaism finally judged Jesus to be a false Messiah. This negative view conceded very little. Jesus was not the only false Messiah in Jewish history; he was neither the first nor the last. In the seventeenth century, Sabbatai Sevi, one of the great false Messiahs of Jewish history, swept the Jewish world. The Jews are still looking for a Messiah. So, if a few Jews followed Jesus, it proved nothing. The Rabbis concluded that Christianity is an alien growth, developed by those who followed a false Messiah.

The Rabbis perhaps erred here. Understandably, they did not do greater justice to Jesus because they were surrounded by an enemy (= Christians) one hundred times larger than Jewry, aggressively proselytizing and persecuting the Jews in the name of Jesus' claims. Out of defensiveness, the Rabbis confused a "failed" Messiah (which is what Jesus was) and a false Messiah. A false Messiah is one who has the wrong values: one who would teach that death will triumph, that people should oppress each other, that God hates us, or that sin and crime is the proper way. In the eighteenth century, a putative Jewish Messiah named Jacob Frank ended up teaching his people that out of sin comes redemption: therefore, one must sin. Such is a false Messiah.

A failed Messiah is one who has the right values, upholds the covenant, only did not attain the final goal. In the first century, 130–135, Bar Kochba, the great Jewish freedom fighter who led a revolt against Rome that temporarily drove Rome out of Jerusalem, sought to free the land. He was hailed by Rabbi Akiva and many great Rabbis as the Messiah. His rebellion was crushed; it did not bring that final step of redemption. It turned out that he was a failed Messiah. But Akiva did not repudiate him. Since when is worldly success a criterion of ultimate validity in Judaism?

Calling Jesus a failed Messiah is in itself a term of irony. In the Jewish tradition, failure is a most ambiguous term. Abraham was a "failure." He dreamt of converting the whole world to Judaism. At the end he ended up barely having one child carrying on the tradition; even that child he almost lost.

Moses was a "failure." He dreamt of taking the slaves, making them into a free people and bringing them to the Promised Land. They were hopeless slaves; they died slaves in the desert; neither they nor Moses ever reached the Promised Land.

Jeremiah was a "failure." He tried to convince the Jewish people that the Temple would be destroyed unless they stopped their morally and politically wrong policies; he tried to convince them to be ethically responsible, to free their slaves, not to fight Babylonia. No one listened.

All these "failures" are at the heart of divine and Jewish achievements. This concept of a "failed" but true Messiah is found in a rabbinic tradition of the Messiah ben Joseph. The Messiah ben David (son of David) is the one who brings the final restoration. In the Messiah ben Joseph's idea, you have a Messiah who comes and fails, indeed is put to death, but this Messiah paves the way for the final redemption.

In fact, Christians also sensed that Jesus did not exhaust the achievements of the final Messiah. Despite Christian claims that Jesus was a total success (the proof being that redemption has been achieved; it is of the otherworldly kind) even Christians spoke of a second coming. The concept of second coming, in a way, is a tacit admission—if at first you don't succeed, try, try again.

One might argue then that both sides claimed—and denied—more than was necessary in order to protect their own truth against the counter claims of the other. Both sides were too close to recognize each other, and too close and too conflicted to come to grips with each other's existence as valid in its own right. Both faiths stepped out of history to protect their own position—Christians denying that anything revelatory further can happen in history because Christ is the final revelation; Jews denying any further revelation in history because Judaism is a covenant that cannot be revoked.

There was even more theological fallout to these moves. Religion tended to abandon the world to Caesar or to Mammon. Religion all too often ended up as an opiate of the masses, i.e., promising people fulfillment in the great by-and-by if they accept suffering and the world as it is. In a way, each group was defining the sacred out of history into another realm.

Placing the sacred beyond history protected faith from refutation and disappointment but the cost was high. It is not surprising then that each faith tended to generate movements from time to time that sought to redress the balance or that sought to bring the "missing" part of redemption into being. What was defined as *"missing"* grew out of the interaction of tradition, local culture and the historical condition of the group. Since the concept of redemption can be pushed toward a spiritual realization or a worldly one, both religions developed parallel responses along a spectrum of positions within each faith. These developments further complicated relationship between the two faiths even as they insured even greater overlap and parallelism between them.

In retrospect, a key moment of division came in the differential response of the two groups to the Destruction of the Second Temple. The Christians reacted to the Destruction as the best proof that the Jews had forfeited their covenant. If the main vehicle and channel of Jewish relationship to God has been cut off and destroyed, is this not decisive proof that God has rejected Jews? In fact, the Jewish Christians left Jerusalem before the final Destruction—as the Jews saw it—thereby abandoning the Jewish people. Christians assumed that Jewry had no future and went off to make their own religion, their own faith, their own home, their own future.

The Christians were wrong. Judaism did not disappear, the Jews did not disintegrate. The Rabbis encountered a crisis equal to the early Christians' experience of the crucifixion, e.g., being cut off from the channel of revelation and connection to God, with the question gnawing at their faith: Why did evil triumph in this world? The same questions that Christians raised, Jews understood, too. Does the destruction mean that the Jews are finished? Does it mean that the covenant is finished? The Rabbis responded in faith in the covenant and trust in God and the goal. The Rabbis answered, as the prophets before them, that the destruction was punishment for sins, and therefore a mark of Divine concern—not rejection.

The most fundamental insight of the Rabbis was: Why did God not vanquish the Romans, even as God had destroyed the Egyptians? The Rabbis concluded that God had "pulled back"—not to abandon Jews and not to withdraw from this world because of some weakening of concern. Instead of splitting the Red Sea again, God was calling the people of Israel to participate more fully in the covenant. Instead of winning the war for the Jews, God was instructing the Jews to participate in redemption themselves. The Jews failed to do so adequately—they engaged in civil war and fought each other instead of the Romans. Since they had timed and conducted their rebellion wrongly, the Jewish failure was the Jewish failure, not God's rejection. The lesson of the Destruction was not that God had abandoned Israel, but that God was deliberately hiding in order to evoke a greater response, a greater participation in the covenantal way.

In the Biblical covenant God was, as it were, the senior partner: the one who took Israel out of Egypt, almost against its will: the one who sternly threatened and punished until Israel awoke and did the right thing. In the new stage of relationship, the Jews would become true partners in the covenant. The Rabbis are the first ones to use the term "partnership." Despite the fact that the covenant is a partnership by definition, nowhere in the Bible is the term "partnership" used. It was the Rabbis who were the first ones to realize the concept of partnership.

What this means was that the Destruction was a revelation, e.g., an event that illuminated the original Exodus. This revelation did not overwhelm the original with a message that death wins, but rather taught a new understanding and a new role for Israel in the covenant. It also dramatized the fact that the covenant itself is a pedagogical model that unfolds the relationship between Israel and God as Israel operates—and matures—in history.

In the course of rabbinic response and leadership, Judaism underwent a kind of "secularization" process. In the Temple, the manifest God showed overwhelming power. In the old Temple, God was so manifest that holiness was especially "concentrated" in Jerusalem. If one went into the Temple without the proper purification ritual, it was like walking into a nuclear reactor without shielding: one would inescapably die. The synagogue is a place one can enter with milder preparation and far less risk. The Divine is present but its power is "shielded."

In "hiding," Divine was calling on Israel to discern the Divine—which was hidden but present *everywhere.* The manifest God is visible in Jerusalem. The hidden God can be found everywhere. One need not literally go to Jerusalem to pray—one can pray anywhere in the world. The synagogue, which was a secondary institution before the Destruction, became a central institution after the Destruction. In the Temple, God spoke—either directly, or through the breastplate, or through the prophet. The synagogue is the place you go to when God no longer speaks to you.

The deepest paradox of the Rabbis' teaching was that the more God is hidden, the more God is present. The difference is that in the good old days one did not have to look—the Divine illumination lit up the world. Now, one must look. If one looks more deeply, one will see God everywhere. But to see God everywhere, one must understand. The key to religious understanding is learning. The Jewish people, which in Biblical times was an ignorant peasantry, awed by sacramental, revelatory experiences in the Temple, was trained by the Rabbis to learn and study. Now that God no longer speaks directly—how would one know what God wants? The answer is: go to the synagogue; there one does not see God visibly, but one prays and asks God for guidance.

God does not speak in a roaring voice from Heaven—"Thus saith the Lord." How does God speak now? Go ask a rabbi. Ask the prophet and the prophet says, "Thus saith the Lord"—it's a clear, unequivocal message, straight from the divine mouth. Ask a rabbi, "What does God want from me?" and the rabbi answers, "I do not have direct access. I will study the record of God's past revelation. I will study the precedents for the situation and give you my best judgment as to what God wants right now." Note that the human agent takes a much more active part in discerning God's will but the answer is much less certain at the end of the process. Whenever one asks a question, rabbis disagree. When there is human participation, there is disagreement—but both views are valid.

The Talmud, in one of its most insightful and humorous moments, tells how Israel adjusted to the shock of the pluralism of rabbinic authority. Initially, individual Rabbis could disagree and one could live with individual cases. Then, whole schools developed—in particular, the school of Hillel and the school of Shammai—and they disagreed on hundreds of cases. The initial reaction was: crisis! The reason for the disagreements was attributed to a failure to learn deeply enough. But then the systematic disagreement added up to the point where it was as if there were two different Torahs. But, then, obviously one of them was a false Torah. This threatened the credibility of both schools and cast doubts on the validity of Judaism. So they prayed: give us one last revelation—which of these schools is teaching the true Torah? So they prayed for two and one-half years, and a voice from Heaven spoke and said, ''Both are the words of the Living God.'' In fact, both could be right, and both *were* right. The disagreement is an argument on how best to get to redemption, not an argument on what God said.

In the triumph of the Rabbis, there was an incredible transformation of Judaism. The manifest, sacramental religion of the Bible was succeeded by the internalized, participatory, more ''laic'' faith of the Rabbinic period. Indeed, the Rabbis came to the conclusion that they had lived through events comparable almost to a reacceptance of the covenant. Even as Christians responded to their great religious experiences by proclaiming its record to be a New Covenant, Jews responded to theirs by affirming a *renewal* of the covenant.

In one classic Talmudic passage, the Rabbis deal with the relationship of redemption and revelation again. If the Exodus was the great redemptive event of the Manifest God, what is the great redemptive event of the Hidden God? The answer is: Purim. As told in the Book of Esther, the Jews were almost destroyed by a threatened genocide. How were the Jews saved? By political action. By court intrigue; one would say, by bedroom intrigue. After they won the king to their side, Jews had to fight to defend themselves. Thousands of people were killed in that fight. This is not clean, not neat, not like the good old days when God did it all. And nowhere in the Book of Esther is the name of God mentioned. But the Rabbis concluded that in those very events, the Hidden God was present. The fact that the Jews had reached the maturity of realizing that the Hidden God, working through human agents, using bedroom and courtroom intrigues, had saved the Jewish people, made Purim their redemptive event comparable to the Exodus.

In short, to reverse a classic Christian explanation of the relationship of Judaism and Christianity, I would argue that both Judaism and Christianity are outgrowths of and continuous with the Biblical covenant; that indeed Christianity is more closely tied to a previous Biblical mode—but not in the triumphalist way that Christianity has always claimed. Christianity is a commentary on the original Exodus, in which the later event—the Christ event—is a manifest, "Biblically" miraculous event—God becoming incarnate and self-validating through miracles. Obviously, many Jews will argue that closing the Biblically-portrayed gap between the human and the divine, between the real and ideal, by Incarnation, is idolatrous or at least against the grain of the Biblical way. But even if Incarnation is contradictory to some Biblical principles, the model itself is operating out of classic Biblical modes—the need to achieve redemption, the desire to close the gap between the human and divine which includes divine initiatives, etc. Thus, a faithful Jew can affirm that Incarnation is improbable and violative of other given Biblical principles and that it is unnecessary in light of the continuing career of the Jewish people; yet such a Divine gesture is not destructive of the original covenant if it was a Divine act intended for the salvation of the Gentiles, and "broadcast" to them rather than to the Jews. This interpretation grants Christianity legitimate roots in the Biblical covenant. And it allows faithful Jews to respect the distinctive theological claims of Christianity—and not just the models and values which Jews and Christians hold in common.

This approach also locks Christianity into a Biblical mode of theological action. This interpretation has been preferred by Christian anti-Jewish polemicists. However, they fail to see the cost to Christianity in this claim. This can be deemed a case of "arrested development." And in an era of secularity and human maturation, there is an additional risk of being identified as a sacramental salvation way which infantilizes people.

By contrast, stimulated by the Destruction, Judaism went into a second stage, continuous but developed out of the Biblical mode. In this stage, God is more hidden, Judaism is more worldly. In this stage, the human matures, and the covenantal model leads to greater responsibility for human beings. I consider the Rabbinic to be a more mature mode of religion. However, I would also affirm that the sacramental mode (Christianity) is most appropriate for Gentiles. This is the first step of Gentile covenantal relationship with God. Jews were in the same mode in their first stage, also. The choice of this mode bespeaks the Divine pedagogy of love which approaches people where they are and, only after they have grown into the covenant, leads them to new levels of relationship. This analysis permits the possibility that sacramental Christianity is in fact an extension of Biblical religion, e.g., one in which God is even *more* manifest and present. The committed Jew need not affirm this, indeed may be convinced it is an erroneous interpretation of God's message. But the committed Jew need not deny this either, need not foreclose any such divine option.

The above model of the relationship of Judaism and Christianity to each other and to Biblical faith is offered with great diffidence. The statement that Christianity is an extension of the Biblical mode can be misused to reassert the old Christian claim that Christianity is the true outgrowth of the Biblical covenant and that Judaism is cut off from its roots. Moreover, the model opens great vistas of Christian legitimacy in Jewish eyes without any guarantee that the ongoing Christian denial of Jewish validity will be stopped. My affirmations, then, may feed Christian triumphalism and supersessionism. I acknowledge the risk but I think it is worth risk to overcome the dismissals and divisiveness which weaken both religions' role. I turn to Christians in trust and love and depend on them to prevent repetition of the old triumphalist abuses. Failure to prevent would only prove that Christianity is not a valid hermeneutic on the Biblical covenant. It would suggest that the sum of woe brought into the world by Christianity will go on and on—which undermines its claim to be a legitimate major step forward on the road to redemption.

By the same token, many Christians will find the concept that God called Jewry to a new level of relationship in the covenant a denial of their own belief in Christ as the ultimate event. I do not underestimate the challenge in giving up the monopoly claims or in recognizing Judaism as a form of independently valid relationship to God. Yet, this model offers the affirmation of the fullest possibilities of Christ: from God incarnate to prophet or Messiah or teacher— freed at last of the incubus of hatred and monopolistic claims of owning God. For this model to work, Jews as well as Christians will have to have faith in the sufficiency of God's capacity to offer love enough for everyone and that the Lord who is the Makom/Place, who is ''the ground of all existence, has many messengers.''

III. IN A NEW ERA: AFTER MODERNITY AND AFTER HOLOCAUST AND REBIRTH OF ISRAEL

The history which both religions denied in order to claim their own absolute validity came back to haunt them. In the modern period, the revolt of humans against oppression, suffering and inequality led to enormous growth of secularism and rejection of religion. The demand for human freedom, for perfection of life, the demand to overcome sickness and death and poverty: all those demands that were central to Judaism and Christianity now took the form: get God (or religion) off our back and we can free humans finally. This theme runs straight through modern culture—be it Marxism in economic theory, or Freud in the psychological area, be it the warfare of science and religion or of critical scholarship and Revelation—free the human from God, and humanity can get that final redemption. Both Christianity and Judaism lost serious ground to revolt in the name of the very goal they were pledged to achieve in the first place. And both faiths were forced back into history by the over-whelming weight of modern culture and scholarship which continually dug at their claimed foundations, e.g., transcendent extra-historical truth. Modern scholarship insisted that the denial of history is false. Revelation is in history. To deny that, one must ignore or contradict archeology, anthropology, soci-ology, philosophy, history—which is to say, to be judged to be false, non-factual, by the standards of modern culture. Reluctantly but inexorably, both religions have been forced to confront their own historicity.

An event of great historical magnitude has now gone beyond modernity in pushing faith back into the maelstrom of history. In the Holocaust, Jews discovered they had no choice but to go back into history. If they did not have power, they would be dead. The only way to prevent a recurrence was for Jews to go to their land, establish a state and protect themselves, to take responsi-bility so that the covenant people could be kept alive. In this generation, the Jewish people—secular as well as religious—took responsibility for its fate, and for the fate of the divine covenant with Jewry. This is the meaning, not always recognized, of the re-establishment of the state of Israel.

Christians also have been forced back into history by the impact of this event. Those faithful Christians realized that the evil portrait of Judaism, the whole attempt to assure Christian triumphalism, had become a source of the teaching of contempt and had convicted Christianity or implicated it in a gen-ocide to which it was indifferent or silent. The Holocaust forced Jews and Christians to see that the attempt to protect faith against history was an error and that both religions can have no credibility in a world in which evil can totally triumph. I have argued elsewhere that the true lesson of the Crucifixion had been misunderstood by Christians because of their past triumphalism. In the light of the Holocaust, one would argue that the true lesson of the Cruci-fixion is that if God in person came down on earth in human flesh and was put on the cross and crucified, then God would be broken. God would be so ex-hausted by the agony that God would end up losing faith, and saying, "My God, my God, why have you forsaken me?" If God could not survive the cross, then surely no human can be expected to. So the overwhelming call for both religions is to stop the Crucifixion, not to glorify it. Just as Jews, in re-sponse, took up arms and took up the power of the state, so Christians are called simultaneously to purge themselves of the hatred that made them indif-ferent to others, and to take up the responsibility of working in the world to bring perfection. This is the common challenge of both faiths; they can ill af-ford to go on focusing on each other as *the* enemy.

There is another possible implication. Destruction of the temple meant that God was more hidden. Therefore, one had to look for God in the more "secular" area. Living after the Holocaust, the greatest destruction of all time in Jewish history, one would have to say that God is even more hidden. Therefore, the sacred is even more present in every "secular" area. Building a better world, freeing the slaves, curing sickness, responsibility for the kind of economic perfection that is needed to make this a world of true human dignity, all these activities pose as secular. But in the profoundest sort of way these activities are where God is most present. When God is most hidden, God is present everywhere. If, when God was hidden after the destruction of the Temple, one could find God in the synagogue, then when God is hidden after Auschwitz, one must find God in the street, in the hospital, in the bar. And that responsibility of holy secularity is the responsibility of all human beings.

Similarly, apply the rabbis' analysis of why God did not stop the Romans to the question of why God did not stop the Holocaust. The question is *not:* Where was God during the Holocaust? God was where God should have been during the Holocaust. God was with God's people—suffering, starving, being gassed and burnt alive. Where else would God be, when God's people are being treated that way?

The real question is: What was God's message when God did not stop the Holocaust? God is calling humans to take full responsibility for the achievement of the covenant. It is their obligation to take arms against evil and to stop it.

The implication of this model is that Judaism is entering a third stage, or at least a new level of covenantal development. This is the ultimate logic of covenant: If God wants humans to grow to a final perfection, then the ultimate logic of covenant is for humans to take full responsibility. This does not mean the human arrogance that dismisses God, the human arrogance that says more human power is automatically good. "Covenantal commitment" implies the humility of knowing that the human is not God. The human is like God but is ultimately called by God to be the partner. This implies the humility of recognizing that one is a creature as well as a creator. Using this covenantal understanding, one can perceive God as the Presence everywhere—suffering, sharing, participating, calling. But trust in God or awareness of God is necessary but not sufficient for living out faith. The awareness moderates the use of power; trust curbs power ethically. But the theological consequence is that without taking power, without getting involved in history, one is religiously irresponsible. To pray to God as a substitute for taking power is blasphemous.

The new human responsibility level implies that the events of our lifetime are revelatory. Therefore, one has to incorporate those events into religion and into our understanding. If we are to be true partners with God, and if we have full responsibility, then we are morally responsible for our own traditions. If there is anything in our own traditions that demeans, or denies, or degrades somebody else, then one cannot answer: it is the Word of God and so be it. One must answer: it is my responsibility. God has given me a call to take responsibility. Even if that means one must argue with God or confront God, that also is responsibility. If, indeed, God said that only a male can stand in for God, then someone who is faithful to God would have to argue with God: "It is not right—woman is also your creature, in your image." If God declared the Jews blind and hateful, to be treated as pariahs, then one must confront God and call God back to the universal love which God has revealed to humanity.

This is a time of major transformation in which the past experiences on the road to perfection are reinterpreted in light of the events of our lifetime for both religions. I believe we are living in an age of the Jewish reacceptance of the covenant. The re-creation of Israel is the classic covenantal symbol. If you want to know if there is a God in the world and is there still hope, if you want to know whether there is still a promise of redemption—the Bible says one goes back to Israel and makes the streets of Jerusalem resound with the laughter of children and the sounds of bride and groom dancing. That is what is happening in Jerusalem right now. This is true notwithstanding all the political, economic, and moral flaws of the new earthly Jerusalem. The flaws, the tragic conflicts with Arabs, the difficulties, all these are part of the fundamental proof that here we have the hidden Presence. This moment of revelation is fully human; this moment of redemption is humanly fully responsible in the presence of God.

One might suggest that the Holocaust has its primary impact on Judaism. Nevertheless, as a Jewish theologian, I suggest that Christianity also cannot be untouched by the event. At the least, I believe that Christianity will have to enter its second stage. If we follow the rabbis' model, this stage will be marked by greater "worldliness" in holiness. The role of the laity would shift from being relatively passive observers in a sacramental religion to full (or fuller) participation. In this stage, Christianity would make the move from being out of history to taking power, i.e., taking part in the struggle to exercise power to advance redemption. The religious message would be not accepting inequality but demanding its correction. The movement is toward learning and understanding as against hierarchy and mystery. Christians—as Jews—will recover the true role of Israel/Jacob who struggles with God and with people, for the sake of God and of humanity.

Unless this shift takes place, those Christians who seek to correct Christianity vis-à-vis Judaism will be blocked by the fact that within the New Testament itself are hateful images of Jews. Therefore, humans must take full responsibility—not out of arrogance, not out of idolatry. It must be done without making God into the convenient one who says what one wants to hear. Out of the fullest responsibility to its covenant partner, Christianity can undergo the renewal which I believe it must undertake.

The unfinished agenda of the Jewish-Christian dialogue is the recognition of the profound interrelationship between both. Each faith community experiencing the love of God and the chosenness of God was tempted into saying: I am the only one chosen. There was a human failure to see that there is enough love in God to choose again and again and again. Both faiths in renewal may yet apply this insight not just to each other but to religions not yet worked into this dialogue. Humans are called in this generation to renew the covenant—a renewal which will demand openness to each other, learning from each other, and a respect for the distinctiveness of the ongoing validity of each other. Such openness puts no religious claim beyond possibility but places the completion of total redemption at the center of the agenda.

Judaism as a religion of redemption believes that in ages of great destruction, one must summon up an even greater response of life and of re-creation. Nothing less than a messianic moment could possibly begin to correct the balance of the world after Auschwitz. This is a generation called to an overwhelming renewal of life, a renewal built on such love and such power that it would truly restore the image of God to every human being in the world.

NOTES

1. cf. I. Greenberg, "Cloud of Smoke, Pillar of Fire: Judaism, Christianity, and Modernity After the Holocaust," in Eva Fleischner, *Auschwitz: Beginning of a New Era?* (New York: KTAV, 1977), pp. 20–22.

2. *Ibid.*, p. 22.

Selected Official Catholic Statements
on Jewish-Christian Relations

EUGENE J. FISHER

This final section includes four addresses. Two are by Pope John Paul II, given in Mainz (1980) and in Rome (1982). These set forth the basic themes of the Holy Father's theological understanding of the Jewish-Christian relationship (Mainz) and its practical implications for the teaching of the Church (Rome).

The second two papers were given by Presidents of the National Conference of Catholic Bishops. Archbishop John R. Roach, addressing the Synagogue Council of America on March 12, 1981, interprets the teaching of the Pope. Bishop James Malone, addressing the National Workshop on Christian-Jewish Relations in St. Louis on October 29, 1984, speaks of the areas of progress that can be discerned in Catholic-Jewish dialogue today, beginning with the series of textbook "self-studies" initiated by the American Jewish Committee in the late 1950's. Bishop Malone's prayer for the "third millennium of our common history" is a fitting note on which to end this volume, with a new beginning.

John Paul II

DIALOGUE: THE ROAD TO UNDERSTANDING

Reprinted with permission from *Origins* (12/4/80).

I thank you for the friendly and sincere words of greeting. This meeting was my desire on the occasion of this apostolic visit and I thank you for responding to my wish. May God's blessing stand over us in this hour.

1. If Christians see each other as brothers and must treat each other ac-

cordingly, how much more should this be true when they stand before the Jewish people.

In the "Declaration on the Relations of the Church to Judaism" in April of this year, the bishops of the Federal Republic of Germany began: "Who meets Jesus Christ, meets Judaism." May I make these words my own.

The faith of the church in Jesus Christ, the son of David and son of Abraham (Mt. 1:1) contains in reality what the bishops in their declaration call "the spiritual legacy of Israel for the church" (Section II), a living legacy that must be understood and treasured in its profundity and its richness.

2. The concrete brotherly relation between Jews and Catholics in Germany takes on a quite special value in the dark background of the persecution and attempted elimination of the Jewish people in this country.

The innocent victims in Germany and elsewhere, the destroyed or dispersed families, the irretrievably lost cultural values and art treasures are a tragic demonstration of where discrimination and contempt for human dignity can lead, especially when this is inspired by perverse theories of the alleged differences in the values of races or the division of mankind into "worthy" and "worthy of life," as opposed to "without value" and "unworthy of life." Before God all men are equally worthy and important.

In this spirit, Christians during the persecution worked, often in danger, to prevent the suffering of their Jewish brothers or to moderate them. I extend to them, at this time, my recognition and thanks.

But there were also others who as Christians went to the end in the affirmation of their adherence to the Jewish people along the road of suffering with their brothers and sisters. Such was the great Edith Stein, in religion Theresa Benedicta of the Cross, whose memory is held justly in high honor.

I would also like to mention Franz Rosenzweig and Martin Buber, who through their creative familiarity with the Hebrew and with the German languages established a truly admirable bridge for a profound encounter between the two cultures.

You yourselves in your greetings mentioned that among the many efforts to create a new common life with Jewish fellow citizens, Catholics and the church have made decisive contributions. This recognition and the corresponding necessary cooperation on your part fills me with joy.

On my part, I must express my grateful admiration for your own related initiatives, including the recent creation of your institute of higher education in Heidelberg.

3. The depth and the richness of our common inheritance bring us together in a friendly dialogue and mutually trustful collaboration. I rejoice that this goes forward in this land conscientiously and with determination.

Many public and private initiatives in the pastoral, academic and social fields serve this end, for example, solemn occasions such as the recent *Kath-*

olikentag in Berlin. An encouraging sign also was the meeting of the International Liason Committee of the Roman Catholic Church and Judaism in the past year in Regensburg.

In all this it is not only a question of correcting a false religious view of the Jewish people, which caused in part the misunderstandings and persecution in the course of history, but above all a question of the dialogue between the two religions which—with Islam—can give to the world the belief in one ineffable God who speaks to us and which, representing the entire world, wish to serve him.

"The first dimension of this dialogue, that is the meeting between the people of God of the old covenant never retracted by God" (Rom. 11:29), on the one hand, and the people of the new covenant, on the other, is at the same time a dialogue within our own church, so to speak, a dialogue between the first and the second part of its Bible.

On this the "Directory for the Execution of the Conciliar Decree *Nostra Aetate*" states: "An effort will be made to acquire a better understanding of whatever in the Old Testament retains its own perpetual values . . . since that has not been cancelled by the later interpretation of the New Testament. Rather, the New Testament brings out the full meaning of the Old, while both Old and New illumine and explain each other" (II).

A second dimension of our dialogue—the real, central consideration—is the encounter between today's Christian churches and today's people of the covenant concluded with Moses. The postconciliar directive mentioned tells us how important it is that Christians tend to understand better the fundamental components of the religious tradition of Judaism and that they learn what fundamental lines are essential for the lived religious reality of Jews, according to their own understanding of it (Introduction).

The road to this reciprocal learning process is dialogue. I thank you, respected brothers, that you too lead the dialogue with the "opening and largeness of the spirit," with that "rhythm" and that prudence which were recommended to us Catholics by the above mentioned directives.

One result of this dialogue, and a sign pointing to its fruitful continuance, is the declaration of the German bishops already cited, "On the Relations of the Church to Judaism," of this past April. It is my earnest wish that this declaration becomes the spiritual property of all the Catholics of Germany!

I would like also to mention briefly a third dimension of our dialogue. The German bishops devote the concluding chapter of their declaration to the tasks that we have in common. Jews and Christians are called, as sons of Abraham, to be a blessing for the world (Gn. 12:2). They engage themselves jointly to work for peace and justice among all men and people and in the fullness and profundity that God himself has disposed for us and with readiness for the sacrifices that this high goal may impose on us. "The more this holy duty inspires our encounter, so much the more will it become for us a blessing."

4. In the light of this promise and this Abraham-like call I look with you toward the destiny and the role of your people among the peoples. I gladly pray with you for the fullness of *shalom* for all your brethren of the same faith and the same people and also for the land to which all Jews look with special reverence.

Our century witnessed the first pilgrimage of a pope in the Holy Land. Here, in concluding, I can repeat the words of Paul VI at his entrance into Jerusalem: "By your wishes and your prayers, invoke with us upon this land, unique in the world, which God has visited, his graces of concord and of peace. Let us here, all together, implore the grace of true profound brotherhood between all men and among all peoples . . . 'May those who love you prosper! May peace be within your walls, prosperity in your buildings; I will say, Peace be within you!. . . I will pray for your good' (Ps. 122,6–9)."

May all the peoples in Jerusalem be blessed and reconciled in Abraham. He, the ineffable, of whom all his creation speaks. He who does not constrain mankind to the good but guides it nevertheless. He who announces our destiny and is silent. He who has chosen us for all to his people. He who guides us on his roads in his future.

May his name be praised. Amen.

Mainz. Nov. 17, 1980

John Paul II

THE IMPORTANCE OF JEWISH-CHRISTIAN RELATIONS

Reprinted with permission from *Origins (3/25/82)*.

You have gathered here in Rome from different parts of the world to explore the important matter of relations between the Catholic Church and Judaism. The importance of this problem is also emphasized by the presence among you of representatives of the Orthodox Churches, the Anglican Communion, the Lutheran World Federation and the World Council of Churches. I am glad to be able to greet all these especially and to thank them for their collaboration.

I likewise express all my gratitude to you who are bishops, priests, religious, Christian laity. Like your commitments in pastoral activities or in the field of biblical and theological research, your presence here shows the degree to which relations between the Catholic Church and Judaism touch on various aspects of the church and her activities.

This is easily understood. The Second Vatican Council said in its declaration on the church's relations with non-Christian religions, *Nostra Aetate* (no. 4): "As this sacred synod searches into the mystery of the church, it recalls the spiritual bond linking the people of the new covenant with Abraham's stock." I myself have had occasion to say more than once: Our two religious communities "are linked at the very level of their identities" (cf. Discourse of March 12, 1979, to representatives of Jewish organizations and communities.) Indeed, and I again quote the text of the declaration *Nostra Aetate* (no. 4):

"The church of Christ acknowledges that, according to the mystery of God's saving design, the beginnings of her faith and her election are already found among the patriarchs, Moses, and the prophets . . . The church therefore cannot forget that she received the revelation of the Old Testament through this people . . . She ever keeps in mind the words of the apostle Paul about his kinsmen, 'who have the adoption as sons, and the glory, and the covenant and the legislation and the worship and the promises; who have the fathers, and from whom is Christ according to the flesh' (Rom. 9:4–5), the son of the Virgin Mary.''

This is as much as to say that the links between the church and the Jewish people are grounded in the design of the God of the covenant, and that as such, they have necessarily left traces in certain aspects of the church's institutions, especially in the liturgy.

Certainly since a new bough appeared from the common root, 2,000 years ago, we know that relations between our two communities have been marked by resentments and a lack of understanding. If there have been misunderstandings, errors and even insults since the day of separation, it is now a question of overcoming them with understanding, peace and mutual esteem. The terrible persecution suffered by the Jews in various periods of history have finally opened many eyes and disturbed many hearts. Thus Christians are on the right path, that of justice and brotherhood, when they seek, with respect and perseverance, to gather with their Semitic brethren around the common heritage which is a treasure to us all.

Is there any need to point out, above all to those who remain skeptical or even hostile, that such rapprochement should not be confused with a certain religious relativism, still less with a loss of identity? For their part, Christians profess their faith without equivocation in the universal salvific character of the death and resurrection of Jesus of Nazareth.

Yes, clarity and awareness of our Christian identity are an essential basis for achieving authentic, fruitful and lasting relationships with the Jewish people. I am happy to know that in this regard you are making many efforts, by studying and praying together, to grasp better and to formulate more clearly the often difficult biblical and theological problems raised by the progress of the Judeo-Christian dialogue. May God grant that Christians and Jews may hold more in-depth exchanges based on their own identities, without ever allowing either one or the other side to be obscured, but always seeking truly for the will of the God who revealed himself.

Such relationships can and ought to help enrich the knowledge of our own roots and to shed more light on certain aspects of this identity which we have. Our common spiritual heritage is considerable. Help in better understanding certain aspects of the church's life can be gained by taking an inventory of that heritage, but also by taking into account the faith and religious life of the Jewish people as professed and lived now as well. This is the case with the liturgy. Its roots have still to be more deeply traced, and above all need to be better known and appreciated by the faithful. This is true at the level of our institutions, for they have been inspired ever since the beginning of the church by certain aspects of the synagogue's community organization. Finally, our common spiritual patrimony is above all important at the level of our faith in one sole and unique God, who is good and merciful, who loves men and makes himself loved by them (cf. Song.' 11:24–26), who is master of history and of men's destinies, who is our Father, and who chose Israel, "that good olive tree onto which have been grafted the wild olive branches of the gentiles" (*Nostra Aetate*, 4; cf. also Rom. 11:17–24).

This is why you have been concerned during your session with Catholic teaching and catechesis in regard to the Jews and Judaism. You have been guided on this point, as on others, and have been encouraged by the "Guidelines and Suggestions for Implementing the Council Declaration *Nostra Aetate* (no. 4)," published by the Commission for Religious Relations with the Jews (cf. Chapter III). It is necessary to get to the point where such teaching at the various levels of religious instruction and in catechesis with children and adolescents will not only present the Jews and Judaism in an honest and objective manner, but will also do so without any prejudice or offense to anyone and, even more, with a lively awareness of that heritage that we have broadly outlined.

Finally, it is on such a basis that close collaboration will be able to be established—it is already making itself very happily felt. Our common heritage impels us toward this, our common heritage of service to man and his immense spiritual and material needs. We shall be able to go by diverse—but in the end, convergent—paths with the help of the Lord, who has never ceased loving his people (cf. Rom. 11:1), to reach true brotherhood in reconciliation, respect, and full accomplishment of God's plan in history.

218   *Eugene J. Fisher*

I am happy to encourage you, dear brothers and sisters in Christ, to continue on the path you have taken, giving proof of your discernment and confidence, as well as your very great fidelity to the magisterium. In this way you provide an authentic service to the church, flowing from her mysterious vocation, and contribute to the good of the church, the Jewish people and all of mankind.

Rome. March 6, 1982

Archbishop John R. Roach

A RENEWED VISION OF CATHOLIC-JEWISH RELATIONS

Reprinted with permission from *Origins* (5/7/81).

Catholic-Jewish relations have progressed remarkably in the few years that have elapsed since the Second Vatican Council in its declaration, *Nostra Aetate,* called the church to a renewed vision of its ancient relationship with the Jewish people.

From the point of view of the church, this renewal in dialogue is much more than simply an exercise in good neighborliness. It is, as Pope John Paul II stated in his first meeting with representatives of the world Jewish community two years ago this month, a "solemn mandate," which reaches the essence of the Christian community's own self-understanding. "Thus," the pope declared, "it (is) understood that our two religious communities are connected and closely related at the very level of their respective religious identities" (NC News, March 15, 1979).

It must be admitted, in deep sorrow, that what the council called "the spiritual bond" linking our two peoples tended to slip from our awareness for long periods in centuries past. Often it was honored more in the breach than in the proper spirit of love. Yet since we believe the link to be divinely forged, out of the very election of our two peoples to serves God's will, the Christian must proclaim that it is a link which can never be wholly broken.

Today, through dialogue, Christians are coming to realize that many of our previous assumptions about the nature of Judaism were, to put it kindly, wrong. Thus we tended to cast what *Nostra Aetate* called, "the spiritual legacy of Israel for the church" almost exclusively in negative terms, deeming that legacy a past reality abrogated by the coming of Christ and superseded by the Christian dispensation. That such a view impoverishes Christianity as well as doing injustice to the integrity of Judaism is now increasingly recognized in our community (cf. "Statement on Catholic-Jewish Relations," National Conference of Catholic Bishops, Nov. 20, 1975). Indeed, the pope, in his most recent statement to the Jewish community on the occasion of his visit to Germany last fall, specifically interpreted *Nostra Aetate* as calling for an appreciation of Judaism as "a *living* legacy" that must be understood by Christians "in its profundity and richness" (NC News, Nov. 20, 1980; italics added).

This statement of the pope in Germany, I believe, deserves closer attention than it has received to date. For in it the pope both consolidates insights gained from the dialogue and projects in a few short paragraphs his own vision of its structure and future possibilities.

The pope discerns three essential and interrelated dimensions in the dialogue. I would like to recall these with some particular references to the situation in our own country.

1. The first dimension flows from the past, from our common origins and the roots of Christianity in Judaism. From this perspective, the pope sees today's dialogue as "the meeting between the people of God of the old covenant never retracted by God (Rom. 11:29) on the one hand, and the people of the new covenant on the other." The phrase "never retracted by God" needs to be underscored. It at once rebuts all old claims of Christian triumphalism (the so-called "teaching of contempt") and opens up the way for an entirely new relationship between two living traditions on the basis of mutual respect for each other's essential religious claims.

Obviously this formulation does not answer all our questions about each other or, frankly, about ourselves. In this context the pope notes that the dialogue with Jews is "at the same time a dialogue within our own church, a dialogue between the first and second parts of its Bible." He cautions Catholics to hold fast to biblical values which "have not been obliterated by later interpretations of the New Testament (cf. "Guidelines and Suggestions for Implementing the Conciliar Decree, *Nostra Aetate*," Rome, Dec. 1, 1974)."

It is good to be able to note here the many dialogues taking place in this country on the academic levels which seek to plumb the mysteries of the unique covenant relationship between our two peoples. One such is the joint "Historical Reflection on the Notion of Covenant" which took place in Los Angeles in March of 1979. Others can be seen in the many dialogues sponsored on the national level by our own secretariat for Catholic-Jewish relations with a variety of Jewish and Protestant agencies.

2. The second dimension of the dialogue for the pope is the encounter in the present between the churches and "today's people of the covenant concluded with Moses." Note again the pope's insistence on the church's acceptance of the continuing and permanent election of the Jewish people. Such a notion calls for Christian appreciation of Judaism's own self-definition and for

an awareness that the church has a very real stake in the survival and prosperity of the Jewish people today.

This second dimension, which the pope terms "a reciprocal learning process," obviously will entail a full-scale engagement of people on all levels of our respective communities, from the local to the international. Here, I believe, is where the uniqueness of the American experience can make a significant contribution to the endeavors of the universal church and world Jewry. Not only is America blessed by being able to count the world's largest Jewish community among its citizens, but its history of pluralism has provided a fit setting for contacts and cooperation all through our shared history on these shores. The Catholic and Jewish Communities in this country have undergone common immigrant experiences and developed remarkably similar patterns of coping with the problems of assimilation and nativist rejection. Such shared experience and common commitment to pluralism provides a solid foundation for further sharing today.

The national workshops on Christian-Jewish relations (the sixth of which will take place in Milwaukee Oct. 26–29, 1981) thus reflect in the diversity and range of topics discussed the manifold concerns of our two communities. We will need to develop ever better educational tools and sources if the fruits of such dialogues are to be passed on to succeeding generations of our youth.

3. The third dimension of dialogue suggested by the pope is oriented from the present into the future. Here, he urges our attention to "the tasks that we have in common . . . to work jointly for peace and justice" in the world. Such joint social action as understood by the pope is not merely a secular enterprise but a properly religious one, a "holy duty." The pope thus finds its source deep within the biblical tradition, in the call to Abraham "to be a blessing for the world" (Gn. 12:1).

Again it is good to be able to note the many steps already being taken in this country to live up to the concreteness of this challenge. Our conference has cooperated with Jewish agencies on a variety of programs, from migration services to action for Soviet Jewry to educational efforts aimed at the elimination of prejudice. Joint or parallel statements on the important social issues of our times continue to mark our cooperative efforts. The ongoing discussion of the religious foundations of social policy in the Catholic and Jewish traditions, sponsored by ourselves and the Synagogue Council at the University of Notre Dame (and aided by a National Endowment for the Humanities grant), have been especially important in achieving the understanding necessary for successful cooperative action.

We do not, of course, always agree on social matters. But we have shown an ability to continue to dialogue despite such differences as, for example, in the meetings held between the Synagogue Council and ourselves concerning abortion over the past several years.

Finally, running through the three-dimensional pattern of dialogue as sketched by the pope, I believe is a sense of hope, one might even say of eschatological longing. This is the longing for the kingdom of God, whose vision we share. Such a vision can provide us with a proper goal for the endeavor of dialogue as a whole. In the perspective of the kingdom we can find a sense of common witness, a witness to the world by Jews and Christians together. In this perspective, past practices of false proselytism are eschewed in favor of a deeper awareness of the nature of our mission.[1] As the pope comments: "In all this it is not only a question of correcting a false religious view of the Jewish people, which caused, in part, the misunderstandings and persecution in the course of history, but above all a question of the dialogue between the two religions which, with Islam, can give to the world the belief in one ineffable God who speaks to us and . . . the entire world."

The pope, who began his talk with a poignant reference to the Holocaust,[2] ended with a moving tribute to Israel, "this unique land visited by God . . . the land to which all Jews look with special reverence."[3] This statement recalls that made by our own conference in 1975:

"Jews have explained that they do not consider themselves as a church, a sect or a denomination as is the case among Christian communities, but rather as a peoplehood that is not solely racial, ethnic or religious, but in a sense a composite of all these . . . Whatever difficulties Christians may experience in sharing this view they should strive to understand the link between land and people which Jews have expressed in their writing and worship throughout two millenia as a longing for the homeland holy Zion" (NCCB, Nov. 20, 1975).

We have, after all, been listening and learning in dialogue. I can only pray that such mutual cooperation will continue. Linked together in the perspective of the past which calls us into being and of the future which gives us our destiny, Catholics and Jews can today work and dialogue together as never before in all the ages of our often troubled yet still common history.

NOTES

1. For a fuller study of this question, see T. Federici, "Study Outline on the Mission and Witness of the Church," presented to the International Vatican-Jewish Liaison Committee Meeting in Venice, March 28, 1977, published in SIDIC journal (Vol. 9:3, 1978) 25–34, and Origins (Vol. 8, 1978) 273ff.

2. The pope's compassionate understanding of the tragedy of the Holocaust was clearly revealed in his pilgrimage to Auschwitz in 1979: "I am here today as a pilgrim. It is well known that I have been here many times. So many times . . . among the ruins of the crematorium furnaces . . . I kneel on this modern Golgotha of the modern world, on these tombs largely nameless like

the great Tomb of the Unknown Soldier. I kneel before all the inscriptions that come one after another bearing the memory of the victims of Oswiecim (Auschwitz) . . . In particular I pause with you before the inscription in Hebrew. This inscription awakens the memory of the people whose sons and daughters were intended for total extermination . . . It is not permissible for anyone to pass by this inscription with indifference'' (Origins, June 2, 1979).

3. In his homily at Otranto the pope specifically linked the Holocaust with the rebirth of the Jewish state of Israel. This is the strongest expression to date of papal recognition of the support for the moral legitimacy of Israel, a fact largely overlooked in the controversy over the second portion of the statement, which some have construed to be a vindication of certain Palestinian claims. "The Jewish people, after tragic experiences connected with the extermination of so many sons and daughters, driven by the desire for security, set up the state of Israel." (L'Osservatore Romano, Oct. 13, 1980).

New York. March 12, 1981

Bishop James Malone

THE STATE OF JEWISH-CHRISTIAN RELATIONS

Reprinted with permission from *Origins* (12/6/84).

I feel privileged as president of the National Conference of Catholic Bishops to be part of this panel. I am happy to join the president of the National Council of Churches and the president of the Synagogue Council of America in this keynote presentation. I do hope that our tripartite presence illustrates the significance we attach to the Jewish-Christian dialogue of this workshop.

In a preliminary remark or two, I want to assure you that I consider this workshop gathering a graced occasion for us to explore further the relationship between the Christian church and the Jewish people.

This workshop has come a long way in about 10 years time. We began as a single local dialogue unit in the early 1970s, and look at our workshop program and its outreach today!

Strange to relate, but 10 years ago "holocaust" was an unusual word to many Christian ears. And many other Christians had a hard time figuring out why they had to face up to the tragic lessons which the Holocaust could teach them.

But, thank God, the climate between Christians and Jews is clearing and improving. As we struggle toward better understanding of one another, we can resonate with the words of Pope John Paul II. He said, ''The terrible persecutions suffered by the Jews in various periods of history have finally opened many eyes and disturbed many hearts.''

I must admit that Pope John Paul's words especially impress me, because he himself personally experienced the horrors of Nazi domination in his native Poland.

On another occasion, the pope spoke to the Jewish community in Mainz, West Germany. He said that our interfaith agenda is a ''holy task which God himself has disposed for us.'' And the pope also asserted that ''Jewish-Christian dialogue can be a sign to the world of belief in the one ineffable God who calls to us.''

Now I am quoting Pope John Paul in these preliminary remarks of mine not only because I consider his words on target for this workshop audience, but also because some other items in his West Germany remarks are so encouraging to us participants in this dialogue.

I like, for example, his exhorting Christians to acknowledge the continuing validity of God's covenant with the Jewish people.

No less do I treasure the pope's call for us Catholics to see the Catholic Church's own mission in the proper context of a joint witness with the Jewish people, to the world, for the upbuilding of God's kingdom among us.

Well, my point is that our workshop convenes us to pursue many of the objectives of which the Holy Father has so persuasively spoken. I note with approval that our 1984 workshop agenda is studded with many examples of Jews and Christians cooperating in examining justice and peace issues.

All in all, I congratulate the planners of this assembly for the substance and scope of the program, and for the sensitivity and creativity which mark their workshop design.

Before indicating what I consider three points of progress in our Christian-Jewish relations from the Catholic point of view, I do want to remark, by way of overview, about the growing number of dialogues and about the increased number of publications on the Christian-Jewish theme.

The dialogues range from a major conference like this to academic symposia, and on to local Catholic-parish and Jewish-synagogue people dialogues.

And the publications are both scholarly and popular. They range in topics from biblical study to shared social goals for the betterment of humankind.

Compared to the deep silence between our communities in days gone by, our current conversations and lively exchanges can be described as a great clamor to give and to receive information about each other's families and traditions.

But can we really count the friendly miles we have walked thus far together? Can we somehow measure our progress in Christian-Jewish relations?

I, for one, think we can, and I want to number three points of progress from a Catholic perspective.

First of all, I cite better-balanced Catholic religious education materials touching upon the Jewish community. Perhaps the clearest example of the impact of the Second Vatican Council on improved Catholic-Jewish relations stands in the area of Catholic religious education materials, the portrayal of Jews and Judaism in Catholic religious textbooks. These studies were then made available to the Catholic bishops at the Second Vatican Council in the early 1960s.

Similarly, as you probably also know, Protestant religious books were scrutinized by the late Dr. Bernhard Olson at Yale University.

About roughly the same time, Jewish religion-teaching materials were examined at Dropsie University and additional Catholic materials here at St. Louis University.

What were the results of these efforts? Well, for one thing, the composite picture of how we Christians and Jews described each other was not flattering and, to say the least, it was an incomplete picture.

But the good news is that by 1977, the picture changed for the better. In 1977, Dr. Eugene Fisher, now on our National Conference of Catholic Bishops staff, analyzed Catholic religious teaching materials published since the close of the Second Vatican Council. Dr. Fisher reported welcome and startling improvement in the ways Jews and Judaism were described in Christian religion texts.

Erased was the notion that Jews collectively could be considered responsible for the death of Jesus. Lifted up in the textbooks was the Jewishness of Jesus and of the apostles.

But let me say—loud and clear—that in the Catholic community, we have set in motion an irreversible dynamic whereby Jews and Judaism are presented and explained in positive fashion. Many Jewish scholars and Jewish leaders helped in the development of that dynamic, and I thank them.

In this connection, I remember in 1975 voting to issue a statement which I reaffirm in the face of this company today. In part it said, ''The clarification of our Catholic teaching about the Jews pertains as much to the purity of the Catholic faith as it does to the defense of Judaism.''

A second benchmark of progress in Christian-Jewish relations can be etched in the record—namely, the growth and the improvement of this very national workshop in which we are engaged.

Begun in my native Ohio in 1973, this enterprise has grown from a baker's dozen participants to 1,200 registrants at the 1983 Boston workshop. They traveled from seven countries and numbered representatives from the World Council of Churches, the International Conference of Christians and Jews, and from the Holy See.

In my judgment, this workshop has earned itself the accolade of "the most significant regular meeting of Christians and Jews in the world today."

Perhaps a more prestigious accolade was bestowed by Pope John Paul on the dialogue concept which permeates our workshop agenda. The pope calls dialogue between the Catholic Church and the Jewish people "a necessity for the full accomplishment of God's plan in history."

And—may I add—when, almost 10 years ago, the Holy See issued guidelines for our Catholic-Jewish relations, they wrote, "It is when pondering her own mystery, that the church encounters the mystery of Israel."

I turn your attention now to the third measure of progress in Catholic-Jewish relations, and that is the many statements on this topic formulated by Catholic bishops worldwide and the additional supportive statements by the popes. They exhibit a gradual and distinct line of developed understanding of the spiritual relationship between the Catholic Church and the Jewish people. I can best describe it as a shift from earlier days when Christian apologists imposed on Judaism a set of ideas alien to Jewish tradition in an effort to prove Christian superiority over it. In its place there stands now the welcome posture of the church in a listening mode, listening to what Jews are saying both in the spheres of religious teaching and of social policy.

As regards a change in Catholic bishops' statements on the Jewish community, I cite, over the past 15 years, the pronouncements of the bishops of Austria, Holland, Belgium, France, Switzerland, Germany, Brazil and the United States.

At the level of the Holy See during the same period, the popes have voiced strong support to the local churches in their efforts to implement the Vatican Council teaching on interfaith relations. In my opinion, no pope has been more outspoken than John Paul II. Nor has any other pope showed himself as ready as Pope John Paul to meet with the leaders of the Jewish community at the Vatican and in his international travels.

But now, having offered my opinion of the three growth areas in our Catholic-Jewish association over the past two decades, I turn our attention to how we Christians and Jews approach certain social questions of our day.

To quote Pope John Paul again, he describes dialogue as a "reciprocal learning process." Further, the Holy Father stresses his sense of a joint witness of Jews and Christians to the world in the name of the one ineffable God who speaks to us both.

Citing the 12th chapter of Genesis, the pope declares, "Jews and Christians are called, as children of Abraham, to be a blessing for the world."

Highly significant, I think, is Pope John Paul's challenge to Christians and Jews that we "engage jointly to work for peace and justice among all people."

Those words focus our attention on the tasks we can work at together, as we develop the kingdom of God which both Jews and Christians await.

The context for our relationship is our sense of common purpose in forming the kingdom. Despite sometimes differing social agendas, Christians and Jews are closely associated by the scriptures we share and by the God who brings us into being. We are united on a level more profound than the contemporary issues which may divide us. As John Paul puts it, "Christians and Jews are linked at the very level of their identities as religious communities."

Frequently, of course, many Catholics and many Jews share similar views of current social issues; for example, international peace and the nuclear arms race or on certain domestic issues such as health care and economic justice and the family.

This convergence of viewpoints is not altogether surprising. On the one hand, we Christians and Jews often ground our social vision in a common source, namely, the Hebrew prophets. On the other hand, we work out our views either halachically in the Jewish tradition or by theological reflection as in the Catholic tradition.

At times, of course, we disagree between us on the specific value applications we make to social questions. But however forcefully we diverge in our viewpoints, may we move apart ever more respectfully. Again in the pope's words, Be aware of the "mutual esteem" that is to characterize our dialogue with each other.

As we try to address social issues, complaints arise now and again. We need to answer them sensitively. For example, certain Catholics occasionally complain that they are tired hearing Jews talk about the Holocaust and about the homeland state of Israel at the very times they want to talk about social topics. By contrast, certain Jews complain that Christians do not want to become involved in dialogue and joint undertakings; they want only to be left alone.

Complaints like these, in my opinion, need to be faced as they are voiced, because they illustrate the continuing need for dialogue between us.

In fact, I think, we Catholics have not yet come to grips with the implications of the Holocaust for ourselves and for our Jewish neighbors. We Catholics are only beginning to learn from Jews about the traumas which the Holocaust has worked on the Jewish community and upon the wider world community.

Attention needs also be given to the revisionists who assert that the Holocaust never happened. Both Christians and Jews can condemn this new anti-Semitic twist for the lie it is.

At the same time, acknowledgment is due that all-too-many Catholics were, in fact, among the executioners of death-camp inmates. But equally to be acknowledged are the millions of Catholics and the thousands of their clergy who were themselves victims of death-camp executioners.

Part of the Christian tragedy is that untold numbers of Christians lost their lives attempting to shelter Jews.

Part of the Christian tragedy, too, is that Christians were numbered both among the executioners and among the victims. At one and the same time, Christians were both oppressor and oppressed.

Trying to piece together the meaning of our Christian-Jewish relationship in the wake of such contradictory realities is a complex and demanding task for Christians and Jews alike. What are we to do? We need to seek reconciliation with each other, patiently and persistently, as sons and daughters of the one God. Reconciliation—our only adequate response.

Another significant topic for us is our attitude toward the state of Israel.

As regards the state of Israel, I can best state my attitude by reaffirming the 1975 statement of our bishops' conference:

"In dialogue with Christians, Jews have explained that they do not consider themselves as a church, a sect or a denomination, as is the case among Christian communities, but rather as a peoplehood that is not solely racial, ethnic or religious, but in a sense a composite of all these. It is for such reasons that an overwhelming majority of Jews see themselves bound in one way or another to the land of Israel. Most Jews see this tie to the land as essential to their Jewishness. Whatever difficulties Christians may experience in sharing this view, they should strive to understand this link between land and people which Jews have expressed in their writing and worship throughout two millennia as a longing for the homeland, Holy Zion."

These sentiments of our U.S. bishops' conference set forth a religious position, not a political one. Our words leave unsaid much more that needs expression between us on the topic of the state of Israel. I, for one, look forward to dialogue in the spirit of Pope John Paul, who said to the Jewish community of Germany:

"I look with you toward the destiny and the role of your people among the peoples. I gladly pray with you for the fullness of *shalom* for all your brethren of the same faith and the same people, and also for the land to which all Jews look with special reverence."

May I conclude my remarks by observing that as the 1980s move to their midpoint, our thoughts and aspirations turn toward the year 2000 and to our entry into the third millennium of our common history.

I pray that together we may share a vision of increased understanding and greater cooperation among Christians and Jews in days to come.

I hope for our children and for our children's children a greater measure of *shalom*.

NOTES ON THE CONTRIBUTORS

JUDITH HERSHCOPF BANKI is Associate National Director of Interreligious Affairs of the American Jewish Committee and works with the leaders of all religious groups to advance communication and understanding between religious communities. She authored *The Image of the Jews in Catholic Teaching* for consideration by the Vatican Council Commission which drafted the historic declaration on the relationship of the Church to the Jews. Her articles have appeared in a variety of publications, including *Religious Education* and the *Journal of Ecumenical Studies*. She is editor of the *Interreligious Newsletter*, a review of trends and developments in interreligious affairs. She planned and coordinated the national "Faith Without Prejudice" conference at St. Louis University and has spoken at various regional and local institutes on this theme.

LAWRENCE BOADT, C.S.P. is Associate Professor of Sacred Scripture at the Washington Theological Union in Washington, D.C., and an editor at Paulist Press. He received his doctorate in Biblical Studies and Near Eastern Languages from the Pontifical Biblical Institute in Rome and is the author of numerous articles and books on the Hebrew Scriptures. His most recent title is *Reading the Old Testament: An Introduction* (Paulist Press, 1984).

MICHAEL J. COOK is Professor of Intertestamental and Early Christian Literature at the Hebrew Union College, in Cincinnati, where he earned his Ph.D. He has served on the Executive Board of the Central Conference of American Rabbis, and as Visiting Professor at Xavier University and textbook consultant for the Archdiocese of Louisville. His books include *Mark's Treatment of the Jewish Leaders* (Brill, 1978) and *The Jewish People in Christian Preaching* (Mellen, 1984); his articles include "Judaism, Early Rabbinic & Hellenistic," in the *Interpreter's Dictionary of the Bible*, Volume 5; "Jesus and the Pharisees: The Problem As It Stands Today," in the *Journal of Ecumenical Studies*, Volume 15 (1978):441–460; "Anti-Judaism in the New Testament," in the *Union Seminary Quarterly Review*, Volume 38 (1983):135–147; and "Samuel Sandmel on Christian Origins," in *Nourished with Peace* (Denver, 1984).

EUGENE J. FISHER is Executive Secretary of the Secretariat for Catholic-Jewish Relations of the National Conference of Catholic Bishops. He holds his Ph.D. from New York University in Hebrew Culture and Education. In 1981 he was named Consultor to the Vatican's Commission for Religious Relations with the Jews by Pope John Paul II, and in 1985 was named a member of the International Catholic-Jewish Liaison Committee. Author of over one hundred articles for scholarly and popular journals, his previous volumes include *Faith Without Prejudice* (Paulist, 1977), *Social Policy in the Catholic and Jewish Traditions* (University of Notre Dame Press, 1980), *Liturgical Foundations in the Catholic and Jewish Traditions* (University of Notre Dame Press, 1983), *Seminary Education and Christian-Jewish Relations* (NCEA, 1983), and *The Challenge of Shalom* (UAHC/NCCB, 1985).

EDWARD H. FLANNERY is Director of Continuing Education of the Clergy of the Diocese of Providence, R.I., member of the Advisory Committee of the Secretariat of Catholic-Jewish Relations (NCCB), and President of the National Christian Leadership Conference for Israel. Rev. Flannery has held posts as Associate Director of the Institute of Judaeo-Christian Studies and member of the faculty of Seton Hall University, Executive Secretary of the Secretariat for Catholic-Jewish Relations, and consultor to the Vatican Secretariat for Catholic-Jewish Relations (1969–74). He is author of *The Anguish of the Jews* (Updated and revised) (Paulist, 1985), and has contributed chapters to *The Sunflower*, edited by Simon Weisenthal (Schocken, 1976), *When God and Man Failed: Non-Jewish Views of the Holocaust*, edited by H.J. Cargas (Macmillan, 1981) and *The Deepening Dialogue*, edited by R. Rousseau (Ridge Row, 1983). He is author of numerous booklets and articles in *The Bridge*, the *New Catholic Encyclopedia*, and many Jewish and Christian journals and magazines.

IRVING (YITZ) GREENBERG is an ordained Orthodox rabbi, scholar and prominent lecturer. He is President of CLAL—The National Jewish Center for Learning and Leadership, an organization providing leadership education and policy guidance through Jewish learning. He earned his Master's and Ph.D. degrees from Harvard University. Rabbi Greenberg has served as Professor at City University of New York, Yeshiva and Brandeis Universities, and as Fulbright Visiting Professor at Tel Aviv University. He has been a seminal thinker in confronting the Holocaust as an historically transforming event, and the creation of the State of Israel as the beginning of the third era in Jewish history. He has written extensively about rethinking the fundamental assumptions of Judaism, Christianity, and modern culture to develop an ethic of power and mutual responsibility in order to prevent a recurrence of catastrophe. His monographs include: "The Third Great Cycle of Jewish History," "Voluntary Covenant," and "Will There Be One Jewish People by the Year 2000?"

GEORGE G. HIGGINS is Adjunct Lecturer at the Catholic University of

America. He received his Ph.D. in 1944 from the Catholic University of America in Economics and Political Science. From that year until his retirement in 1980, Rev. Msgr. Higgins served on staff of the National Catholic Welfare Conference, which became the U.S. Catholic Conference, as Director of its Social Action Department and Secretary for Research. Currently, he chairs the Advisory Committee to the Secretariat for Catholic-Jewish Relations of the National Conference of Catholic Bishops, is a consultant to the Bishops' Committee on Farm Labor, and is a member of the Bishops' Committee on Catholic Social Teaching and the U.S. Economy. He is the author of the weekly syndicated column, "The Yardstick" and has contributed articles to numerous journals and volumes.

JOHN T. PAWLIKOWSKI, O.S.M. is Professor of Social Ethics at the Catholic Theological Union, a constituent school of the Chicago Cluster of Theological Schools. For over a decade he has been a prominent figure in the Christian-Jewish dialogue as lecturer, writer, advisor to the American Bishops' Secretariat for Catholic-Jewish Relations and a member of the Israel Study Group of Christian scholars. In 1980 he was appointed by President Carter to the United States Holocaust Memorial Council, a position he continues to hold. He is the author of *What Are They Saying About Christian-Jewish Relations?* (Paulist, 1980), and *Christ in the Light of the Christian-Jewish Dialogue* (Paulist, 1982).

A. JAMES RUDIN is the National Interreligious Affairs Director of the American Jewish Committee. He works with all religious groups to secure greater understanding of Jews and Judaism and to promote good human relations among people of all races and creeds. Rabbi Rudin is a founder of the National Interreligious Task Force on Black-Jewish Relations, and a member of the Martin Luther King, Jr. Federal Holiday Commission. He is an acknowledged expert on the contemporary religious cult movement, and a member of the Executive Boards of the American Family Foundation, the New York City Interfaith Coalition of Concern About Cults, the New York City Jewish Community Relations Council Task Force on Missionaries and Cults, and the Editorial Board of the CULTIC STUDIES JOURNAL. He is the author of *Israel for Christians: Understanding Modern Israel* (Fortress Press, 1983). Rabbi Rudin has participated in interreligious seminary conferences, served in the Executive Council of the American Jewish Historical Society, and is a member of the National Council of Churches' Committee on Christian-Jewish Relations.

ROBERT M. SELTZER is Associate Professor in the History Department of Hunter College and the Graduate School of the City University of New York, Director of the Mazer Institute for Advance Study in Judaica of the CUNY Graduate Center, and coordinator of Hunter's interdisciplinary program in Jewish Social Studies. He holds his Ph.D. from Columbia University in Jewish and East European history. He is author of articles on modern Jewish intellectual history, Jewish historiography, and the rise of Jewish nationalism in late Tsarist Russia; his *Jewish People, Jewish Thought: The Jewish Experience in History* is a comprehensive survey of the development of Jewish life and ideas. Professor Seltzer is an editor of the forthcoming sixteen-volume *Encyclopedia of Religion,* has acted as consultant for the National Educational Television series *Heritage: Civilization and the Jews,* and has served on the executive boards of the Association for Jewish Studies and the Central Conference of American Rabbis.

MARC H. TANENBAUM is Director of International Relations of the American Jewish Committee, and has had a long and distinguished career in international human rights, world refugee, world hunger, and foreign relations concerns. Dr. Tanenbaum has served as a member of the Human Rights Research Committee of the Foreign Policy Association's Study of Priorities for the 1980's. President Carter invited him as the American Jewish leader to discuss "the State of the Nation" at Camp David summit meetings in 1979. He was also appointed as a member of the Advisory Committee of the President's Commission on the Holocaust. He is a founder and leading member of the joint liaison committee of the Vatican Secretariat on Catholic-Jewish Relations and the International Jewish Committee for Interreligious Consultations (IJCIC), and of a similar body with the World Council of Churches. He is a founder and co-chairman of the National Interreligious Task Force on Soviet Jewry, which aids oppressed Jews and Christians in the Soviet Union and Eastern Europe. Rabbi Tanenbaum is the author or editor of several published books and of numerous articles.

ROYALE M. VADAKIN is the Rector of the Cathedral of St. Vibiana in Los Angeles, and chairs the Los Angeles Archdiocesan Ecumenical, Interreligious Affairs Committee, the Archbishops' Committee on Peace and Justice, and the Commission on Women in the Church and Society. Rev. Msgr. Vadakin was active in establishing the Los Angeles Priest-Rabbi Committee and in the publication of Archdiocesan Guidelines for Catholic-Jewish Relations, Lenten Meditations, liturgical readings to ameliorate anti-Jewish passages in pre-Easter New Testament lessons, and joint Catholic-Jewish statements on "Abortion" and "The Nuclear Reality." He is a member of the Advisory Committee to the Secretariat for Catholic-Jewish Relations of the National Conference of Catholic Bishops and past Vice-President of the National Association of Diocesan Ecumenical Officers.

ALFRED WOLF, Ph.D. D.D. is Rabbi Emeritus of Wilshire Boulevard Temple and Director of the Skirball Institute on American Values of the American Jewish Committee. He has served the Wilshire Boulevard Temple of Los

Angeles since 1949 and joined the staff of the American Jewish Committee in 1985. He is active and holds office in a number of local, regional and national, civic, religious and interfaith organizations. He is also co-author of the book *Our Jewish Heritage* (Wilshire, 1978) and lectures extensively at universities. He is married and has three children and three grandchildren.

INDEX OF TOPICS

INDEX OF NAMES